The WI
Diamond Jubilee
Cookbook

The WI
Diamond Jubilee
Cookbook

Edited by
BEE NILSON

HEINEMANN : LONDON

William Heinemann Ltd
15 Queen Street, Mayfair, London W1X 8BE
LONDON MELBOURNE TORONTO
JOHANNESBURG AUCKLAND

434 51400 4

Printed Offset Litho and bound in Great Britain by
Cox & Wyman Ltd
London, Fakenham and Reading

Contents

INTRODUCTION

The recipes in this book have been chosen from thirty-five cookery books compiled by members of the National Federation of Women's Institutes.

In making the choice I was not looking for the 'best' recipes—a subjective and impertinent exercise anyway. Rather I wanted a selection which reflected the great variety of tastes, both traditional and modern, among members of the Women's Institutes.

Everyone knows that country women are good cooks but not everyone knows that through these books Women's Institute members have been preserving traditional recipes, not as museum pieces but as practical recipes for modern cooks. Naturally I have included many of these.

For the rest of the book I have chosen recipes for a variety of reasons. Many have been used for their clear instructions with quantities carefully prescribed when this is important, so that the user will have a reasonable chance of success. Some very interesting recipes were obviously written for experienced cooks and with these I have taken the liberty of adding a 'Note for Beginners'. In some others I have inserted information on temperatures and cooking times I used when testing them. I hope the owners of the recipes will not mind.

Some recipes I tried because the names intrigued me—Sly Cakes, King George First's Christmas Pudding, Buttery Dick, Guernsey Bean Jar, Oozie-woozie Tart, Australian Jack, Stone Cream, Cawl Mamgu, Fat Rascals, Lord Welby's Sauce, to mention but a few.

I was also guided by the preference for certain types of foods as shown by the large number of similar recipes. For example, the undoubted preference for soup as a first course; the importance of pork and bacon recipes and the interesting recipes for using cheaper cuts of other meats; the importance of yeast cookery; the delicious home-made biscuits and cookies; and in the cake section the preference for fruit cakes, gingerbreads and cakes using pastry.

I found some interesting regional differences of opinion on the best way of cooking certain foods and have included a number of these, for example, on how to cook salmon; on cooking vegetables; on stewing rhubarb; and on making a fruit salad.

To help the reader identify the origin of each recipe they are all labelled with the name of the county from whose book I took the recipe. They are the old county names because the books were published before the formation of new boundaries.

The whole collection is unique among cookery books and brings to a wider public the good cooking of the country women of England, Wales and the Island of Guernsey. I am honoured and privileged to have been asked to make this selection.

Bee Nilson
London, 1975

WEIGHTS, MEASURES & TEMPERATURES

I

Quantities in the recipes are in both ounces, pounds or pints and the metric grams, kilograms or litres.

16 ounces (oz)	= 1 pound (lb)	
20 fluid ounces (fl oz)	= 1 pint	
1,000 grams (g)	= 1 kilogram (kg)	= approximately 2 lb 3 oz
1,000 millilitres (ml)	= 1 litre (l)	= approximately $1\frac{3}{4}$ pints

Cake tin sizes are given in both inches and the metric centimetres or millimetres.

100 millimetres (mm) = 1 centimetre (cm) = approximately $2\frac{1}{2}$ inches

When a definite size of mould or pie-dish is recommended in a recipe, this is given in volume measures of pints with the metric equivalent in millilitres or litres.

TEMPERATURES are in both Centigrade (°C) and Fahrenheit (°F) followed by the equivalent number on a gas cooker.

When translating ounces, pounds and pints into their metric equivalents certain compromises have to be made in order to produce quantities which can be weighed on domestic scales or measured with spoons and jugs. To take one example: an ounce equals 28·35 grams but this is an impossible quantity to weigh on domestic scales. These usually do not weigh less than 5 grams; so we have the choice of counting an ounce as either 25 grams or 30 grams. In most of these recipes an ounce has been taken as 25 grams.

In the same way larger quantities have to be adjusted to give metric quantities which are multiples of 5 grams. In doing this it is important to keep the same balance of ingredients as in the original recipe which is why sometimes you may, for example, find 4 ounces translated as 100 grams and sometimes as 125 grams; or 8 ounces as 200 grams or 225 grams. Which of the two alternatives is the better choice depends on the quantities of other ingredients in the recipe.

To complete the metric conversion, spoon measures have been given as millilitres. The British Standards Institution recommended spoon measures include 20, 15, 10, 5 and $2\frac{1}{2}$ millilitres; but are not given specific names. In translating these recipes a level tablespoon has been taken as 15 millilitres (the same as a medicinal tablespoon or an average table tablespoon). A level dessertspoon has been taken as 10 millilitres and a level teaspoon as 5 millilitres.

In the original recipes spoon measures may be level, rounded or heaped and this has been taken into account in giving the millilitre equivalents.

In general the metric version is a trifle smaller than the original recipe but this is not usually enough to significantly alter sizes of tins required or recommended cooking times.

The original recipes from which this book has been compiled were tested by members of the Women's Institutes; with the exception of the preserve recipes, they have all been tested again using the metric quantities.

FIRST COURSES
2

Soups

Garnishes and Accompaniments for Soups

This list has been compiled from information in books from Cumberland, Durham and Yorkshire.

ALMONDS, shredded, roast.
APPLE, diced raw.
BACON, chopped, grilled or fried.
BUTTER BALLS to thicken and add richness to purées. They are made from equal quantities of flour and butter blended together and made into small balls about the size of a marble, dropped into the boiling soup one at a time, before serving.
CHEESE, grated. Use dry cheese and grate it finely. Serve it separately or sprinkle on the soup before serving. As an alternative garnish, mix it with chopped parsley or watercress.
CHEESE STRAWS.
CHIVES, chopped.
CORNFLAKES, crushed.

CREAM, seasoned, whipped.

CROÛTONS. Toasted bread cut into small dice; or cut small dice and either bake until crisp and brown or fry them.

CUCUMBER, sliced.

DUMPLINGS, small ones, plain or with herbs, in broth.

EGG, chopped hardboiled.

FRANKFURTER SAUSAGES, sliced.

HERBS, chopped green—added at last minute.

LEEKS, chopped, fried.

LEMON, sliced.

MUSHROOM SHREDS. This garnish is suitable for thick soups. Cut mushrooms and stalks across into shreds and fry lightly.

OLIVES, chopped.

ONION, raw grated.

ONION RINGS. Cut an onion into thin rings, soak in milk and fry in a little fat until brown and crisp. Add to soup just before serving.

ORANGE, grated rind or slivers of rind.

PASTA. Specially suitable for minestrone or any thin clear soup. Break in small lengths and add to the soup, allowing 20–30 minutes for macaroni to cook, less time for small shapes.

POTATO CRISPS, crushed.

POTATO RINGS. Cream 1 lb mashed potatoes (500 g), with 1 oz margarine (25 g), 1 tablespoon milk and 1 egg. Pipe on to a greased tin and cook for 5–10 minutes in a hot oven, or until crisp.

RADISHES, sliced.

Artichoke Soup

1 lb Jerusalem artichokes (500 g)
1 stick celery
1 potato
1 oz lean ham (25 g) or rinds of bacon
1½ pints of water (800 ml)
½ pint milk (300 ml)
1 oz butter (25 g)
1 dessertspoon flour (20 ml)
Salt, pepper and nutmeg to taste

Put the artichokes, celery, potato and ham into an enamel, aluminium, or stainless steel saucepan. Cover with the water and boil until cooked. Put all through a hair or nylon sieve, add the milk and butter, thicken with flour, bring to boiling point and add seasoning—serve.

Serves 4–5.

Note for Beginners

Wash and peel the artichokes and cut them up before cooking. Slice the celery. If the artichokes are prepared some time before cooking, cover them with cold water to which a tablespoon of vinegar has been added—this keeps them white. Allow about ½ hour for cooking the vegetables. This may be done in advance and the soup completed just before serving.

Somerset

Cawl Mamgu

Granny's Broth

Cover meat with cold water in pan. Add salt and pepper. Bring to boil, skim. Add swede, carrots, white of leeks. Simmer 2–2½ hours.

Add potatoes, simmer another 30 minutes. When potatoes almost cooked, thicken with flour and a little water. Lastly add green of leeks and parsley (chopped) and simmer further 10 minutes. Serve in basins while hot.

Serves 8.

2 lb best end of neck (Welsh lamb) (1 kg)
Salt and pepper
1 small swede, sliced
8 oz carrots (250 g), cut in half
2 large leeks
1 lb potatoes (500 g), cut in quarters
½ oz flour (15 g)
1 oz parsley (25 g)

Pembrokeshire

Celery Cream Purée

Wash celery and cut into 2 inch (5 cm) pieces. Prepare onion and chop. Place vegetables in pan with stock, bouquet garni and seasoning. Simmer gently after bringing to boiling point. Pass through a sieve.

Melt the butter in the stewpan, add flour and cook together. Add the milk gradually and the purée and stir until boiling. Boil for 5 minutes, cool slightly, add cream and serve.

Serves 6.

1 or 2 heads of celery (about 500 g),
    according to size
1 small onion
1 pint white stock (600 ml)
Bouquet garni
Seasoning
1½ oz butter (40 g)
1½ oz flour (40 g)
1 pint milk (600 ml)
¼ pint cream (150 ml)

Note for Beginners

Start making the soup at least 1 hour before serving time. The celery will take about 45 minutes to soften sufficiently for sieving.

Cumberland

Cheese Soup

Gently fry onion in butter until tender but not brown. Stir in milk and water. When nearly boiling stir in eggs, cheese and seasoning. Heat gently but do not boil.

Garnish
Cut small rings or crescents from bread and fry in hot butter until golden brown, drain.

Ladle soup into bowls, add 3–4 rings of bread and serve at once.

Serves 6.

1 medium onion (finely chopped)
1 oz butter (25 g)
1 pint water (600 ml)
1 pint milk (600 ml)
2 eggs (lightly beaten)
8 oz grated Cheddar cheese (200 g)
Salt and pepper

Garnish
4 slices thin white bread
2 oz butter (50 g)

Cumberland

Cock-a-Leekie Soup

12 prunes steeped overnight in warm
  water
8 or 10 leeks
4 pints chicken stock (2¼ l)
Salt and pepper

Surrey

Stone prunes, remove the green from the leeks, wash the white stems and shred. Put prunes and shredded leeks into the chicken stock, add salt and pepper to taste. Bring to the boil and simmer for ¾ hour.

Serves 6.

Conger Soup

1 conger head and good tail piece or a
  piece of conger
Parsley
Bay leaf
Chopped onion
1 lb shelled green peas (300 ml shelled)
1 finely diced carrot
Marble-sized dough balls (2 per person),
  small dumplings
1 pint milk (600 ml)
1 sprig thyme
Bay leaf to taste
2 flower heads of soucis (marigold
  petals)
Seasoning

Guernsey

Clean and wash fish, cover with cold water, add seasoning, thyme, parsley, bay leaf, chopped onion. Simmer 2 hours. Strain.

To fish stock add the peas, carrot, dough balls and boil 30 minutes. Then, about 15 minutes before serving, add milk and marigold petals. Taste for seasoning.

Serves 8–10.

Curried Apple Soup
Cold

2 shallots, chopped
2 tablespoons butter (25 g)
1 pint stock (600 ml)
1 level tablespoon curry powder (15 ml)
1 tablespoon arrowroot (30 ml)
2 apples, pippins are best
2 egg yolks
¼ pint single cream (150 ml)
1 tablespoon lemon juice (15 ml)
Salt and pepper

Hampshire

Sizzle the chopped shallots in the butter until transparent. Add the curry powder and stock. Stir well and bring to the boil. Make the arrowroot into a smooth cream with water and stir into the soup. Simmer for 5 minutes. Take off the heat, cool for a few minutes and then put it in the liquidizer with one apple peeled, cored and diced, the egg yolks and the cream. Put to cool.

Peel and core the second apple, dice it, and cover with lemon juice to stop it going brown. Stir into the soup just before you serve it. Check for seasoning.

Serves 4 (at a pinch).

Iced Cucumber Soup

Cut the cucumber into small cubes. Keep an inch or two back. Chop up the onion and simmer it in the stock. Add the cucumber and about 10 mint leaves, simmer again until the cucumber is soft.

Purée this in the blender, or use a small mouli-legume, and return to the saucepan. Mix the cornflour to a smooth paste with the cream and a tablespoon of the soup. Stir it into the soup and bring to the boil while stirring. Taste it and season with salt. Take it off the heat and when cold put it in a basin or jug in the refrigerator. It will take several hours to chill completely unless you turn your refrigerator to the coldest position. Garnish it with very small sticks of cucumber.

Lettuce soup can be made in the same way, and this is a good use of a glut lettuce. Garnish with a little pinch of finely chiffoned lettuce leaf.

Serves 4–6.

2 washed but unpeeled cucumbers (500 g)
1 small onion
1½ pints stock (900 ml) (a white Oxo cube or two serves the purpose well)
10 mint leaves
1 dessertspoon cornflour (20 ml)
½ gill single cream (75 ml)
Salt

Hampshire

Mushroom Soup

Cold

Melt butter, add flour, cook without colouring, add stock gradually and boil. Wash mushrooms and press through a fine wire sieve. Add to soup along with cream and milk. Simmer 3 minutes, pour into bowl, whisking frequently until quite cold.

Serves 6.

1 oz butter, good weight (30 g)
1 oz flour, good weight (30 g)
1½ pints chicken stock (900 ml), bouillon cubes are good
6 oz light coloured mushrooms (175 g)
¼ pint milk (150 ml)
¼ pint cream (150 ml) or ½ pint single cream (300 ml)
Salt and pepper

Note for Beginners

The mushrooms can be processed in the electric blender, with the milk.

Westmorland

Mushroom Soup

Hot

Wash and peel mushrooms, including stalks, chop mushrooms and onion and cook gently in the butter 10 minutes.

Stir in flour and mix well, add stock and bay leaf. Stir until boiling. Add milk, simmer 15 minutes.

Rub through a sieve, re-heat and season to taste. Serve very hot.

Especially good if 2 or 3 tablespoons cream added after removed from heat.

Serves 4–6.

8 oz mushrooms (200 g)
1 onion
2 oz butter (50 g)
1½ oz flour (40 g)
1 pint stock (600 ml)
1 bay leaf
1 pint milk (600 ml)
2 or 3 tablespoons cream (optional) (30–45 ml)
Salt and pepper

Westmorland

Onion Soup

1 oz butter (25 g)
1 lb onions (500 g)
2 slices stale bread
1 pint milk (600 ml)
½ pint water (300 ml)
Seasoning
Bouquet garni
Grated cheese
Chopped parsley

Cumberland

Melt butter in pan. Add sliced onion and cook gently for 15 minutes without burning.

Remove crusts from bread and add bread, milk and water to pan. Add the bouquet garni and seasoning. Boil for 5 minutes, then simmer for approximately 40 minutes. Sieve, return to rinsed pan and reheat.

Serve sprinkled with grated cheese and a little parsley.

Serves 4.

Parsnip Soup

4 parsnips
1 onion
2 sticks celery
Butter or dripping
2 pints stock (1¼ l)
1 pint milk (600 ml)
Salt and pepper
Juice of 1 small lemon, optional

Westmorland

Clean and slice vegetables, fry in butter or dripping for 5–10 minutes, then add stock. Simmer until vegetables are tender, about 30 minutes. Rub through a sieve and return purée to pan. Add milk and seasoning to taste. Re-heat to just under boiling point.

If wished, juice of 1 small lemon can be added to lessen sweetness.

Serves 6.

Pea Soup

½ pint dried peas (300 ml)
1 onion
1 ham bone or hock end with more
   bone than meat
2½ pints water (1½ l)
Nut of butter
Seasoning

Hampshire

Soak peas overnight. Rinse and strain. Cut onion up roughly. Put peas into saucepan. Add ham bone and onion and water. Simmer gently until peas are soft. Remove the bone. Sieve if necessary. Stir in a nut of butter and season to taste.

Serves 4–6.

Variation
Herbs may be added if liked. Mint, fresh or dried, may be sprinkled over before serving. Lentils may be used in place of dried peas (no need to soak). Split peas may be used.

Note for Beginners

The cooking time for dried peas averages about 2 hours, lentils and split peas about 1 hour. Do not skimp the cooking time as the ham bone needs time to flavour the soup. Bits of meat left on the bone can be diced and added to the soup.

Purée of Brussels Sprouts

Boil sprouts till tender, keep them very green, pass through hair sieve. Then put into a saucepan with the boiling stock and cream. Season with pepper and salt. Get it quite hot but do not allow it to boil or the colour will be spoilt. Serve with sippets of toast.
    Serves 8.

1 lb sprouts (500 g)
3 pints boiling white stock (1¾ l)
1 gill thick cream (150 ml)
Pepper and salt
Sippets of toast

Note for Beginners

Instead of passing the cooked sprouts through a hair sieve they may be processed in the electric blender with a little of the stock.

Northamptonshire and Soke of Peterborough

Sorrel Soup

Melt butter and add finely chopped onion. Cook over low heat for a few minutes. Add washed and chopped sorrel leaves and thinly cut potatoes. Cook all together in the butter for 5 minutes, stirring all the time. Cover with water or stock, add seasoning and simmer until tender. Sieve if preferred, and if too thick add more stock, or if water has been used, a little milk. Serve with chopped watercress.
    Serves 4.

1 oz butter (25 g)
1 large onion
1 good handful of sorrel leaves (to be found in the fields in late spring or early summer)
3 large potatoes
Water or stock
Seasoning
Watercress

Note for Beginners

It is advisable to strip the leafy part of the sorrel from the stalks and centre ribs and discard these.

Yorkshire

Tomato and Carrot Soup

Cut up vegetables and brown lightly in butter or margarine, add stock, and cook until vegetables are tender, approximately ½ hour. Sieve or put through a blender. Then thicken with the flour mixed with milk and boil for 3 or 4 minutes. Season to taste. Very delicious.
    Serves 4.

4 large tomatoes
1 large carrot
1 onion
1 oz butter or margarine (25 g)
1 pint stock or water (600 ml)
½ pint milk (300 ml)
1 oz flour (25 g)
Salt and pepper

Shropshire

Tripe Soup

2 lb fresh tripe (1 kg)
2 quarts white stock (2¼ l)
2 onions, minced
2 potatoes, sliced
1 oz butter (25 g)
1 oz flour (25 g)
Small teacup milk (100 ml)
Salt and pepper
Chopped parsley

Northumberland

Cut tripe into small pieces and put it into stock; add onions and potatoes, cook slowly together for about 1 hour, then thicken with the butter well rubbed into the flour. Add a small teacup of milk, some chopped parsley and pepper and salt to taste just before serving.

Serves 8.

Turkey Corn Soup

1 tin creamed sweet corn (283 g)
1 onion
½ red pepper
1 bay leaf
1 pint turkey stock (600 ml)
Salt and pepper
2 tablespoons cornflour (20 ml)
¼ pint milk (150 ml)

Garnish
Chopped chives, parsley and rings of
   red pepper. Sprinkle with paprika.

Surrey

Place sweet corn, finely chopped onion, sliced red pepper, bay leaf and stock into pan with seasoning. Bring to the boil and simmer gently 15–20 minutes, then sieve. Return to pan and add the cornflour blended with a little of the milk. Add remaining milk. Boil 3 or 4 minutes. Adjust seasoning. Garnish and serve.

Serves 3–4.

Starters

Cucumber Cocktail

1 clove garlic, finely chopped
Juice of 1 lemon
5 tablespoons salad oil (75 ml)
1 teaspoon salt (5 ml)
1 dessertspoon made mustard (10 ml)
Black pepper
Brown sugar
½ honey-dew melon, diced
½ cucumber, diced
2 pears, diced
½ bunch watercress

Cumberland

Mix all ingredients together, except fruit and vegetables, to make a dressing. Marinade the melon, cucumber and pears in the dressing for at least ½ hour.

Remove and drain, place in individual dishes. Serve chilled, topped with watercress clusters.

This looks marvellous in tall stemmed hock glasses.

Serves 8.

Devon Trout and Mushroom Pâté

Clean the trout but do not remove the heads.

Put a knob of butter into the slit stomachs, wrap in grease-proof paper and steam for ½ hour.

While the fish is cooking, chop the mushrooms (including stalks) very small and fry in butter.

When fish is ready, carefully remove all bones, skin and heads, but retain any liquid, melted butter, etc. from the paper.

Mash the meat with a fork, add the liquid and the fried mushrooms together with any butter left in the pan, add a dash of anchovy sauce and pepper and salt.

Melt remaining butter and mix.

Beat the mixture with a fork until smooth and creamy, then place in pots (empty meat paste pots are ideal), packing the pâté down well. Fill nearly to the top, then seal with a small amount of melted butter.

Put in a cool place, preferably a fridge, to set.

When cold cover as jam. (Makes about 12 oz or 400 g.)

This pâté can also be made with salmon or peal (sea trout). It is delicious eaten on hot toast, or in sandwiches, or makes an unusual hors d'oeuvre.

1½ lb fresh-caught trout (700 g)
(either one large fish or several small)
4 oz farm butter (100 g)
2 oz field mushrooms (50 g)
Salt and pepper
Dash of anchovy sauce

Devon

Fish Cocktails

Shake well and serve over any cooked flaked fish or shellfish.

6 tablespoons tomato ketchup (100 ml)
1½ tablespoons wine vinegar (40 ml)
½ teaspoon Worcester sauce (2½ ml)
2 tablespoons wine (30 ml)
Juice of half lemon
Cayenne and salt to taste

Cheshire

Fruit Cocktails

Serve the fruit cocktails in glasses using:
1 Cubed apples, pears and peaches garnished with cherries.
2 Grapefruit sections or halved grapefruit garnished with a cherry.
3 Avocado pear and pineapple.
4 Fresh strawberries, grapes and orange slices.
5 Watermelon cut into balls.

Dress with either of the following dressings:
(a) 4 oz sugar (100 g), ⅛ pint sherry (75 ml), 2 tablespoons lemon juice (30 ml).

(b) Mix together lemon and orange juice and sweeten with sugar.

Cheshire

Chill and serve over fruit and sprinkle with chopped nuts.

Grapefruit Cocktail

1 grapefruit
1 tablespoon stock syrup (15 ml)
½ orange
1 lemon
1 tablespoon sherry (15 ml)

Squeeze the grapefruit—add the syrup. Add orange and lemon juice. Cover and chill well.

Strain and add sherry just before serving. Serve in small glasses (never overfill).

Serves 4–6.

Stock Syrup
4 oz sugar (100 g).
¼ pint water (150 ml).

Cumberland

Boil 3 minutes. Use as required.

Ham and Pineapple Cocktail

6 oz cooked ham (lean) (150 g)
1 slice pineapple
2 tablespoons cream (30 ml), whipped
1 dessertspoon tomato ketchup (10 ml)
Juice of ½ lemon
Shredded lettuce
Paprika to garnish

Cut the ham and pineapple in fine shreds. Mix together the cream ketchup and lemon juice. Mix together the ham, pineapple and dressing.

Arrange a little shredded lettuce in the base of individual glasses. Spoon mixture on top. Garnish with paprika.

Serves 4.

Cumberland

Note: Prawns may be used instead of ham.

Liver Pâté

8 oz pig's liver (250 g)
1 small onion
Sliver of garlic, if liked
3 oz butter (75 g)
1 dessertspoon tomato purée (10 ml)
Seasoning

Chop the liver, onion and garlic. Melt the butter in a pan. Add the onion, garlic, liver and tomato purée. Cook gently, stirring often, until tender. Season. When cool, put all through a sieve or the fine plate of a mincer twice. Put into small pots and cover with melted butter.

Serves 4.

Variations
Herbs to taste may be added or a little red wine used to assist in cooking.

This mixture is suitable for pulping in an electric blender. Do this while the mixture is still warm.

Hampshire

Prawn Cocktail

Shell the prawns. Mix all ingredients together, chill and serve on a lettuce leaf with chopped lettuce for decoration.
 Serves 4.

1 pint shrimps or prawns (500–600 ml)
2 tablespoons thick mayonnaise (30 ml)
3 tablespoons double cream (45 ml), whipped
1 tablespoon tomato ketchup or purée (15 ml)
1 tablespoon Worcester sauce (15 ml)
1 tablespoon lemon juice (15 ml)
1 teaspoon finely chopped onion (5 ml)
1 teaspoon finely chopped celery (5 ml) or $\frac{1}{2}$ teaspoon celery salt ($2\frac{1}{2}$ ml)
Salt to taste
Lettuce

Northumberland

Shropshire Pâté

Put all ingredients in pan (except spices and sherry or brandy). With enough water to cover, simmer for 35–40 minutes, allow to cool in juices, remove herbs, then put all in a liquidizer with a little of the stock. Blend finely, add nutmeg, mace, pepper, salt and sherry or brandy to taste. Put in a crock and seal with melted butter. This freezes very well.
 Serves 8.

8 oz chicken livers (250 g)
Onion or shallot
8 oz streaky bacon (250 g)
Bouquet garni
Spices (nutmeg, mace)
Pepper
Sherry or brandy (optional)

Shropshire

Skipper Pâté

Mash skippers with juices from can until fairly smooth.
 Blend in remaining ingredients, mix well.
 Turn into small serving dish, cover with foil lid, chill in refrigerator until required.
 Serve with warm toast and unsalted butter as a starter or snack.
 Serves 4.

$3\frac{3}{4}$ oz John West Skippers in oil (106 g)
3 oz packet Philadelphia cream cheese spread (85 g)
Juice of $\frac{1}{2}$ lemon
Few drops tabasco
Freshly ground black pepper

Note for Beginners

This recipe can be made with any full-fat soft cheese.

Derbyshire

Taramasalata

8 oz smoked cod's roe (175 g) (can be
 bought at most big fish shops)
4 oz cream cheese (125 g)
1 tablespoon chopped chives (30 ml)
1 tablespoon lemon juice (15 ml)
Sprigs of watercress
Twists of lemon
Dry toast

Hampshire

This is a smoked cod's roe pâté. Serve in little pots. Individual porcelain soufflé cases are a very useful buy.

Skin the cod's roe and mash it and all the other ingredients with a fork. Pile it casually but tidily into the little dishes and garnish with a small sprig of watercress and a twist of lemon. Serve with dry toast. About 2 tablespoonsful each will be enough.
 Serves 6.

FISH
3

Baked Fish

Wash and drain the fish but do not dry it.

Melt sufficient fat in a pie-dish to well cover the bottom. When hot dip the fish into the hot fat so that each piece is coated on both sides. Lay the fish back in the dish with the halved tomatoes at the sides, add pepper and salt and a little sugar on the tomatoes.

Place the bacon rashers on the top and bake in a moderate oven, 375°F (190°C) Gas 5, for about 20–30 minutes or until the fish is cooked through and the bacon crisp.

This is very good served with Chinese Sweet Sour Sauce.
Serves 4.

As many fillets as required
A little fat or dripping
3 or 4 rashers of streaky bacon
2 or 3 tomatoes
Pepper and salt and a little sugar

Devon

Baked Fish with Mushrooms and Bacon

Whole bream, hake or fresh haddock or
use fillets
Mushrooms
Lemon juice
Salt and pepper
Streaky bacon

Oxfordshire

If the fish is cooked whole, clean well and stuff with mushrooms sprinkled with lemon juice.

If fillets are used place mushrooms round them. In either case place the fish and mushrooms in a greased baking dish, season well and cover with strips of streaky bacon.

Bake without a lid in a moderate oven, 350°F (180°C) Gas 4, for 20–30 minutes, according to the size of the fish.

Barbecue Fish Steaks

3 tablespoons oil or margarine (45 ml)
4 steaks of cod, haddock or any firm
white fish
1 small onion
1 small green pepper
Parsley
2–3 mushrooms
1 small tin or ½ lb tomatoes (225 g)
2 tablespoons tomato ketchup (30 ml)
½ teaspoon dry mustard (5 ml)
Salt and pepper

Cumberland

Heat the oil or margarine in a heavy frying pan. Brown fish quickly on both sides—lower heat. Remove the fish from pan and place on a fireproof serving dish. Chop onion. De-seed pepper and chop finely with parsley and mushrooms. Fry gently until soft. Add tomato ketchup and mustard. Season well and pour over the fish. Bake in a moderate oven 20–30 minutes at 375°F (190°C) Gas 5.

If fresh tomatoes are used add 2 teaspoons water (10 ml).

Fish and Egg Mornay

8 oz cold cooked white fish (225 g)
2 hard boiled eggs
Chopped parsley
½ pint thick cheese sauce (300 ml)
Grated cheese

Gloucestershire

Put the fish and halved eggs in a fireproof dish. Mix chopped parsley with cheese sauce, and pour over eggs and fish. Sprinkle grated cheese over the top, and put into the oven to heat thoroughly until it is crispy brown on top, 400°F (200°C) Gas 6, for about 20 minutes.

Serves 4.

Fish Dish

Place fillets in greased fireproof dish. Mix sauce ingredients smoothly. Spread sauce over fish. Slice onion thinly and lay on top. Add halved tomatoes. Cover with greased paper, bake ½ hour or less, according to thickness of fish, in moderate oven, 375°F (190°C) Gas 5.

Serves 4.

1 lb fillet of cod or other white fish (500 g)
1 onion
A few small tomatoes

Sauce
1 teaspoon curry powder (10 ml)
¼ teaspoon dry mustard (2½ ml)
2 teaspoons salad oil or dripping (10 ml)
2 teaspoons vinegar (10 ml)
2 teaspoons tomato sauce (10 ml)
1 teaspoon mushroom ketchup (5 ml)
Salt

Cambridgeshire

Fish Envelope

Roll pastry into an 8 inch (20 cm) square. Trim edges if necessary. Flake fish, mix with sauce, egg, parsley and seasonings and place on centre of pastry. Moisten edges of pastry and fold into an envelope shape. Seal edges well and flute. Brush with egg wash. Decorate with leaves from pastry trimmings. Bake in a hot oven, 425°F (220°C) Gas 7, for ¾ hour reducing heat after first 10 minutes to 350°F (180°C) Gas 4.

Serves 4.

8 oz flaky pastry (250 g)
8 oz cooked white fish (250 g)
2 tablespoons thick white sauce or top of bottle of milk (30 ml)
1 hard boiled egg
1 teaspoon chopped parsley (10 ml)
1 teaspoon chopped gherkins or capers (10 ml)
Salt and pepper

Durham

Fish Pie

Wash fish and put in greased dish, pour over ¼ pint (150 ml) milk and cook in moderate oven, 350°F (180°C) Gas 4, for 20 minutes. Strain off liquid and make up to ½ pint (300 ml) with rest of milk.

Melt margarine in pan, blend in flour, add milk gradually and cook until sauce is smooth. Stir in cheese, chutney and sultanas, and season to taste.

Flake fish in dish, pour over sauce mixture, sprinkle top with breadcrumbs and return to oven to cook for 10 minutes.

Serves 4.

1 lb cod fillet (500 g)
½ pint milk (300 ml)
½ oz margarine (15 g)
½ oz flour (15 g)
3 oz grated cheese (75 g)
1 tablespoon chutney (30 ml)
2 oz sultanas (50 g)
Salt and pepper
1 tablespoon breadcrumbs (30 ml)

Northumberland

Fish Soufflé

Steamed or Baked

1 oz butter (25 g)
1 oz flour (25 g) or ¾ oz if baked (20 g)
1 gill milk (150 ml)
8 oz cooked white fish (225 g), flaked
Pepper and salt
2 eggs
2 tablespoons cream (30 ml)
Juice of ½ lemon
Sauce for coating

Cheshire

Melt butter in pan, add flour, cook for a minute or two, stirring; draw aside and add milk, stir till it boils. Remove from heat, then add fish and seasonings, 1 whole egg and 1 yolk. Rub through wire sieve, stir in cream and lemon juice. Beat white stiff and fold in. Pour into greased 1 pint (600 ml) mould and steam very gently till firm from 1 to 1¼ hours. Turn out and coat with sauce and decorate to taste.

If baked, serve in dish in which it is cooked. Cook at 375°F (190°C) Gas 5 for about 30 minutes.

Serves 3.

Fish with Capers

3 or 4 onions (small)
Fat for frying
1½ lb any white fish (700 g)
Salt and pepper
6 tablespoons sour milk or cream (100 ml)
Juice of 1 small lemon
1 teaspoon grated lemon rind (5 ml)
Chopped parsley
2 or 3 tablespoons capers (40 ml)

Oxfordshire

Brown the onions in a frying pan in hot fat, add the fish cut into 2 inch (5 cm) lengths, season, add sour cream, lemon juice and rind, a little chopped parsley and the capers. Mix well and simmer gently until the fish is tender, 5–10 minutes.

Serves 4.

Pickled Fish

Delicious Hot or Cold

1 lb white fish (500 g)
1 teaspoon cornflour or flour (15 ml)
Fat for frying
2 or 3 sliced onions
½ tablespoon curry powder (10 ml)
Salt
½ tablespoon sugar (10 ml)
¼ pint malt vinegar (150 ml)

*Northamptonshire and
Soke of Peterborough*

Flour the cut fish and fry in fat. Remove from pan. Fry onions, add curry powder, salt and sugar; mix well, stir in vinegar. Cook for a few minutes and pour over fish.

The flavour of this dish is improved with keeping and may be served 48 hours after making.

Devilled Grilled Cod

Place the prepared fish in a greased ovenproof dish and grill quickly for 2–3 minutes on one side.

Cream the softened margarine and chutney, curry powder, salt and pepper and mustard together, adding the anchovy essence if liked.

Turn the fish over and spread the uncooked side with the devilled mixture. Return to the grill. Reduce the heat slightly and cook for a further 10–12 minutes until the coating is browned and the fish is cooked through. Serve at once.

Cod fillets can be used instead of cutlets. Allow 1–1½ pounds fish (500–750 g) and cut into four portions before cooking.

4 cutlets or steaks of cod about 1 inch (2½ cm) thick
1 oz margarine (25 g)
1 level teaspoon chutney (5 ml)
1 level teaspoon curry powder (5 ml)
Salt and pepper
1 level teaspoon dry mustard (5 ml)
1 teaspoon anchovy essence (optional) (5 ml)

Derbyshire

Oven-fried Cod Cutlets or Fillets

Fish cooked in this way looks and tastes like fried fish, but uses very little fat, and causes no smell in the kitchen.

Season fish and dip in milk, and then coat with brown crumbs. Lay on well greased tin, dot with fat and cover with greased paper. Cook 15–20 minutes, according to thickness of fish, in a moderate oven, 375°F (190°C) Gas 5. This method can be used for any white fish.

Fish cutlets or fillets
Seasoning
Milk
Brown breadcrumbs
Fat

Gloucestershire

Cheese and Crab Ramekins

Chop eggs coarsely. Add crab meat, butter and eggs to the sauce. Heat gently. Do not allow to boil.

Transfer to buttered ramekin dishes or individual fireproof buttered dishes. Sprinkle tops with cheese. Brown under a hot grill.

Garnish with watercress. Serve with hot buttered toast.

Serves 3–4.

3 hard boiled eggs
4 oz cooked crab meat (100 g)
1 oz butter (25 g)
¼ pint cheese coating sauce (150 ml)
1 oz grated cheese (25 g)
Watercress
4 slices hot buttered toast

Derbyshire

To Boil a Crab

Have a large pan of boiling water and a handful of salt, and plunge the crab into it. Let it boil quickly for about 20 minutes. It is better to lay the crab on its feet while boiling.

Cornwall

Stewed Eels

Isle of Ely

Cut eels into pieces and wash well. Place in pan with enough water to cover and simmer for about 20 minutes. Strain the water from them and add them to a white or parsley sauce. Put into a casserole and cook in the oven for 1 hour at 375°F (190°C) Gas 5. Serve in the casserole.

Talmousse of Finnan Haddock

Pastry
2 oz flour (50 g)
1 oz margarine (25 g)
1 oz grated cheese (25 g)
Seasoning
Water to mix

Filling
4 oz shredded cooked finnan haddock (100 g)
1 tablespoon white sauce to moisten (15 ml)
1 tablespoon cheese (30 ml)
Pepper to season
Beaten egg to bind
Parsley to garnish

Yorkshire

Make pastry and cut into two rounds. Put a little of the filling in centre, wet edges of circle and pinch up over the filling (as for a Cornish pasty). Bake in a hot oven, 425°F (220°C) Gas 7, for 15 minutes. Garnish with parsley.
Serves 1.

A New Way for Fresh Herrings

Fresh herrings
Cooking salt
Onions
Butter for frying

Herefordshire

Clean and thoroughly dry the fish—they must be dry. Sprinkle a little cooking salt in a heavy frying pan and, when extremely hot, put the herrings in and cook until a crisp golden brown each side.

In another pan, fry some sliced onions in a little butter. Lay herrings in a shallow dish and smother in the rich brown onion rings.

Baked Herrings Normande

4 herrings
1 onion
1 large apple
1 dessertspoon chopped herbs, parsley, chives, thyme (20 ml)
Salt and freshly ground black pepper
1 oz butter (25 g)
2 tablespoons vinegar (30 ml)

Durham

Split and bone herrings. Wash, dry and lay flat. Chop the onion very finely, dice apple and mix all together with herbs. Season the inside of herrings with salt and black pepper, and sprinkle on the onion mixture. Roll up head to tail. Melt butter and brush inside of fireproof dish with it, put in herrings and the rest of the butter with vinegar. Bake in a slow oven for 45–50 minutes at 325°F (160°C) Gas 3.

Margareta Herring

Clean, wash and fillet herrings. Place a butter knob on each fillet and roll, skin out. Pack into casserole and sprinkle with salt.

Mix mustard, tomato purée and cream and spread over the top.

Bake, 400°F (200°C) Gas 6, for about 30 minutes.

Serve with mashed potatoes.

4 large herrings
2 oz butter (50 g)
Salt
4 tablespoons French mustard (60 ml)
4 tablespoons tomato purée (60 ml)
4 tablespoons cream (60 ml)

Pembrokeshire

Limpets

Carefully wash the sand off the limpets, put on the fire in a pan of cold water, and boil until they slip out of their shells. Serve cold with vinegar and pepper.

Cornwall

Marinated Mackerel

Clean and prepare the mackerel and arrange in a pie-dish, chop the onion and parsley and sprinkle over the fish. Add other ingredients with salt to taste. Pour over sufficient vinegar to cover well and bake in a moderate oven, 350°F (180°C) Gas 4, for 40 or 50 minutes.

When cooked put fish carefully on a dish and strain vinegar over them. Leave until cold and serve.

4 or more mackerel
1 onion
1 sprig parsley
2 chopped bay leaves
6 cloves
Blade of mace
10 peppercorns
Salt
Vinegar

Cornwall

Roast Mackerel

Roast them with fennel; after they are toasted open them and take out the bone; then make a good sauce with butter, parsley and gooseberries, all seasoned; soak your mackerel a very little with your sauce, then serve them hot.

Mackerel
Sprigs of fennel
Butter
Chopped parsley
Gooseberry purée
Salt and pepper

Note for Beginners

Put fennel sprigs inside the mackerel, and on top as well for good flavour. Roast at 375°F (190°C) Gas 5 for 20–30 minutes, depending on size (no fat required).

To make gooseberry sauce for 4, use not less than 8 oz (225 g) green gooseberries or ¼ pint (150 ml) purée; add butter, parsley and seasoning to taste.

Cornwall

Casseroled Ormers

Ormers
Flour
Fat for frying
Slice of bacon
Small sprig parsley
Salt
Thick gravy

Guernsey

Roll ormers in flour, fry till brown. Place in casserole with slice of bacon, small sprig of parsley, salt to taste. Pour over thick gravy. Bake in slow oven for 4 hours, the longer the better.

Note: The ormer is a species of univalve mollusc abundant in Guernsey.

Savoury Plaice

4 fillets plaice
4 oz mushrooms (100 g)
Little butter for frying
½ pint cheese sauce (300 ml)
4 oz tomatoes (100 g)
Sugar
Breadcrumbs
Parsley to garnish

Cheese sauce
1 oz margarine (25 g)
1 oz flour (25 g)
½ pint milk (300 ml)
2 oz grated cheese (50 g)
Pepper and salt

Yorkshire

Skin plaice and roll each fillet skin side inside. Put on a greased plate and steam for 20 minutes. Place in a greased fireproof dish.
  Fry mushrooms and place at ends of dish.
  Make the cheese sauce by melting the margarine in a pan, adding the flour and cooking for a minute or so. Gradually add the milk and stir till it thickens. Add the grated cheese and pepper and salt to taste. Pour this sauce over the fish and mushrooms. Slice the tomatoes and fry. Lay them gently at both ends of the dish, sprinkle with sugar. Sprinkle a few breadcrumbs over the whole, brown under a grill and garnish with parsley.

Quick Method of Boiling Salmon

Cheshire

Wrap salmon in piece of muslin and place in a pan of boiling water with a close fitting lid and keep at a full rolling boil for 5 minutes. Remove from heat and leave in liquor till cold.

Salmon

Any size from whole fish to steak for one
Oil or melted butter
Salt and pepper

Devon

Wipe fish all over with oil and sprinkle with salt and pepper. Wrap in foil. Place in saucepan with cold water to cover. Bring slowly to the boil and simmer for 5 minutes. Leave in water to cool.

Tweed Salmon

The cooking of Tweed Salmon is peculiar to the Tweed Valley. Take a whole fresh salmon and weigh it. Cut it down the back and lay it open on a board. Clean the fish, saving roe and liver. Cut the fish across from side to side in strips 1 inch (2½ cm) wide. The fish is placed on the tray taken from the fish kettle, being careful to keep the fish skin-side up and in the shape of the fish. The tray is now lowered into the fish kettle, which should have been filled with enough well salted boiling water to cover the fish. Bring to the boil. Boil rapidly allowing 1 minute for every 1 pound (½ kg) of fish. Remove tray from pan and drain.

Salmon should be served cold with a little of the water (called Dover) in which it has been cooked.

Northumberland

Salmon Cream

Dissolve gelatine in hot water. Mash salmon well, removing skin and bones. Mix with mayonnaise and season well. Fold in stiffly whipped cream and dissolved gelatine. Pour into a wetted 6 inch (15 cm) cake tin and allow to set. Turn out on to a bed of lettuce and garnish with overlapping pieces of cucumber.

Serves 6.

½ oz gelatine (15 g)
3 tablespoons hot water (45 ml)
8 oz tin salmon (226 g)
¼ pint mayonnaise (150 ml)
Salt and pepper
½ pint double cream (300 ml)
Cucumber and lettuce to garnish

Durham

Trout with Almonds

Wash trout and wipe dry. Mix flour, salt and pepper and coat fish.

Put 3 oz butter (75 g) and the oil into a pan and fry trout until golden and cooked through—approximately 5 minutes on each side. Remove to serving dish and keep warm.

Add remainder of butter to pan and fry the almonds gently until golden. Pour hot butter and almonds over fish. Garnish with lemon and parsley.

4 trout
4 level tablespoons flour (60 ml)
½ level teaspoon salt (2½ ml)
Shake of cayenne pepper
4 oz butter (100 g)
2 teaspoons corn oil (10 ml)
3 oz blanched almonds (75 g)
Lemon wedges
Parsley

Cumberland

Trout with Mint

3 frozen or fresh trout
Salt and pepper
3 sprigs fresh mint or 1 teaspoon dried
    mint
2 oz butter (50 g)
Juice of 1 lemon
½ lemon thinly sliced
Sprigs of mint to garnish

Cumberland

Trim tail and fins and remove eyes—wash. Sprinkle inside with seasoning, place sprig of mint inside fish. Arrange in an oven-proof dish—dot with butter and pour over the lemon juice.

Cover with kitchen foil—cook at 375°F (190°C) Gas 5 for 20–30 minutes.

Garnish with lemon butterflies and mint.

MEAT
4

Beef Recipes

Beef with Green Vegetables

Cut the beef in small pieces and coat well with the cornflour. Slice the shallots and most of the cucumber thinly (do not peel). Remove all seeds from the pepper and cut in thin strips.

Sauté the meat, vegetables and almonds in the oil for 10 minutes or until the meat is well browned. Put in a casserole, add the stock to the frying pan, simmer gently for 1 minute then pour over the meat etc. in the casserole. Stir in the soy sauce, cover and cook at 350°F (180°C) Gas 4 for 1½ hours until meat is tender.

Garnish with the fresh cucumber.

Serves 2.

8 oz casserole steak (250 g)
2 teaspoons cornflour (20 ml)
4 shallots
½ cucumber
1 small green pepper
1 oz blanched almonds (25 g), halved
2 tablespoons oil (30 ml) or 1 oz margarine (25 g)
¼ pint stock (150 ml)
1 dessertspoon soy sauce (10 ml)
Salt

Cumberland

Beefsteak Pudding

1 lb stewing steak (500 g)
4 oz kidney (100 g)
Flour
Salt and pepper
8 oz suet crust pastry (225 g flour)

Cut steak into thin strips, and roll in seasoned flour. Line a well greased basin, 1½ pint (900 ml) size, with ⅔ of the pastry. Put in steak and kidney cut in small pieces. Season each layer. Half-fill basin with water. Cover with lid of pastry. Cover with two thicknesses of greased paper. Steam for 3 hours.

Alternatively, the meat can be stewed for 1½ hours and then made into pudding, steaming 1½–2 hours. Reserve some of the gravy to serve with the pudding.

Serves 4.

Yorkshire

Braised Brisket

1 tablespoon dripping (25 g)
3–4 lb middle cut of brisket (1½–2 kg)
Onion to taste
6 or 8 carrots
Other root vegetables (optional)
Salt and pepper
Bouquet garni
Few potatoes
½–1 pint water (300–600 ml)

Melt fat in thick saucepan and brown joint lightly on both sides. Remove meat and put in onions and carrots (cut if large), and brown these lightly. Any other root vegetables can be added if liked. Season with salt and pepper and replace meat, putting the bone down the side. Add bouquet garni if liked. Cover the top with small slices of potato and season well. Add ½ pint (300 ml) of water, cover pan tightly and bring to simmering point. Let it braise slowly, simmering all the time for 2½–3 hours. If necessary, add more water as cooking proceeds.

Note for Beginners

Cooking can be done on top or in the oven at about 325–350°F (160–180°C) Gas 3–4. When the meat is cooked, lift it out and keep hot. Lift the vegetables out with a strainer or perforated spoon and serve them with the meat. Remove surplus fat from the top of the gravy and serve it with the meat.

Yorkshire

Danish Circles

1 oz rice (25 g)
4 oz minced beef (100 g)
1 tablespoon fresh breadcrumbs (30 ml)
1 small onion
Salt and pepper
1 small egg
4 rashers streaky bacon
Cocktail sticks
1 oz dripping (25 g)

Cook rice and strain, add to minced beef, breadcrumbs and finely chopped onion, season and bind with beaten egg. Make into four rounds flattened to about 1 inch (2½ cm) in depth. Wrap round each with streaky bacon and secure with cocktail sticks.

Bake in dripping, 375°F (190°C) Gas 5, for 20 minutes, turn when half cooked. Serve with mashed potatoes or potato nests.

Serves 4.

Denbighshire

26

Potato Nests

Creamed potatoes piped into neat shapes. Fill with cooked peas.

Denbighshire

Galantine

Put the beef and bacon through a mincer, add breadcrumbs, seasoning and a dash of any thick sauce. Mix in the well-beaten egg and milk.

Place in a greased 1½ pint (850 ml) basin, cover with greaseproof paper and steam for 3 hours. Press, but leave in basin until quite cold.

Turn out and serve slices with any green salad or the following dressing:

> 2 tablespoons vinegar (30 ml)
> 2 teaspoons sugar (10 ml)
> 1 small onion
> 1 small lettuce

Place vinegar in small bowl, add sugar and stir till dissolved. Chop the onion and lettuce finely and add to the vinegar.
Serves 6–8.

1 lb stewing steak (450 g)—fresh and lean
8 oz bacon (225 g)—collar is suitable
1 thick slice of bread (50 g) rubbed into breadcrumbs
Salt and pepper
2 eggs or 1 egg and 3 or 4 tablespoons milk (45–60 ml)
A little thick sauce (optional)

Herefordshire

Savoury Meat Squares

Mix all together except dripping and breadcrumbs. Pack in well greased tin. Sprinkle top with breadcrumbs and cover with pats of dripping. Bake in a slow oven for 1½–2 hours, 325°F (160°C) Gas 3.

Cut into squares.
Serves 4–6.

8 oz minced beef (200 g)
8 oz grated raw potato (200 g)
6 oz grated raw carrot (150 g)
4 oz minced onion (100 g)
¼ pint water (125 ml)
1 teaspoon marmite (5 ml)
Pinch mixed herbs
Salt and pepper
3 oz white breadcrumbs (75 g)
1 oz dripping (25 g)

Denbighshire

Spiced Beef

Place beef in baking tin. Stick half the cloves into it and put the rest in the tin with the peppercorns and the mace. Almost fill tin with water and enough salt to make it rather briny.

Cover with another baking tin. Put in a fairly slow oven until it boils, then keep to moderate heat till done.

A nice economical joint to be eaten cold.

Brisket of beef
16–20 cloves
8–10 peppercorns
Small piece of mace
Water
Salt

Note for Beginners

This can be cooked in a casserole instead of a baking tin, adding about 1½ inches (4 cm) water. Do the main cooking at about 325°F (160°C) Gas 3, first bringing the water to the boil at a higher temperature or on the hotplate. Use the same times as for boiling beef: for a piece weighing 2–3 lb (1–1½ kg) allow 2–3 hours; for 4–5 lb (2–2½ kg) allow 3–4 hours.

The stock will be spicy and salty but is good mixed with unsalted stock or water for a soup or sauce.

Somerset

Steak and Kidney Pie

1 lb stewing steak (450 g)
4 oz kidney (100 g)
Flour
Salt and pepper
8 oz flaky pastry (using 200 g flour)

Cut up steak and kidney and roll in seasoned flour. Place in a pan or casserole with cold water barely to cover and stew gently for 1½–2 hours. Allow meat to cool. Put it in a 1 pint (600 ml) pie-dish or an 8 inch (20 cm) pie plate. Wet the edges of the pie-dish and put strips of pastry on. Wet the lined edges slightly and cover with the crust taking care to cut crust larger than the dish. Make hole in the middle and flake edges, and brush over with egg or milk. Bake in a hot oven, 425°F (220°C) Gas 7, for about 30 minutes.

Serves 4–5.

Yorkshire

Lamb and Mutton

A New Way with Lamb Breasts

1 large sliced onion
2 sliced carrots
Bouquet of herbs
1 breast of lamb
Seasoning
½ pint stock or water (300 ml)
Egg
Fine breadcrumbs
Melted margarine
Lemon or Tartare sauce

Arrange onion, carrots and bouquet in a large flat baking dish. On top lay a breast of lamb cut in two. Add seasoning and stock or water. Cover and cook in a very slow oven for 3 hours, 250°F (120°C) Gas ½.

Remove meat and when cool cut out bones. Cut meat on the slant into strips about an inch (2½ cm) wide. Coat with beaten egg and breadcrumbs. Leave on a wire rack for coating to set. Then put in a grill pan, sprinkle with melted margarine and grill gently on both sides until outside is crisp. Serve with lemon or Tartare sauce.

Serves 6–8 depending on size of breast.

Note for Beginners

The preliminary cooking can be done the day before, at the same time as some other dish needing long, slow cooking. What many butchers call a breast of lamb is in fact a half breast so ask for a whole one if you want it to serve 6–8.

Oxfordshire

Fresh Meat Curry

Slice onions and heat butter and oil. Cook but do not brown. Keep lid on pan and cook gently for 15 minutes.

Add curry powder and when well mixed with onion add cut up apple and cook until tender. Add stock and all other ingredients except meat and cook gently for 20 minutes.

Add the fresh cut up meat and cook for 1½ hours.

Serves 3–4.

2 onions
2 oz butter (50 g)
1 tablespoon oil (15 ml)
2 level tablespoons curry powder (30 ml)
2 cooking apples
1 pint stock (600 ml)
2 tablespoons chutney (60 ml)
Juice of 1 lemon
1 oz sultanas (25 g)
1 teaspoon salt (5 ml)
1 bay leaf
1 lb lamb (500 g)

Side Dishes
4–6 oz cooked rice (100–150 g)
Mango chutney
Coconut
Lemon wedges
Sliced banana
Sliced tomato

Durham

Grilled Lamb Cutlets with Mint Butter

Pound the mint in a mortar, add the butter and pound to a smooth ointment; season with salt (very little if salt butter is being used), ground black pepper, a squeeze of lemon juice. This quantity will make enough for eight cutlets.

2 large tablespoons fresh mint leaves (100 ml)
2 oz butter (50 g)
Salt
Ground black pepper
A squeeze of lemon juice

To Grill the Cutlets
Score the meat lightly on both sides and coat it with the butter. Leave for an hour.

Grill the cutlets, first on each side close to the grill, then turn them over twice again, cooking farther away from the flame. They will take about 10 minutes altogether.

At the same time, if there is room, grill some half tomatoes and serve with some of the butter poured over them.

Berkshire

Mock Bacon Roll

Skin and bone breast, trim rashers and lay neatly on, putting lean part of rasher to fat of lamb. Roll and tie securely. Cook slowly in a little salted water until tender. Leave to cool before

1 unchopped breast of lamb
2 or 3 rashers bacon, bacon pieces or end of ham

taking it from the saucepan, cut into rings, arrange it suitably on dish, dressing it attractively with snippets of salad for table. (Economical with decided flavour of bacon.)

Serves 4.

Note for Beginners

Tie the roll at about 1 inch (2½ cm) intervals using a fine white string. Cooking time for an average breast will be about 1½ hours.

Do not allow it to cool completely before taking it from the pan, about half an hour is long enough. It is dangerous to leave meat in a warm stock. When the roll is completely cold, store it in cold larder or refrigerator.

Oxfordshire

Squab Pie

Ingredients according to size of pie:
Mutton chops, all fat removed, bones boiled separately for stock
Apples, chopped fine
Onions, chopped fine
Currants
Sugar (brown, sprinkled thinly)
Spice, very little
Salt
Stock
Pastry

As taught by the Phoenicians when they mined tin in Cornwall.

Pie-dish, brown earthenware preferred.

Put layers of mutton, about 3 inches square (8 cm), over bottom of pie-dish. Put layer of apple 1 inch thick (2½ cm), sprinkle sugar. Put layer of onions ½ inch (1 cm), only one layer, salt. Put layer currants, ½ inch (1 cm), sprinkle spice or layer of apples. Then put layer of mutton as at first. Finish with layer of apples. Pour on small quantity of stock. Boil uncovered (except a dish on top) 1½ hours on slow fire.

Make light, thin pastry, put on and bake 1 hour in oven.

Note for Beginners

Cook the filling in advance and allow it to become cold before covering with pastry. It may be cooked in a slow oven as for a casserole, covering the top with another pie-dish or a loose lid of foil. Before covering with pastry, make sure the filling is piled up enough to support the pastry; or use a pie funnel. Bake at 425°F (220°C) Gas 7.

Cornwall

Bacon, Ham, Pork

Bacon and Pineapple

Simmer the gammon in water for $\frac{3}{4}$ hour. Lift and remove skin. Lay in a shallow baking dish and sprinkle with the sugar and lay pineapple (rings or bars), 1 or 2 per person on top. Brown lightly under grill.

Cover with foil and place in oven, 275°F (140°C) Gas 1, for about $\frac{3}{4}$ hour.

Gammon or similar rasher cut 1 inch ($2\frac{1}{2}$ cm) thick
1 tablespoon Demerara sugar (15 ml)
Pineapple rings or bars

Devon

Baked Forehock with Apple Rings

Soak forehock 3–4 hours and rinse well. Simmer for $1\frac{1}{2}$ hours. Allow to cool a little, but remove skin while still hot. Place in baking tin. Heat syrup, butter and stock till blended and pour over bacon. Bake in a moderate oven 1 hour, basting often until the fat is golden brown. Core, but don't peel, apples, and cut into slices $\frac{1}{4}$ inch (6 mm) thick. Place on top of bacon, brush over with syrup from tin and sprinkle with brown sugar. Return to oven 10–15 minutes until apples are soft and lightly browned.

Garnish with Duchesse potatoes and serve with peas and green salad.

1 whole and boned forehock
4 tablespoons golden syrup (60 ml)
1 oz butter (25 g)
2 tablespoons bacon stock (30 ml)
3 medium sized apples
1 tablespoon brown sugar (30 ml)

Note for Beginners

A forehock of bacon weighs about 4 lb (2 kg) before boning. A gammon hock is about the same size but is more expensive. A suitable temperature for the baking would be 350°F (180°C) Gas 4.

Isle of Ely

Ham and Pineapple

Slightly grill the ham, then place slice of pineapple on each slice of ham. Place in shallow fireproof dish and pour in the cider. Cover with lid or foil and cook in slow to moderate oven, 350°F (180°C) Gas 4, for $\frac{3}{4}$ hour.

4 thick slices raw ham
4 slices pineapple
About $\frac{1}{4}$ pint cider (150 ml)

Denbighshire

Somerset Dinner

A piece of streaky bacon or ham
Cabbage or sprouting or broad beans
Dry boiled potatoes

Take a piece of streaky bacon or ham, place in cold water, bring steadily to the boil, gently simmer until cooked, then take out on dish.

Then cook any cabbage or sprouting in the water the meat has been cooked in—also broad beans are nice cooked in the same way.

Serve with dry boiled potatoes.

This should take about 2 hours according to size of bacon or ham.

Somerset

Stuffed Bacon

3 back rashers of bacon
4 oz sausage meat (100 g)

Divide the sausage meat into three and spread rasher with it to within 1 inch (2½ cm) of the end. Roll up and put the rolls in a baking tin. Bake in moderate oven for 20 minutes.

Note for Beginners

These are very good indeed but I prefer them cooked for longer than 20 minutes; for my taste 30 minutes at 400°F (200°C) Gas 6 was about right, cooking them until the fatty ends look crisp.

Allow one or two per person.

Yorkshire

Various Methods of Cooking Hams and Boiling Joints

In Casserole

Place washed and soaked joint into casserole. Add a bay leaf, some black peppercorns, and 6 berries of allspice, and 3 cloves. Pour water on to about two-thirds depth of joint. Cover closely and cook in fairly hot oven, 375°F (190°C) Gas 5, about 30 minutes per pound (½ kg).

To Bake in Foil

Soak gammon or ham for 24 hours, changing water two or three times. Drain well and scrape to remove any 'bloom'. Have ready a sheet of foil large enough to envelope joint completely. Put joint on to foil and add 6 berries of allspice, 4 cloves, 6 peppercorns and 2 bay leaves. Wrap up neatly, making a double fold at top, and turning ends up to retain juices. Cook in moderate oven, 375°F (190°C) Gas 5. Cooking times: 20 minutes per pound (½ kg) for large joints: 20 minutes per pound (½ kg) plus 20 minutes for smaller joints.

Place wrapped joint in meat tin and put in centre of oven. When cooked remove foil, skin joint and cover with brown crumbs.

Note: The liquor from the joint should be strained into a basin. Use the fat for frying and add the jelly underneath to the water for cooking greens. This is especially delicious with sprouts.

To Glaze a Boiled Joint
After removing skin, score fat with a sharp knife.

Make a syrup from 2 tablespoons (30 ml) golden syrup, 4 tablespoons (60 ml) brown sugar, 2 tablespoons (60 ml) flour.

Brush over well, stick a clove at each line. Bake in moderate oven, 375°F (190°C) Gas 5, for 30–40 minutes.

To Cook with Black Treacle and Beer
Wash ham well. Rub with treacle. Soak overnight. Drain and rub again with treacle. Place in water in pan. Add beer and vegetables. Simmer about 20 minutes to the pound ($\frac{1}{2}$ kg) plus 20 minutes.

One ham or piece of bacon
1 lb black treacle (450 g)
1 small bottle dark beer
8 oz carrots (225 g)
8 oz onions (225 g)

To Cook with Pineapple
Put bacon—shoulder is very good—into pan, and bring to boil. Drain. Put into casserole. Pour over $\frac{1}{4}$ tin pineapple juice (125 ml). Cover closely and cook in slow oven, about 250°F (120°C) Gas $\frac{1}{2}$, for 3 hours. May need basting.

Hampshire

Casserole

Cheap and Tasty

Peel and slice apple and onion and place in bottom of casserole. Put meat on top. Dissolve stock cube in hot water and pour in casserole. Season and bake at 350°F (180°C) Gas 4 for 2 hours.
Serves 4–6.

1 apple
1 onion
1½–2 lb belly of pork ($\frac{3}{4}$–1 kg)
1 beef stock cube
$\frac{1}{4}$ pint hot water (150 ml)
Salt and pepper

Durham

Cheese and Pork Casserole

Season the pork and fry until well-browned on both sides. Grate a little bed of cheese into the bottom of a tin into which the pork will fit. Lay the pork on this, then the onion and apple finely chopped. Season with a little salt and pepper. Cover with a thick layer of cheese.

Cover with foil and cook in a moderate oven for 40–45 minutes, 375–400°F (190–200°C) Gas 5 or 6.

Remove the foil and cook for a further 10 minutes.

1 pork chop or a slice of shoulder pork
 per person
Salt and pepper
Fat or oil for frying
1 oz cheese per piece of pork (25 g)
1 small onion per slice of pork
1 large cooking apple

Derbyshire

33

Continental Pork Casserole

1½ lb spare rib of pork (700 g)
1 oz seasoned flour (25 g)
2 tablespoons cooking oil (30 ml)
½ oz butter (15 g)
2 medium onions, thinly sliced
1 green pepper
10 oz tin consommé soup (284 g)
½ pint chicken stock (250 ml)
1 level tablespoon chopped parsley
    (15 ml)
1 red skinned apple

Derbyshire

Cut the meat from the bone and remove any fat before cutting the meat into 1 inch (2½ cm) pieces. Toss the pork in seasoned flour until it is well coated.

Heat the oil and butter in a pan, and fry the meat until it is light golden brown. Add the sliced onions and continue frying for a further 2–3 minutes.

Meanwhile cut the pepper in half, remove the core and seeds and cut the flesh into strips. Add the pepper strips, consommé, parsley and stock to the pork and, stirring all the time, bring them back to the boil for 2 minutes. Transfer the ingredients to a 3 pint (1½ l) casserole and cook it covered for about 1½ hours at 325°F (160°C) Gas 3. Ten minutes before the cooking time is completed, quarter and core the apple, cut in small pieces and stir into the casserole.

Serves 4–6.

Pork Chops in Savoury Sauce

Using 4 pork chops or cutlets
Savoury Sauce made with:
1 oz butter or margarine (25 g)
1 oz flour (25 g)
2 tablespoons concentrated tomato
    purée (30 ml)
¾ pint water (400 ml)
2 tablespoons chopped gherkins (60 ml)
2 tablespoons cocktail onions (60 ml)
1 tablespoon chopped capers (30 ml)
Salt and pepper
1 tablespoon French mustard (15 ml)
1 teaspoon tarragon vinegar (5 ml)
A few onions or gherkins to garnish

Trim the fat off the chops and plunge them into boiling salted water for 5 minutes. Remove and drain.

Prepare the sauce. Melt butter in a fairly large pan. Draw aside and add the flour. Mix well, cook slightly, then add the tomato purée together with the water. Add all other ingredients with the exception of the mustard and vinegar. Bring slowly to simmering point. Put the chops or cutlets into the pan and cover with greaseproof paper and the lid. Cook over gentle heat or in the oven for 20–25 minutes.

Just before serving, stir in the French mustard and vinegar. Arrange the chops slightly overlapping in a serving dish and garnish with a few onions or gherkins. Serve very hot.

Note for Beginners

The cooking time given above is for small cutlets or thin chops, larger and thicker ones will need 45 minutes cooking or even longer. The pork will come to no harm while cooking gently in the sauce and it is better to overcook than undercook.

Berkshire

Pork Crisps

Bone the pork and cut it into fairly thin slices with a sharp knife.
Beat the egg and put on a plate.
Mix together the breadcrumbs, lemon rind, salt and mustard.
Dip the pork slices into the egg then coat with the bread-crumb mixture. Put the slices into a roasting tin, and bake in the oven at 400°F (200°C) Gas 6 for the first 15 minutes, then reduce to 350°F (180°C) Gas 4 for approximately 45 minutes until crisp.
Serves 3–4.

1 lb belly of pork (500 g)
1 large egg
4 oz browned breadcrumbs (100 g)
Grated rind of 1 lemon
Salt
1 level tablespoon dry mustard (15 ml)

Derbyshire

Pork Ribs—Chinese Style

Heat all sauce ingredients in saucepan. Put joint into casserole, pour sauce over. Cover with lid and bake in slow oven, 300°F (150°C) Gas 2, for 3 hours. Serve with rice.
The sauce is enough for 4–6 portions.

Pork ribs (according to number of people)

Sauce
1 dessertspoon honey (10 ml)
4 tablespoons vinegar (60 ml)
1 medium chopped onion
2 tablespoons Worcester sauce (30 ml)
1 teaspoon salt (5 ml)
1 teaspoon dry mustard (5 ml)
1 teaspoon paprika pepper (5 ml)

Isle of Ely

Pork that Really Crackles

Score pork finely, rub in 3 parts salt to 1 part pepper and slow roast at 350°F (180°C) Gas 4, allowing 25 minutes per pound ($\frac{1}{2}$ kg).
Step up heat to 425°F (220°C) Gas 7. Baste well; roast for 15 minutes. Baste again and roast for a further 15 minutes.

Cambridgeshire

Traditional Brawn

Ask your butcher to salt the half head and trotters for you. Soak for 2 hours or so, according to degree of saltiness liked. Put into large pan with the spices and fresh cold water to cover. Bring up to boil, and then simmer until all meat will fall off bones, about 4 hours. Cool until able to handle.
Remove meat from bones, and cut into pieces, but do not mince. Wet a deep pie-dish or other suitable dish. Ornament bottom and sides with slices of hard boiled egg. Put in meat pieces.

$\frac{1}{2}$ pig's head
2 pig's trotters
Spices – bay leaf (or 2 small ones), peppercorns, whole allspice, a few cloves
Hard boiled eggs

Boil liquor again to reduce by a third or half. Skim and strain sufficient of the liquor from pan. Cover meat with this. Leave overnight. Turn out to serve.

Note: Some butchers salt meat more than others. If in doubt, do not add spices at first, but simmer for 30 minutes and then throw that water away and re-boil, adding spices. Continue to cook as above. Extra trotters improve stiffness of jelly and are usually easily obtained.

Variations
1   Add onion and root vegetables instead of spices, and serve top of head separately with these while hot.
2   Some recipes add ½ lb (250 g) shin of beef, or other stewing beef.

Hampshire

Veal

Goulash

An Austrian Recipe

5 medium-sized onions
6 oz butter (150 g)
4 teaspoons paprika (20–40 ml)
2 lb pie veal or stewing steak (1 kg)
Seasoning
A little stock

Fry the finely chopped onions in the butter to a golden brown—add the paprika—stir well. Put in the meat cut in cubes and seasoned. Let it stew a little, then add the stock a little at a time until the meat is tender. This should only be simmered and therefore takes several hours (about 3). The sauce by then should be nice and thick.

Pie veal is by far and away the best meat to use for this, although one can use stewing steak.

Serves 4.

Berkshire

Veau Chasseur

1–1½ lb stewing veal (500–750 g)
Seasoned flour
1½–2 oz butter (40–50 g)
1 tablespoon oil (15 ml)
1 small onion
1 teaspoon flour (10 ml)
1 teaspoon tomato purée (concentrated)
   (10 ml)
1 gill white wine or dry cider (150 ml)
½ pint stock (300 ml)

Chop the meat into convenient sized pieces, discarding fat and gristle. Dip each piece into seasoned flour. Put 1½ oz butter (40 g) and the oil into a thick sauté pan. When it is hot, add the veal and turn quickly until it is brown on all sides. Remove from the pan—add a little more butter if needed. Then brown the finely chopped onion.

Stir in the flour and tomato purée. Mix well—add the wine and stock, together with the bouquet garni, seasoning and crushed clove of garlic. Bring it to simmering point.

Return the veal to the pan. Cover with greaseproof paper and the lid. Place on a very low heat or in a moderate oven, 375°F (190°C) Gas 5, for 1 hour. At the end of that time, add the mushrooms cut in slices. Cook for a further 10 minutes. Serve in a hot dish. Sprinkle lightly with finely chopped parsley. Arrange fried croûtons round the sides and serve at once.

Serves 3–4.

Bouquet garni
Salt and pepper
1 clove garlic
4 oz mushrooms (100 g)

To finish
Fried croûtons
Finely chopped parsley

Berkshire

Veal Escalopes with Cucumber Sauce

Have veal beaten thinly, dip in seasoned flour. Heat all but ½ oz (15 g) of butter in frying pan, add meat and fry for about 8 minutes, browning both sides. Remove and keep hot.

Add peeled and chopped cucumber (deseeded) to hot butter with seasoning. Fry gently until tender. Stir in cream and one rounded teaspoonful of seasoned flour creamed with remaining butter. Stir over low heat until sauce thickens. Replace veal in sauce and allow to heat through. Check seasoning, sprinkle chopped parsley. A delicious special occasion dish.

Serves 4.

4 veal escalopes
Salt and black pepper
2 oz butter (50 g)
1 small cucumber
¼ pint single cream (150 ml)
1 rounded teaspoon seasoned flour
    (10 ml)
Chopped parsley

Cambridgeshire

Various

Bobotee

This is a variation of the Indian curry dish.

Soak the bread in half the milk. Fry the onion gently in butter or margarine till cooked, stir in the curry powder, sugar, salt and pepper. Mix meat and bread together and add to onion. Put in a greased pie-dish and pour over the beaten egg with remainder of milk. Lastly add lemon juice. Bake in a moderate oven, 375°F (190°C) Gas 5, about 20 minutes. Serve with boiled rice.

1 slice white bread (25 g)
1 teacup milk (170 ml)
1 small onion, chopped
1 oz butter or margarine (25 g)
1 teaspoon curry powder (10 ml)
1 teaspoon sugar (10 ml)
Salt and pepper
8 oz cold meat, minced (225 g)
1 egg
1 dessertspoon lemon juice or vinegar
    (10 ml)

Westmorland

Curry with Cold Meat

2 oz butter or dripping (50 g)
1 chopped onion
½ oz flour (15 g)
½ oz curry powder (15 g)
1 apple or peeled tomato
½ pint stock (250 ml)
Salt to taste
8 oz cooked meat (200 g)
⅛ pint cream or top milk (75 ml)
1 oz chutney (25 g)
1 teaspoon lemon juice (5 ml)

Melt butter or dripping from the cooked meat. When smoking hot add onion and flour mixed with the curry powder. Cook slowly for a minute or two, stirring constantly.

Peel and chop apple or tomato, add to pan with stock, and salt to taste. Stir till sauce comes to the boil, lower heat and cover. Simmer gently for 30 minutes, stirring occasionally. Cool.

Add meat. Stand for 30 minutes, then reheat. Stir in cream and chutney. When almost boiling, add lemon juice. Arrange on hot dish. Serve with boiled rice.

Serves 3–4.

Note for Beginners

Start making the sauce well in advance so that it can be cooled before the meat is added. When re-heating the curry it is wise to boil it for a few minutes before serving. If the meat is cut in fairly small cubes this will ensure that it heats through quickly and thoroughly.

Cumberland

Liver Casserole

8 oz lamb's liver (250 g)
3 rashers bacon
3 medium onions
2 carrots
Flour
2 oz butter (50 g)
Water
Salt and pepper
2 lamb's kidneys (optional)

Chop liver, bacon, onions and carrots and roll all in flour. Fry lightly in butter. Add water to cover and bring to boil, add seasoning. Turn into casserole and cook slowly for 1½ hours, 350°F (180°C) Gas 4.

Two lamb's kidneys may be added to liver for extra richness.
Serves 4.

Pembrokeshire

Oxtail Shape

1 oxtail
1 small onion
4 cloves
Salt and pepper
2 hard boiled eggs

Wash and joint the oxtail, put in pan or stew jar with the onion stuck with cloves and cover with water. Simmer gently for 3 hours. Remove the onion, take all the meat from the bones and cut into pieces. Strain the liquor and return meat and liquor to pan. Season with salt and pepper and bring to the boil. Halve the two hard boiled eggs and place them cut sides to bottom of a mould. Put in meat mixture and leave overnight to set.

Yorkshire

38

Savoury Sausage Casserole

Peel and chop the onion and mix it with the sausage meat and herbs, and plenty of salt and pepper. Divide the mixture into 16 pieces, roll each piece into a ball and toss them in the seasoned flour.

Melt the lard in a frying pan, add the meat balls and fry them quickly to brown all over. Transfer them to a plate.

Stir the curry powder and the rest of the flour into the fat in the pan and cook for a few seconds, then remove the pan from the heat and gradually stir in the stock. Return the pan to the heat and stirring all the time bring the sauce to the boil for 2 minutes to thicken.

Peel the carrots and cut them into small sticks and wipe and roughly chop the mushrooms; stir them both into the sauce with the meat balls.

Cover the pan with a lid or a piece of kitchen foil and simmer the casserole on a low heat for about $\frac{1}{2}$ hour until the meat balls are cooked. Serve the casserole with rice.

Serves 4.

1 large onion (175 g)
1 lb pork sausage meat (500 g)
Pinch of mixed herbs
Salt and pepper
1 level tablespoon plain flour seasoned with salt and pepper (15 ml)
1 oz lard (25 g)
1 level dessertspoon curry powder (10 ml)
$\frac{3}{4}$ pint stock (400 ml)
4 oz carrots (100 g)
4 oz mushrooms (100 g)
Rice

Derbyshire

Stewed Tripe and Onions

Wash the tripe in cold water, drain and cut into small pieces. Peel and slice the onions. Put tripe and onions into a pan, cover with the milk. Simmer for 1 hour. Strain the tripe into a hot dish, keeping the milk. Rinse out the pan and melt the butter in the pan, stir in the flour, keep stirring until it turns yellow. Add the milk and stir until it boils. Boil gently for 5 minutes, adding salt and pepper to taste. Add the tripe and reheat. Serve sprinkled with chopped parsley.

Serves 4.

1 lb dressed tripe (500 g)
4 onions
1 pint milk (600 ml)
1 oz butter (25 g)
1 oz flour (25 g)
Salt and pepper
Chopped parsley

Yorkshire

39

POULTRY & GAME
5

Poultry

How to Joint a Chicken

1 Place chicken on chopping board and with sharp knife cut through and along length of breastbone. Use poultry scissors if preferred.
2 Open bird out, then cut through along length of backbone. If liked, backbone can be removed entirely by cutting along close to either side. Tap back of knife sharply with heavy weight to cut through bony sections. Bird is now in two halves.
3 Lay halves of chicken skin side up on board and divide each in half again by cutting diagonally across between wing and thigh. Bird is now in four quarters, two wing and breast joints, two thigh and drumstick joints. Joints are neater if leg shanks and wing tips are removed.
4 To make six joints divide each thigh and drumstick portion in half by cutting through at ball and socket joint.

Surrey

Chicken and Ham Pancakes

Sieve together salt and flour. Add egg then gradually add half the milk, beating well into a smooth batter. Stir in remaining milk and oil.

Put a little oil into the frying pan and heat. Pour off surplus oil. Pour about 2 tablespoons batter into frying pan and tilt so that the batter covers the base thinly. Cook until underside is golden. Toss or turn pancake and fry other side. Turn out of pan and keep hot. Repeat with remaining batter to give 8 pancakes.

Filling
Melt butter in pan, add flour and cook for a minute. Remove from heat and gradually stir in milk. Return to heat and bring to boil, stir until it thickens. Add chopped ham and chicken and season well. Divide filling between pancakes and roll up. Serve garnished with grilled tomato slices and parsley sprigs.

Serves 4.

4 oz plain flour (100 g)
Pinch of salt
1 egg
½ pint milk (250 ml)
1 tablespoon oil (15 ml)
Oil for frying

Filling
1½ oz butter (40 g)
1½ oz flour (40 g)
¾ pint milk (400 ml)
6 oz cooked ham (175 g)
6 oz cooked chicken (175 g)
Salt and pepper
Tomato slices
Parsley sprigs

Yorkshire

Chicken and Ham Roll

Mince chicken and ham together. Add chopped pineapple and cream cheese and blend well together. Season to taste.

Roll out pastry in oblong approximately 6 × 12 inches (15 × 30 cm). Place mixture on pastry in a sausage shape, roll up and seal edges. Brush top with beaten egg and slash about 1 inch (2½ cm) apart.

Bake at 450°F (230°C) Gas 8 for 20–25 minutes. Can be served either hot or cold. Very good for picnics or buffet snacks.
Serves 4.

4 oz cooked chicken (100 g)
2 oz cooked ham (50 g)
3 oz chopped pineapple chunks (75 g)
3 oz cream cheese (75 g)
Salt and pepper
4 oz puff pastry (125 g)
Little beaten egg for glazing

Cumberland

Chicken in Brandy

A Luxury Dish

Season chicken with salt and pepper. Cook in the butter in a heavy pan, over moderate heat for 30 minutes, until brown and tender. Add the sliced mushrooms and cook for another 5 minutes. Pour in the warmed brandy and set alight. Remove the chicken and mushrooms, and keep hot. Blend flour in the pan, stirring in the tomato sauce, cream, and seasoning, if necessary. Simmer for 10 minutes and pour over the chicken.

Allow approximately 1 hour total cooking time.
Serves 4.

1 young chicken, jointed
Salt and pepper
4 oz butter (100 g)
8 oz sliced mushrooms (200 g)
1 tablespoon brandy (20 ml or more)
1 tablespoon flour (15 ml)
1½ teaspoons tomato sauce (15 ml)
¾ pint cream (400 ml)

Northumberland

Chicken Pilaf

3 tablespoons butter (40 g)
2 cups hot cooked rice (250 g)
½ cup fresh or canned tomatoes (75 g), cut up
½ cup diced cooked chicken (75 g)
Veal or chicken stock, highly seasoned
Salt and cayenne

Melt butter in omelet pan and add rice. Cook 3 minutes. Add tomatoes, chicken and enough stock to moisten. Cook 5 minutes and season lightly with salt and cayenne. Add more butter if desired.

Serves 3–4.

Note for Beginners

About 1 cup (125 g) of raw rice will give 2 cups when boiled.

Herbs can be used for flavouring the stock, for example, bay leaf, rosemary or tarragon or add fresh chopped herbs to the cooked dish.

It is also very good made with other left-over poultry and the appropriate stock.

Cheshire

Chicken Roasted in Wine with Oranges

A Simple Dish with the Luxury Flavour

1 chicken
2 oranges
Honey
¼ pint white wine (150 ml)

Stuff the chicken with one whole orange. Cut the other orange and rub over the skin of the chicken. Spread a little honey over the chicken and roast. Fifteen minutes before end of cooking time pour the wine over the bird.

The oranges give the chicken an unusual flavour, and the honey gives a sweet and crisp flavour to the skin.

Surrey

Chicken with Almonds

1 oz blanched and toasted almonds (25 g)
1 small chopped onion
2 oz sliced mushrooms and stalks (50 g)
1 oz butter (25 g)
1 level dessertspoon cornflour (10 ml)
¼ pint milk (150 ml)
½–¾ lb cooked chicken (200–300 g)
¼ level teaspoon ground ginger (1 ml)
¼ level teaspoon grated nutmeg (1 ml)
5 oz carton natural yogurt (140 ml)
2 egg yolks
Salt and pepper

Cut almonds into strips.

Fry onions and mushrooms in butter in a saucepan until pale gold. Add cornflour. Cook 1 minute. Gradually blend in milk. Cook, stirring until sauce comes to the boil. Add chicken (in bite sized pieces), ginger and grated nutmeg. Heat gently 5–7 minutes.

Beat yogurt and egg yolks well together. Add to chicken mixture. Cook very slowly, without boiling, until thickened. Season to taste. Pour into warmed serving dish. Scatter almonds over the top.

Serves 4.

Cumberland

Cock-a-Leekie

Wash the leeks and cut into pieces 1 inch (2½ cm) long. Put into pot with trussed fowl and stock; add seasoning. Simmer gently for 4 hours. Skim occasionally; half an hour before serving, add prunes.

When ready to serve, take out fowl and cut into pieces. Place in a tureen and pour the broth over it.

3 large leeks
1 fowl
Stock
Seasoning
8 prunes

Berkshire

Crunchy Crisp Baked Chicken

Pre-heat oven to 350°F (180°C) Gas 4.

Mix flour, salt and curry powder. Crush the potato crisps with a rolling pin. Coat the chicken joints with the seasoned flour. Dip the joints in the milk, and coat thickly and evenly with potato crisp crumbs. Arrange skin side up on a baking sheet. Bake for 40–45 minutes.

Serve hot or cold with green salad and sauté or fried potatoes. Serves 4.

This tasty crisp chicken is excellent cold for picnics.

2 rounded tablespoons flour (60 ml)
1 rounded teaspoon salt (10 ml)
¼ rounded teaspoon curry powder (2½ ml)
2 packets potato crisps (50–60 g)
4 chicken quarters
A little creamy milk

Surrey

English Farmhouse Chicken

Fry the shredded bacon lightly. Lift it out and keep it hot. Add the margarine or chicken fat to the frying pan—fry the jointed chicken until lightly browned and keep it hot.

Half stew the shredded vegetables in the fat with the seasoning and a little sugar. Mix in the bacon and turn all into a casserole dish. Lay the chicken on top. Cover the dish and complete the cooking in the oven at 350°F (180°C) Gas 4, for about an hour. Just before serving sprinkle on the chicken stock.

Allow about 1½ hours total cooking time.

2 bacon rashers
1–2 oz margarine (25–50 g) or chicken fat
A jointed chicken—to serve 4–6 people
3 oz shredded carrot (75 g)
3 oz shredded turnip (75 g)
2 oz celery heart (50 g), sliced
½ onion, sliced
Salt, pepper and a little sugar
4 or 5 tablespoons hot chicken stock (60–75 ml)

Berkshire

Fried Chicken with White Wine Sauce

4 chicken joints
2 oz butter (50 g)
1 oz chopped onion or shallot (25 g)
⅛ pint cheap white wine (75 ml)
½ pint stock (300 ml) (can be made with
  chicken cube)
Tomato with skin and pips removed
Salt and pepper
Chopped parsley
4 oz button mushrooms (100 g)
Fat for frying

Isle of Ely

Wash, dry and season chicken.

Melt butter in pan, add chicken and fry lightly. Cover pan with a lid, lower heat and fry very gently until chicken is cooked (about 40–45 minutes).

Remove chicken from pan, place on serving dish and keep warm. Put shallots or onions in pan. Cover with lid and fry gently until cooked (about 5 minutes).

Drain off surplus fat, add white wine and boil rapidly for 1 minute. Add stock and tomato, simmer for 5–10 minutes.

Correct seasoning and pour over chicken. Sprinkle with chopped parsley and garnish with lightly fried mushrooms.

Hindle Wakes Fowl

1 old boiling fowl
1 lemon
Cider and water mixed

Berkshire

Rub the outside of the fowl with a cut lemon. Put the lemon inside the bird, place in a casserole, half cover with a mixture of cider and water. Put on lid and simmer very slowly for at least 8 hours in a cool oven, 200°F (100°C) Gas LOW.

How to Take Years Off an Old Hen

Leicestershire and Rutland

Put a trussed old hen into a small pan full of cold water with a teacupful of vinegar (150 ml). The pan should be sufficiently deep to enable the cold water and vinegar to cover the hen. Soak overnight.

The next day wash the hen under the cold tap to remove all trace of vinegar, and dry thoroughly.

Roast in the ordinary way. The vinegar makes the flesh white and tender, and it will taste like a roast chicken.

Poulet Sauté Normand

1 small chicken, jointed
2 tablespoons corn oil (30 ml)
1 cup apple juice (200 ml)
2 cups water (400 ml)
2 dessertspoons cream (20 ml)
Salt and pepper
Stuffed olives

Durham

Fry chicken joints in oil until golden brown—about 10 minutes. Add apple juice and water and cook for ½ hour. Remove chicken, add cream and seasoning to liquid. Pour over chicken and decorate with stuffed olives. Serves 4.

Note for Beginners

Should there be rather too much liquid left when the chicken is cooked, after removing it, boil the liquid rapidly to reduce it before adding seasoning and cream. If you cook the chicken in a pan with a lid, add only half the amount of water.

Roast Chicken and Accompaniments

Cooking time: 18–20 minutes per lb (450 g), plus 20 minutes. Prepare the bird and stuff with sausage forcemeat or a simple herb forcemeat. Lay one or two fat rashers bacon over breast and place the bird on a trivet in a roasting tin containing some dripping. Cook in a hot oven 1½–2 hours, 450°F (230°C) Gas 8, for 15–20 minutes then reduce the heat to 375°F (190°C) Gas 5. Remove the bacon 15 minutes before cooking is completed to allow the breast to brown.

The breast may be frothed (i.e. dredged with flour and basted) when the bacon has been taken off.

Sausage Forcemeat
Melt the dripping, chop the onion finely and mix with the sausage meat. Lightly sauté the sausage meat and onion in the dripping for a few minutes to give a good flavour, mix in the other ingredients and use as required.

Bread Sauce
Peel the onion and stick the cloves into it, place in a saucepan with the milk, salt and peppercorns, bring almost to boiling point and leave in a warm place for about 20 minutes in order to extract the flavour from the onion. Remove the peppercorns and add the butter and breadcrumbs. Mix well and allow to infuse for about 15 minutes, then remove the onion.

If preferred the onion may be removed before adding the breadcrumbs, but a better flavour is obtained by allowing the flavour of the onion to penetrate the breadcrumbs by infusing them together.

4 lb chicken (2 kg)

Sausage Forcemeat
1 oz dripping (25 g)
1 large onion
1 lb pork sausage meat (450 g)
4 tablespoons breadcrumbs (125 ml)
½ teaspoon mixed herbs (5 ml)
1 teaspoon chopped parsley (10 ml)
Seasoning

Bread Sauce
1 medium sized onion
2 cloves
¾ pint milk (425 ml)
Salt
A few peppercorns
¾ oz butter (20 g)
3 oz breadcrumbs (75 g)

Accompaniments
Chipolatas
Bacon rolls
Roast potatoes
Gravy

Surrey

Spring Chicken with Mushrooms

Cut chicken into joints and fry in butter until brown. Season and add chopped onion, mushrooms and ham. Cover with milk and simmer slowly for 25 minutes. Remove chicken and thicken milk with a little cornflour and serve poured over the chicken.

Serves 4.

1 small chicken
1 oz butter (25 g)
Seasoning
1 small onion
2 oz mushrooms (50 g)
2 oz chopped ham (50 g)
Milk to cover
Little cornflour

Yorkshire

To Use Up Cooked Chicken Legs

Make cuts in the legs, marinate in the liquid for at least 1 hour, spooning it into the cuts. Grill and pour any liquid that remains over before serving.

Mix together:
2 tablespoons Worcester sauce (30 ml)
1 tablespoon vinegar (15 ml)
2 tablespoons melted butter (30 ml)
2 teaspoons dry mustard (20 ml)

Berkshire

Devil Mixture for Legs of Poultry, etc.

Equal quantities of:
Dry mustard
Chutney
Anchovy sauce

Twice as much:
Salad oil
   and
A pinch of cayenne

Berkshire

Mix all this together, score legs and insert mixture. It is better prepared early and allowed to soak into the meat. Grill until brown and heated through.

Braised Duck

1 duck
1 large onion
2 medium carrots
2 oz mushrooms (50 g)
1 rasher bacon, roughly chopped
2 oz butter (50 g)
1 orange
Bouquet garni
Seasoning
Stock
1 gill red wine (150 ml)
Flour
Croûtons of bread
Parsley
Orange rings

Joint the duck. Prepare vegetables and cut up roughly. Heat butter in a large pan and lightly brown vegetables and bacon. Add grated orange rind, herbs and seasoning and put in enough stock to barely cover vegetables. Put in duck joints, cover with grease-proof paper and a tightly fitting lid. Cook gently for about 45 minutes.

Remove lid, pour in wine and cook uncovered in oven for about 35 minutes. Arrange joints on a heated serving dish.

Strain liquid and make a gravy allowing a heaped tablespoon of flour (40 g) to 1 pint (500 ml) of liquid. Add orange juice. Strain gravy over duck and garnish with orange rings, croûtons of bread and parsley.

Note for Beginners

To allow plenty of time for dishing up and thickening the gravy begin cooking the braised duck about 2 hours before serving time. After the preliminary frying, cooking can be in the oven at about 350°F (180°C) Gas 4.

To avoid having the dish too fatty, trim some surplus fat from the joints before cooking; or even remove skin and fat entirely.

The quantities in this recipe are enough for a 4 lb (2 kg) duck which will serve 5–6, depending on its condition.

Shropshire

Roast Duckling with Stuffed Apples

Duckling
Sage and onion stuffing
Cooking apples
Sausage meat, well seasoned

Stuff duckling with sage and onion stuffing, cook in hot oven according to size.

Twenty-five minutes before serving add as many cooking apples as required, cored and stuffed with a very well seasoned

46

sausage meat. Serve at table with cooked apples round duck, 400°F (200°C) Gas 6, allowing 15–20 minutes per pound (½ kg).

Pembrokeshire

Roast Turkey

The Traditional Way

Both crop and body can be stuffed, the crop with sage and onion stuffing, the body with pork sausage meat.

When crop is stuffed draw the flap back and skewer or sew in position to hold stuffing neatly. Spread a little seasoned, softened butter over the turkey then place in roasting tin, cover with aluminium foil.

Get the oven really hot before putting in the bird, then set oven at 325°F (160°C) Gas 3. Baste every ½ hour, at the same time turning bird from side to side.

Leave off covering for the last 30 minutes. Serve with giblet gravy, bread sauce, cranberry jelly, roast potatoes, Brussels sprouts.

Note: If the bird is stuffed with sausage meat, weigh the whole bird as extra cooking time is needed.

Guide to Roasting Time

6 to 8 lb (2¾ to 3½ kg)	2½ to 3 hours approx.
9 to 12 lb (4 to 5½ kg)	3½ to 4½ hours approx.
13 to 16 lb (5¾ to 7¼ kg)	4½ to 5 hours approx.
17 to 20 lb (7¾ to 9 kg)	6 to 6½ hours approx.

Surrey

Turkey Salad

Prepare the peppers and shred finely. Mix all the ingredients well together except for the cucumber which is used for decoration. (The sweet corn may be fresh, tinned or frozen.)

Red and green pepper
8 oz cooked Patna rice (200 g)
8 oz cooked diced turkey (200 g)
1 oz walnuts (25 g), chopped
1 oz sultanas (25 g)
Sweet corn
French dressing
Seasoning
Cucumber

Surrey

Game

To Prepare Game for Roasting

Game birds should be hung by the neck in a cool, airy place to develop flavour and to ensure the flesh being tender. To prevent them becoming too 'high', examine occasionally. For most people, the bird is sufficiently mature when tail or breast feathers can be easily plucked.

Pluck and draw the bird as for chicken, but do not draw any sinews and leave on the feet (remove the claws). Wipe inside the bird with a clean damp cloth and insert a piece of rump steak or butter to keep the bird moist. Cut off the wings at the first joint and truss as for roast chicken. Cover the breast with strips of fat bacon in order to prevent the flesh of a game bird drying up and losing flavour.

Cooking
Young birds should be roasted, older birds should be braised or cooked in a casserole. The length of time for cooking will depend on time of hanging and age of bird.

Gloucestershire

Fried or Browned Crumbs to Serve with Game

2 oz breadcrumbs (50 g)
1 oz butter (25 g)

Gloucestershire

Heat the butter without discolouring. Add the breadcrumbs and stir over a moderate heat until brown, being careful to have them all of a uniform shade. Season and use.

Crumbs can also be done in the oven.

Roast Grouse

Season: 12th August to 15th December

Grouse
Salt and pepper
Thin slices fat pork or bacon
½ oz butter per bird (15 g)
⅛ pint stock per bird (75 ml)
Buttered toast
Bread sauce
Red currant jelly

Cumberland

Prepare the grouse, wipe well, season with salt and pepper and wrap in thin slices of fat pork or bacon. Roast in a very hot oven 450°F (230°C) Gas 8, for 10–15 minutes.

Remove the birds and skim off all the fat from the pan juices. Add butter and stock. Reduce this sauce very quickly, stirring and scraping the pan. Place each bird on a piece of buttered toast. Serve with bread sauce and red currant jelly.

48

Roast Guinea Fowl

Season: February to August

Draw and truss the guinea fowl. Cover the breast with fat bacon and place some inside. Roast for ¾–1 hour at 375°F (190°C) Gas 5. Serve with watercress, gravy and salad.

Guinea fowl
Fat bacon
Gravy
Watercress
Orange or pineapple salad

Cumberland

Roast Partridge

Season: 1st September to 1st February

Draw and truss the bird. Cover the breast with bacon. Roast for 30–45 minutes at 425°F (220°C) Gas 7. Serve with gravy, game chips, fried crumbs and green salad.

Partridge
Fat bacon
Butter for basting
Gravy
Game chips
Fried crumbs
Green salad

Cumberland

Pheasant in Madeira

Pluck and draw the pheasant and place in a pan with the bacon, ham, onion, celery, parsley, carrot, butter and seasonings. Cook together slowly until the pheasant begins to brown then add the madeira and stock. Cover and allow the bird to finish cooking for about 45 minutes.

Place the bird on a hot dish, strain the fat from the sauce, sieve it and pour over the bird. Send to the table garnished with the croûtons of fried bread.

Serves 2–4, depending on size of bird.

1 pheasant
4 slices fat bacon (cut small)
2 slices ham (cut small)
¼ onion (cut small)
1 stick celery (chopped fine)
1 teaspoon chopped parsley
1 carrot diced
1 oz butter (25 g)
Pepper, salt, dash of nutmeg
¼ pint madeira (125 ml)
¼ pint stock (125 ml)
Garnish—croûtons of fried bread

Yorkshire

Roast Pheasant (1)

Season: 1st October to 1st February

Sprinkle the pheasant with salt and pepper to taste and rub well with butter. Wrap in a thin sheet of larding pork or fat bacon. Roast in a moderate oven 375°F (190°C) Gas 5, for 40 minutes (approximate).

Remove the fat and arrange bird on a dish garnished with watercress. Arrange pieces of pâté de foie gras over the pheasant on the dish. Serve with the pan juices, partially free from fat and strained. Accompany with boiled rice and a tart jelly.

Pheasant
Salt and pepper
Butter
Larding pork or fat bacon
Watercress
Pâté de foie gras
Boiled rice
Tart jelly

Cumberland

Roast Pheasant (2)

1 pheasant
Slices of fat bacon
Small piece of rump steak or butter
2 oz dripping or butter (50 g) for
   basting
Flour

Put the steak or butter inside the bird and cover it with fat bacon and thickly greased paper. Place in a roasting pan. Cook in a moderate oven 375°F (190°C) Gas 5, for 45–60 minutes according to the age of the bird. Ten minutes before the bird is ready, froth the breast. To do this, remove paper and bacon, and baste the breast with melted dripping or butter, dredge it with flour and baste again. Return to the oven heated up to 425°F (220°C) Gas 7, and leave until it is a good brown colour and frothy.

Decorate the cooked pheasant with tail feathers and serve with accompaniments; gravy, bread sauce, browned crumbs, chip potatoes, French salad or watercress.

Gloucestershire

Casserole of Pigeons with Steak and Mushrooms

2 pigeons
8 oz steak (200 g)
1 rasher bacon, chopped
Butter or margarine
½ pint stock (300 ml)
2 oz mushrooms (50 g)
Salt and pepper
1 tablespoon red currant jelly (30 ml)
1 tablespoon lemon juice (15 ml)
1 tablespoon flour (15 ml)
Milk

Cut pigeons in halves and steak in neat pieces. Fry pigeons, steak and bacon in fat. Place in casserole with stock, mushrooms (sliced) and seasoning. Cover and simmer 2½ hours.

Add jelly, lemon juice and flour blended with a little milk. Simmer for another 15 minutes.

Serves 4.

Durham

Roast Pigeon

Young pigeon
Butter
Gravy
Orange salad
Red currant jelly

Draw and truss the pigeon, cover with buttered paper, baste with butter. Roast for 20–30 minutes at 425°F (220°C) Gas 7. Serve with gravy and other accompaniments.

Cumberland

Roast Plover, Snipe, Quail or Woodcock

Roast for 20–30 minutes at 425°F (220°C) Gas 7, and serve with gravy, fried breadcrumbs and chipped potatoes.

Cheshire

50

Roast Ptarmigan

Roast for ½ hour at 425°F (220°C) Gas 7. Serve with gravy, bread sauce, fried breadcrumbs, chipped potatoes.

Cheshire

Roast Wild Duck

Young

Roast for 40–50 minutes at 375°F (190°C) Gas 5, and serve with gravy, orange salad and chipped potatoes.

Cheshire

Rook Pie

Method for Skinning
Cut the skin down the centre of the breast, draw the skin off the breast in the direction of the wing, pulling it up to the first joint, cut the wing at the joint and discard the end part, then draw the skin from the legs and cut off at the shank joint; cut the legs off at the joint where they join the body, then insert the first finger at the breast cavity with one hand and take hold of the lower portion of the neck with the other hand and pull apart. This leaves the breast in one hand and the remainder of the body in the other hand—the latter being discarded. Wash the breast and legs thoroughly in cold water and rinse several times in cold water. (The definition of a rook for this purpose is a young bird, recently left the nest and just able to fly.)

Method for Cooking
Stew the breasts and the legs gently until tender (a small pro-portion of steak and a tablespoon of beef dripping is an improve-ment). When cool, take the meat from the bones and place in a pie-dish, season well with salt and a shake of cayenne, add a little of the gravy and cover with short crust pastry and bake until brown and attractive in appearance. This can be made with a pastry base and covering if desired and can be eaten hot (or cold with salad).

(Rooks are usually available about the second week in May in the North of England.)

Note for Beginners

Quantities usually recommended are 1 rook per person and 4 oz steak (100 g) for 4 rooks.

Yorkshire

Hare Jugged

1 hare
3 oz butter (75 g)
Salt
1 onion
2 shallots
1 small sprig thyme
Parsley
1 bay leaf
4 cloves
12 peppercorns
Small piece mace
1 tablespoon lemon juice (15 ml)
1½ pints good stock (850 ml)
1 oz flour (25 g)
1 glass port or claret (150 ml)
Forcemeat balls
Red or white currant jelly

Shropshire

Cut hare flesh into pieces size of a small egg—heat 2 oz (50 g) butter, fry pieces of hare brown, put them into stew jar with little salt, onion, shallot (parsley, thyme, bay leaf, cloves, peppercorns and mace should be tied together in muslin), lemon juice and stock (previously made hot). Cover jar closely—cook in moderate oven, 300–325°F (150–160°C) Gas 2–3, or the jar may be stood in saucepan of water on stove. About ½ hour before serving, knead the remaining ounce of butter (25 g) and the flour together, stir into stock, add wine.

Make the forcemeat, shape into balls, fry in hot fat. Pile hare on hot dish with the strained gravy and forcemeat balls around. Serve jelly separately. Allow 3–4 hours for cooking.

Serves 6–8.

Roast Saddle of Young Hare

1 young hare
Savoury stuffing
Slices of fat bacon or larding fat
Dripping
Brown gravy
Red currant jelly

Roast only the body of the hare—the neck, legs and head can be jugged or converted into soup. Put the stuffing into the saddle, fold skin over and secure well at the ends. The flesh of the back may either be larded or have slices of fat bacon laid over. Cover with greased paper and roast with dripping 30–40 minutes in hot oven. Baste frequently.

Serve with brown gravy and red currant jelly.

Serves 3–4.

Note for Beginners

For larding, a special larding needle is used, threaded with thin strips of fat pork. Strips of fat are threaded through the flesh of the hare at close intervals.

Roast the hare at about 400°F (200°C) Gas 6, or at a lower temperature for a longer time.

A suitable stuffing would be Forcemeat (Veal), see page 112.

Cheshire

Hot-pot of Rabbit and Sausages

1 rabbit
Flour
Fat for frying
8 oz sausages (250 g)
2 onions
Pepper and salt

Joint, flour and lightly fry the rabbit, also sausages and onions (cut up). Pack all these in a fireproof casserole. Make a gravy in the frying pan with flour, pepper and salt and stock or cold water, boil up and pour over the meat. Put in a few forcemeat balls. Cover with potatoes and cook in oven for about 2 hours,

350°F (180°C) Gas 4. About 20 minutes before serving take off the lid and brown the potatoes.

Serves 6.

Stock or water, about ¾ pint (400 ml)
A few forcemeat balls
2 lb potatoes (1 kg), cut in pieces

Northamptonshire and
Soke of Peterborough

Stewed Rabbit

Cut the onion in thin slices and fry in a stewpan. Cut up the rabbit, wash well and dry in a cloth. Mix the flour with pepper and salt and dip in the pieces of rabbit. Fry them with the onion until a nice brown colour. Pour off any surplus fat and add the hot stock or water, carrot and bay leaf. Simmer gently for 1½–2 hours. Mix remainder of flour with cold water and add to the stew, stirring well. Arrange the rabbit in hot dish and pour gravy over. Delicious hot or cold.

Serves 4–6.

1 large onion
Dripping
1 rabbit
1½ oz flour (40 g)
Pepper and salt
1½ pint stock or hot water (800 ml)
1 carrot
1 bay leaf

Cheshire

Roast Venison

Season: Buck, June to September; Doe, October
to December

Brush the venison with melted butter and wrap it in greased paper, then in a paste of flour and water. Roast haunch will take 4–5 hours in a slow oven 325°F (160°C) Gas 3.

Venison joint
Melted butter
Flour and water paste
Brown gravy flavoured with red wine
Gooseberry or cranberry sauce
Green salad

Cumberland

Venison Casserole

Brown the meat in the dripping. Remove it and fry the prepared vegetables and bacon with a pinch of sugar. Remove vegetables. Add a tablespoon of flour to the pan, stir it round and add the stock and wine. Let it thicken. Put the venison in the casserole with the vegetables, seasonings and herbs. Pour the liquid over it. Seal closely and cook in a moderate oven, 375°F (190°C) Gas 5, for 2½ hours. Add the red currant jelly just before serving.

Hare, chicken or beef can be cooked like this. It is a good basic casserole.

Serves 6.

2 lb venison haunch (1 kg)
2 oz dripping (50 g)
2 onions
3 carrots
2 oz bacon (50 g)
Pinch of sugar
1 tablespoon flour (15 ml)
1 gill stock (150 ml)
1 gill red wine (150 ml)
Seasoning
Bouquet garni
Rosemary
Allspice (*not* cake spice)
2 tablespoons red currant jelly (60 ml)

Hampshire

53

SUPPER DISHES
6

Appledore

Sausage

2 oz butter (50 g)
2 large sliced onions
1 lb cooking apples, sliced (450 g)
1 large red pepper (from can)
Salt and pepper
1 lb Cumberland sausage (500 g)

Cumberland

Melt butter in pan and fry off onions until tender but not coloured. Add apples and sliced red pepper, cover pan and cook gently until apples are just soft. Season to taste.

At the same time fry off sausage either in oven or pan—rather nice in a whirl. Place sausage in centre of dish with apple sauce around. Cooking time about ¾ hour.

Serves 3–4.

Cumberland Sausage

9 lb lean pork (4½ kg)
3 lb pork fat (1½ kg)
3 oz salt (75 g)
1 oz pepper (25 g)

Cumberland

Cut lean and fat into small pieces. Add seasoning. Mix well. Mince fairly finely and fill into prepared skins. Hang for 24 hours before using.

Bacon and Apple Skewers

*May be Eaten Cold for Picnics or Useful Hot
for Barbecues*

Trim rind from bacon. Mix grated cheese with yolk of egg and
seasoning. Spread on rashers. Roll each rasher round quarter
of an apple. Stick skewer through and grill for approximately
10 minutes.

(If eaten at home serve on a bed of savoury rice.)

For each person take:
2 rashers bacon, back or streaky
Half apple
1–2 oz grated cheese (25–50 g)
Salt and pepper
Egg yolk

Hampshire

Bacon Casserole

Slice potatoes ¼ inch (6 mm) thick. Slice onions. Arrange
alternate layers of potatoes and onion, smeared with chutney
and seasoning. Pour over egg and milk, add dabs of butter.

Make rolls from the bacon and place on top of casserole.
Cover and bake at 350°F (180°C) Gas 4, for 1¼ hours, the last
15 minutes without lid to brown bacon.

Serves 4.

12 oz potatoes (350 g)
1 large onion
2 tablespoons chutney (30–60 ml)
Seasoning
½ egg beaten in ¼ pint milk (150 ml)
½ oz butter (15 g)
8 oz shoulder bacon (225 g) rashers

Cumberland

Broccoli with Bacon Sauce

Cut broccoli into sprigs, wash well and cook in ½ pint (300 ml)
boiling salted water.

Cut chopped bacon with onion and cook gently without
browning, add curry powder, pepper and flour, cook for 2
minutes. Use water from broccoli and make up to ½ pint
(300 ml) with milk, add to sauce, gently stirring till thick.
Pour over broccoli.

Serves 4.

1 medium sized broccoli

Sauce
2 oz bacon, chopped (50 g)
1 tablespoon onion (30 ml), chopped
¼ teaspoon curry powder (2½ ml)
Pepper and salt
2 level tablespoons flour (30 ml)
A little milk

Shropshire

Cheese and Carrot Savoury

Cook carrots till tender, preferably in a steamer or a pressure
cooker. Mash well, add fat, breadcrumbs, cheese and seasoning.
Place in a greased pie-dish and bake at 375°F (190°C) Gas 5, till
golden brown, about 20–30 minutes.

It may be steamed for 1 hour.

Serve with jacket potatoes, gravy and Brussels sprouts.

Serves 4–6.

2 lb carrots (1 kg)
1½ oz fat (40 g)
2 oz brown breadcrumbs (50 g)
8 oz grated cheese (200 g)
Seasoning, mace and nutmeg

Westmorland

Cheese Pancakes

4 oz self-raising flour (100 g)
Salt and pepper to taste
1 egg
½ pint milk (250 ml)
4 oz finely grated cheese (100 g)

Gloucestershire

Mix and fry as ordinary pancakes. Makes 8 pancakes.

Cheese Pinwheels

8 oz plain soft flour (200 g)
Salt
½ teaspoon dry mustard (5 ml)
2 oz lard (50 g)
2 oz margarine (50 g)
4 oz strong cheese (100 g)
½–¾ lb sausage meat (200–300 g)

Derbyshire

Sieve the flour with the salt and mustard. Rub in the lard and margarine until the mixture resembles breadcrumbs. Add the cheese, grated coarsely. Add approximately 8 teaspoons (40 ml) water to bind. Turn out of bowl and knead very lightly. Roll out into an oblong approximately 11 × 8 inches (28 × 20 cm).

Spread the sausage meat over the pastry, leaving about ¾ inch (2 cm) at the top edge. Moisten the edges with water, and roll the pastry up as for a Swiss roll. Firm the roll. Take a sharp knife and cut about 12 slices from the roll, round them up and place on a baking tray. Bake in a moderately hot oven about a third of the way from the top at 400°F (200°C) Gas 6, for 20–30 minutes, or until lightly browned.

These are delicious eaten hot with baked beans and grilled tomatoes or cold, served with green salad. Makes 12 pinwheels.

Cheese Savoury

2 rounds of bread, buttered
3–4 oz grated cheese (75–100 g)
2 eggs
Pepper, salt and a little made mustard
½ pint milk (300 ml)
A little more grated cheese

Denbighshire

Cut crusts from bread and dice. Place in greased ovenware dish, 1 pint size (600 ml), add cheese. Beat eggs with seasonings, add milk, pour over the bread. Leave to soak ½ hour at least. Sprinkle with a little more cheese. Bake in a moderate oven, 375°F (190°C) Gas 5, for about ½ hour until firm and golden brown.

Can be served alone, or with peas, baked beans or spaghetti in tomato sauce, or a thick onion sauce.

Serves 4.

Cheese Snack

Oxfordshire

Cut ordinary cheese sandwiches then fry them in pan till both sides are crisp and brown.

Cheese Whirls

Use the flour and lard to make short pastry in the usual way. Roll out thinly into a rectangle and spread lightly with butter. Cover with grated cheese and roll up as for a Swiss roll. Cut into slices and place on a baking sheet. Bake in a hot oven, 425°F (220°C) Gas 7, for 15–20 minutes or until the pastry is lightly browned.
Serves 4–6.

8 oz plain flour (200 g)
4 oz lard (100 g)
A little butter
Grated cheese (about 150 g)

Westmorland

Chicory and Ham in Cheese Sauce

Grease a casserole, put in the washed heads of chicory, pour over the water to which a few drops of lemon juice have been added, cover with a buttered paper and the lid. Braise the chicory in a moderate oven, 350°F (180°C) Gas 4, for 50–60 minutes until tender.

Drain well, then wrap each in a slice of cooked ham. Arrange neatly in a fireproof dish and coat with the cheese sauce. Reheat in a moderate oven for 15–20 minutes, and serve with crisp toast.
Serves 4.

8 small heads chicory
$\frac{1}{4}$ pint water (150 ml)
Few drops lemon juice
8 thin slices cooked ham (approx. $\frac{1}{2}$ lb or 200 g)

Cheese Sauce
$1\frac{1}{2}$ oz butter (40 g)
$1\frac{1}{2}$ oz flour (40 g)
$\frac{3}{4}$ pint milk (450 ml)
6 oz grated cheese (175 g)
Pinch salt and cayenne pepper

Oxfordshire

Country Flan

Sieve flour, salt and pepper together in a bowl. Rub in margarine. Stir in the cheese. Add egg yolk and water and mix with a knife to a firm dough. Turn out on to a lightly floured board. Roll out thinly and mould into a 7 inch (18 cm) flan ring, placed on a baking sheet. Bake in a fairly hot oven, 400°F (200°C) Gas 6, for approximately 20 minutes.

Prepare the filling by cutting the bacon into small pieces, fry gently. Skin and chop the tomato. Wash, peel and chop the mushrooms. Beat the eggs in a basin. Add tomato, mushrooms, fried bacon, grated cheese, milk and seasoning. Pour into flan case. Return to middle shelf of oven for 15–20 minutes, until golden brown and set. Garnish with parsley. Eat hot or cold.
Serves 4–5.

Cheese Pastry
6 oz plain flour (150 g)
Pinch salt
Pinch cayenne pepper
3 oz margarine (75 g)
2 oz grated cheese (50 g)
1 egg yolk
1 tablespoon cold water (15 ml or more)

Filling
2 rashers bacon
1 tomato
2 oz mushrooms (50 g)
2 eggs
1 oz grated cheese (25 g)
1 tablespoon top of milk (15 ml)
Parsley

Northumberland

Country Omelette

1 slice of fat bacon
1 potato
2 eggs
1 dessertspoon cold water (10 ml)
Salt and pepper
A large piece of butter

Quantities for one omelette.

Cut the bacon and potato into small dice, fry and keep hot. Season.

Thoroughly mix the eggs but do not beat to a froth. Add water and seasoning. Put a large piece of butter in a frying pan and make very hot, then pour in the eggs and stir them quickly round and round. Allow to set, keeping in a round shape. When the mixture begins to set, spread the bacon and potato on top. Serve flat and the top should be moist.

Note for Beginners

The potato and bacon will take about 20 minutes to fry until the potato is tender. It is better to do this in a separate pan from that to be used for cooking the eggs.

Berkshire

Durham Woodcock

1½ oz butter (40 g)
2 eggs
Seasoning
1 dessertspoon cream (10 ml)
Toasted bread
Anchovy fillets
Capers or olives
Sprigs of parsley

Melt butter in a saucepan, add the beaten seasoned egg. Stir until thickened. Remove from heat. Add cream and stir. Arrange in shapes on toasted bread. Garnish with trellis pattern of anchovy fillets and capers or olives. Arrange on a hot dish on a plain doyley and garnish with sprigs of parsley.

Serves 2.

Durham

Egg Savoury

Thick pieces of bread
Eggs
Grated cheese

Cut for each person a thick piece of bread (this should be at least 1 inch or 2½ cm thick). Toast one side. On the untoasted side, scoop out a hole and break into that an egg. Cover the egg and bread with grated cheese and brown under grill.

Herefordshire

58

Farm Cheese Patties

A Kirkcudbright Recipe at Least 155 Years Old

Line 18–24 patty tins with pastry. Grate cheese and breadcrumbs, beat eggs, oil the butter. Mix all together, and put a little into each patty tin. Bake at 400°F (200°C) Gas 6 for 15 minutes.

This can be made in a large tin, 8 inches (20 cm), and baked about 25 minutes. A touch of garlic or grated onion can be added.

Any type of pastry
8 oz mild cheese (200 g)
2 eggs
1 tablespoon breadcrumbs (30 ml)
½ oz butter (15 g)
½ gill thick cream or evaporated milk (75 ml)
Salt, pepper, and a few grains cayenne
Garlic or grated onion (optional)

Northumberland

Fitchett Pie

Make an ordinary plate pie with short pastry and for filling put in a layer of grated apple, then a layer of grated cheese and finally a layer of grated onion. If necessary repeat all three layers. It makes a delicious supper dish.

Short pastry
Grated apples
Grated cheese
Grated onion

Cheshire

Gruyère Surprise

Line a sandwich tin or flat plate with rough puff pastry. Shave Gruyère cheese all over, as much as you can spare. Scatter a very little shaved butter over and seasoning too, if liked. A few drops of white wine is also added as a tasty extra. Cover with a thin layer of pastry. Seal edges and lightly cut either sections or a pattern on top. Brush over with beaten egg or milk and bake in a hot oven until golden brown, 450°F (230°C) Gas 8, for 15–20 minutes.

Rough puff pastry
Gruyère cheese
Butter
Salt and pepper
Few drops white wine
Beaten egg or milk for brushing

This was served to us in a tiny little hotel in the wilds of central France. It makes a tasty luxury supper dish.

Berkshire

Italian Risotto

Fry the onion in the butter, add the rice and stir carefully over a gentle heat. Season to taste and add the stock by degrees. Cover and cook slowly, stirring frequently to prevent burning. When the rice is soft and all the liquid absorbed remove from the heat and add the grated cheese. Reheat and serve on a hot dish, accompanied if liked by grilled tomatoes or mushrooms, or a green salad. Cooking time about ½ hour.

Serves 2–3.

1 onion, chopped finely
1 oz butter (25 g)
6 oz Patna rice (175 g)
Salt and pepper
1 pint stock (600 ml) or 1 meat cube dissolved in 1 pint hot water
2 oz grated cheese (50 g)

Westmorland

Leek and Egg Bake

2 eggs
1 leek
½ oz margarine (15 g)
1 level tablespoon plain flour (15 ml)
¼ pint milk (150 ml)
1 oz grated cheese (25 g)
Salt and pepper
Little extra grated cheese

Yorkshire

Put eggs into pan of cold water, bring to boil and boil 10 minutes. Wash leek well and cut into 1 inch (2½ cm) lengths. Cook in salted boiling water for 5 minutes. Make a roux sauce and take off the heat and beat in the grated cheese, season with salt and pepper. Shell the hard boiled eggs; drain the leeks and divide between two individual fireproof dishes. Put an egg on top of each and coat them with cheese sauce. Sprinkle the rest of the cheese on top and brown surface quickly under the grill.
Serves 2.

Leek Pasty
Traditional Recipe

Short Pastry
12 oz flour (350 g)
1 teaspoon salt (5 ml)
1 teaspoon baking powder (10 ml)
6 oz lard (175 g) or 3 oz lard and 3 oz margarine

Filling
1 lb leeks (500 g)
8 oz ham or bacon (250 g)
2 eggs beaten up with 4 tablespoons milk (60 ml)
Salt and pepper to taste

Northumberland

Wash the leeks and cut them into 1 or 2 inch (2½–5 cm) pieces. Pour boiling water over them and leave for 5 minutes. Drain off water.

Make shortcrust pastry. Grease a Swiss roll tin, then line with pastry.

Cut the ham into small pieces and put a layer into the pastry and add the leeks and beaten eggs. Add seasonings. Cover with pastry, sealing the edges well. Brush with a little milk and egg. Put in a hot oven, 425°F (220°C) Gas 7, for 20 minutes, then reduce heat to 350°F (180°C) Gas 4, but allow plenty of time to cook through, about 40 minutes total.
Serves 6.

Note for Beginners

Weigh the leeks after trimming. Allow time for them to cool after blanching and before putting them in the pastry.

Pan Haggerty
Traditional Recipe

8 oz onions (225 g)
1 lb potatoes (450 g)
1 tablespoon dripping (25 g)
4 oz grated cheese (100 g)
Pepper and salt

Northumberland

Cut vegetables into very thin slices and dry in a cloth. Heat dripping in a heavy frying pan, and put vegetables and cheese in the pan in layers. Season each layer. Fry gently until cooked, about 45 minutes, then brown under grill.
Serves 4.

Pizza

Cream yeast with a little milk; sieve flour and salt. Add yeast, milk and beaten egg to the flour, blend in softened but not melted butter, beat well with the hand until mixture comes away from the fingers. Cover with a cloth. Leave to prove for 40 minutes in a warm place. Grease a large baking tray. Pat out dough with hands to 9 inch (23 cm) round.

To prepare the filling melt fat, fry chopped onion until tender and golden. Add skinned tomatoes with 2 tablespoons water, purée, sugar, seasoning, bay leaf, oregano. Simmer 10–15 minutes until thick. Cool.

Cover dough to within ½ inch (1 cm) of edge with filling. Decorate with anchovies thinly sliced, grated cheese and olives. Prove in a warm place for 15 minutes.

Place in centre of oven, 425–450°F (220–230°C) Gas 7–8, for 25–30 minutes. Serve hot or cold.

Serves 6.

For the Dough
½ oz yeast (15 g)
¼ pint lukewarm water (150 ml)
8 oz plain flour (250 g)
1 teaspoon salt (5 ml)
1 oz butter or margarine (25 g)
1 small egg

Filling
½ oz vegetable cooking fat (15 g) or 1 tablespoon oil
1 small onion
8 oz tomatoes (250 g)
2½ oz tomato purée (75 g)
1 teaspoon sugar (5 ml)
Seasoning
1 bay leaf
Pinch of oregano
Small tin anchovy fillets (56 g)
1 oz cheese (25 g)
4–6 olives

Note for Beginners

Allow at least 1½ hours for making the pizza from start to finish. The filling can be prepared in advance of making the dough if that is more convenient.

Lincolnshire

Risotto

Boil rice.

Chop onion and fry lightly in dripping. If using bacon cut into small pieces and fry with onion.

Peel tomatoes, quarter and add to onion and bacon. Cook gently, then add cooked rice, chopped hard boiled eggs and chopped ham, if used instead of bacon. Season. Heat gently till hot through, cover with chopped parsley and serve.

Serves 4.

4 oz long grain rice (100 g)
1 medium-sized onion
Dripping
4 oz bacon or cooked ham (100 g)
4 tomatoes
2 hard boiled eggs
Seasoning
Chopped parsley

Cumberland

Sardine Pie

Drain off as much as possible of the oil from the sardines. Dip each sardine in flour mixed with the curry powder. Arrange on fireproof plate, about 8 inch size (20 cm), tails to centre. Cover with pastry and cook in a hot oven until well browned, 450°F (230°C) Gas 8, about 15–20 minutes.

Serves 4.

Short pastry (one part fat to two parts self-raising flour)
2 tins sardines (240 g)
2 teaspoons curry powder (10–20 ml)
2 teaspoons flour (10–20 ml)

Berkshire

Sardine Snack

1 tin sardines (120 g)
1 oz melted margarine (25 g)
1 oz grated cheese (25 g)
Fingers of bread fried in the sardine oil
Paprika pepper
Chopped parsley

Cumberland

Remove sardines carefully from the tin so that they remain whole and drain off the oil.

Remove the tails from the fish and then dip each sardine in the melted margarine and then in the cheese.

Place one fish on each finger of fried bread. Brown under the grill. Garnish with paprika and chopped parsley in alternate lines.

Sausage Rolls

Hampshire

These are universal favourites, but the following hints may help:
1 If you want your sausage rolls to gain a reputation and to be a little different, try mincing an onion and adding to the sausage meat.
2 They are much quicker to make if you roll the sausage meat into long rolls and wrap it in equally long strips of pastry, and then cut to size required.
3 When making quantities for the Village Do it is a good idea to make the long rolls beforehand and leave them in the fridge or cool place and cook at the last minute. This makes for fresher rolls, and less rush.
4 Short pastry rolls are easier to handle than the richer pastries.
5 See that your sausage rolls really are *sausage* rolls and not mostly pastry!

Savoury Beans

Traditional Recipe

8 oz butter beans (225 g)
Boiling water
2 rashers ham
1 large onion
2 tomatoes
1 pint water or stock (500 ml)
Salt and pepper
2 dessertspoons golden syrup (20 ml)

Durham

Steep beans overnight in boiling water, then par-boil for about an hour. Drain.

Lightly fry ham and cut in small pieces.

Chop onion and tomato.

Place all in a casserole with one pint of stock or water (500 ml). Season to taste and cook for 1 hour at 350–375°F (180–190°C) Gas 4–5, or until the beans are tender. Ten minutes before serving add golden syrup. Serve hot.

This is a real Durham supper dish and is delicious served with toast.

Serves 4.

Supper Savoury

Put the cheese on the bread, then the seasonings. On the cheese place slices of tomato, then a slice of bacon. Place on a hot baking tin and bake in a hot oven until the bacon is crisp, 400°F (200°C) Gas 6, for about 15–20 minutes.

For each person:
A thick slice of buttered bread
A thin slice of cheese
Salt, mustard and a dash of Worcester
Sliced tomato
A slice of rather fat bacon

Herefordshire

Swiss Eggs

Grease a gratin dish, cover bottom with cream or top of the milk, and a little grated cheese. Break in as many eggs as required, sprinkle over salt and pepper to taste, and a little more cream or top of milk, and grated cheese. Bake in oven, 350°F (180°C) Gas 4, until set, about 15 minutes.

Fat
Cream or top of milk
Grated cheese
Eggs
Salt and pepper

Gloucestershire

Tomato and Mushroom Flan

Line a 7 inch (18 cm) plate or sandwich tin with pastry and bake blind.

Wash and peel mushrooms and skin tomatoes. Put in a small pan and cook in margarine for about 10 minutes, remove mushrooms and mix in flour with remaining margarine and cook 2 minutes. Add 3 tablespoons water and a meat cube and cook till it thickens, add more water if needed to thin the sauce.

Arrange mushrooms and tomatoes over cooked pastry, season and sprinkle with grated cheese. Pour sauce over and bake in moderate oven, 350°F (180°C) Gas 4, for 15 minutes.

Serves 4.

4 oz rough puff pastry (100 g flour)
4 oz mushrooms (100 g)
2 tomatoes
1 oz margarine (25 g)
1 teaspoon flour (10 ml)
Salt and pepper
Meat cube
1 oz cheese (25 g)

Somerset

Tatie Stovies

Melt dripping in large stew pan. Add sliced potatoes, meat and onion in layers with seasoning. Almost cover contents of pan with stock or water. Cook slowly until potatoes are soft and floury and moisture almost absorbed, $\frac{1}{2}$–$\frac{3}{4}$ hour.

Serves 4.

Diced carrot and/or turnip can be added if desired. A suet crust can also be cooked on top of the mixture.

1 level tablespoon meat dripping (15 g) (from roast beef)
4–6 large potatoes
4 oz meat (100 g) (preferably cold roast beef in small pieces)
1 large onion
Salt and pepper to taste
Stock or water
Diced carrots and/or turnips (optional)
Suet crust (optional)

Northumberland

The Cornish Pasty

The Cornish pasty is, and has been since time immemorial, the staple dish of the county, and in giving various recipes for making it, it may be noted that the method does not vary, but the nature of the pasty varies according to the filling, or inside.

Therefore, the general method of making has been given, and a list of various kinds of pasties afterwards.

It is said that the Devil has never crossed the Tamar into Cornwall, on account of the well-known habit of Cornishwomen of putting everything into a pasty, and that he was not sufficiently courageous to risk such a fate! However that may be, the Cornish pasty, in its various forms, is a delectable dainty and deservedly world-famous.

When the pasties are being made, each member of the family has his or hers marked at one corner with the initial of the prospective owner. In this way each person's tastes can be catered for.

The true Cornish way to eat a pasty is to hold it in the hand, and begin to bite it from the opposite end to the initial, so that, should any of it be uneaten, it may be consumed later by the rightful owner. And woe betide anyone who takes another person's 'corner'!

Pasty

Any good pastry may be used, but it should not be too flaky nor too rich. A very useful pastry is:

> 1 lb flour (500 g)
> 8 oz lard and suet (250 g)
> ½ teaspoon salt (5 ml)
> Mix with water

When pastry is made, roll out about ¼ inch (6 mm) thick, and cut into rounds with a plate to the size desired.

Lay the rounds on the pastry board with half of the round over the rolling pin and put in the fillings, damp the edges lightly and fold over into semi-circle. Shape the pasty nicely and 'crimp' the extreme edges where it is joined between the finger and thumb. Cut a slit in the centre of the pasty, lay on a baking sheet and bake in a quick oven, so that it keeps its shape.

Apple Pasty

Peel apples, slice thinly, and lightly sprinkle with brown sugar. In summertime, blackberries are usually mixed with the apple.

Chicken Pasty

Chicken cut up in small pieces.

Date Pasty

Stone dates and fill in the usual way.

Eggy Pasty

Bacon cut in dice, parsley and one or two eggs, according to size of pasty required.

Jam Pasty

These are usually made smaller than a savoury pasty, and any kind of jam may be used.

Mackerel Pasty

Allow one or two mackerel to each pasty, and clean and boil them in the usual way. Then remove skin and bones, and lay on pastry; fill up with washed parsley, and add pepper and salt. Finish as above.

Meat and Potato Pasty

Always use fresh steak, potatoes cut small, salt and pepper, flavoured with onion.

Parsley Pasty

Parsley and lamb or mutton.

Pork Pasty

Fresh pork, and potatoes, flavoured with onion, sage or thyme.

Rabbitty Pasty

Use fleshy part of rabbit cut the same as meat, fairly small.

Sour Sauce Pasty

Gather a quantity of sour sauce (sorrel) leaves. Shrink them by pouring boiling water and use the leaves in a pasty. Serve with sugar and cream.

Windy Pasty

Take the last bit of pastry left over from making pasties, roll it into a round, fold over and crimp as for ordinary pasty. Bake in oven and when done (whilst still hot) open out flat and fill each side with jam. It may be eaten hot or cold.

Note for Beginners

1 lb flour (500 g) makes enough pastry for 8 small pasties. For a meat filling allow 1–1½ lb meat (500–750 g). Cook them at 400–425°F (200–225°C) Gas 6–7 for 30–40 minutes.

Cornwall

Decker Sandwiches

These substantial sandwiches, which are made with 3–4 slices of bread and 2–3 different fillings, are very suitable for lunch or supper snacks. To make them, spread one piece of bread and butter with one of the fillings, and cover with a second slice of bread, buttered side down. Butter the top of the piece, spread with the second filling and cover with a slice of bread. Press together.

Good combinations for these sandwiches are:

Ham or bacon with seasoned scrambled egg.
Ham, green salad and sliced hard boiled egg.
Flaked salmon or haddock, moistened with a little mayonnaise, with thin slices of cucumber, seasoned with salt and pepper.
Grilled ham or bacon with sliced sausage, spread with mustard.
Cream cheese with chopped celery, and sliced chopped ham or meat loaf.

Yorkshire

Open Sandwiches

The base of these sandwiches is usually brown, rye or white bread; this is thickly buttered, and on it the fillings and garnishes are arranged to give an attractive appearance, as well as an appetizing flavour. The sandwiches may be either made immediately before serving, or the guests may make up their own sandwiches, choosing from amongst a selection of attractively displayed ingredients. Set out a variety of breads and butter, and try to offer some fillings from each of the following groups:

Anchovy fillets	A variety of cheeses
Sliced smoked salmon	Hard boiled eggs
Smoked eel	Scrambled eggs
Sardines	
Prawns and shrimps	

Cold roast meats	Sliced cucumber
Sliced ham and tongue	Sliced tomato
Cooked bacon rashers	Onion rings
Salami	Lettuce
Liver sausage	Watercress
Liver pâté	Fried apple
	Russian salad

Garnishes Orange and lemon slices. Gherkin fans. Sliced pickled beetroot. Radish roses. Celery curls. Red or green pepper rings.

Yorkshire

Toasted Sandwiches

Toasted sandwiches are very good. Almost any sandwiches, stale or fresh, can be used. Cheese, egg, sardine, ham are particularly good, but not cucumber. Toast under grill or in electric toaster (flatten well first) and serve at once.

Oxfordshire

Toasted Sandwiches

Dutchie Mushroom Toasties
Toast the bread on one side. Butter other side, cover with sliced Gouda cheese and grill until it melts. Cover with fried sliced mushrooms, season and top with another slice of toast.

Mushroom Club Sandwich

Toast the bread on one side. Turn and cover with streaky bacon and grill till crisp. Cover with raw sliced mushrooms marinated in lemon juice. Cover with watercress and spread with mayonnaise. Top with second slice of toast.

Buttered Shrimps and Mushroom Toasties

Toast the bread on both sides. Spread one side with buttered shrimps and grill till butter melts. Sprinkle with lemon juice and cover with grilled mushrooms and remaining slice of toast.

Yorkshire

Sandwich Fillings

Savoury

1 Chicken chopped and mixed with chopped fried bacon and moistened with mayonnaise.
2 Cream cheese mixed with watercress or chopped chives, chutney, chopped chicken or ham, chopped olives or nuts or both.
3 Mushrooms chopped, dredged with flour, sautéed in butter and moistened with top of milk.
4 Hard boiled egg chopped and mixed with tomato and Worcester sauce and chopped parsley.

Sweet

1 Banana mashed with lemon juice, a few dates and honey.
2 Mint and raisins, equal quantities minced and moistened with water.
3 Dates chopped and moistened with lemon juice.
4 Orange marmalade—especially good with nut breads.

Oxfordshire

Sandwich Hint

To cut a tidy sandwich use a very sharp knife and cut from the centre of the pile of sandwiches outward in each direction, having removed the crusts first.

Oxfordshire

68

Anchovy Spread

Melt butter over slow heat, add anchovy essence and stir well, add well beaten egg. Stir over slow heat until the mixture thickens. Will keep two weeks.

  Delicious in sandwiches, or on toast or crumpets.

1 oz butter (25 g)
1 tablespoon anchovy essence (15 ml)
1 egg

Oxfordshire

Sardine Spread

Mash together sardines and scrambled egg—adding seasoning to taste.

1 scrambled egg
1 tin sardines (120 g)
Seasoning

Oxfordshire

Small Savouries for Picnic or TV Evenings

Mix as for pastry. Roll out to $\frac{1}{8}$ inch (3 mm) and cut into circles for patty tins and small fancy biscuit shapes. Bake in hot oven, 400°F (200°C) Gas 6, for 15 minutes or until lightly browned.

Cheese Pastry
4 oz plain flour (100 g)
Pinch cayenne
Salt and pepper
3 oz margarine (75 g)
3 oz grated cheese (75 g)
1 yolk of egg
1 tablespoon milk (15 ml)

Fillings for Cases
Flaked white or smoked fish bound with a light sauce.
  Chopped shellfish in a light sauce.
  Any kind of diced cooked or canned meat with a little chutney.
  Cooked diced vegetables.
  A little minced curry (think of the scope from left-overs).

Spreads for Fancy Shaped Cheese Biscuits
Anchovy paste with a little flaked fish—garnish with parsley.
  Finely chopped egg yolk, chutney and creamed butter.
  Chopped sardine mashed with a little cheese, flavoured with lemon juice.
  Shrimps pounded in parsley sauce, garnish with parsley and one shrimp.
  Cream cheese sprinkled with finely chopped mint.
  Diced cold chicken in mayonnaise, garnish with cress.
  Minced fried mushrooms in egg sauce, garnish with parsley.
  Finely chopped celery and cream cheese with creamed cayenne butter.

Cumberland

Cheese Butterflies

½ cheese pastry recipe above

Filling
1 oz margarine (25 g)
½ oz grated cheese (15 g)
Pinch cayenne
Chopped parsley
        or
Primula cheese spread
Salt and pepper
Green colouring if liked

Cumberland

Roll out pastry ⅛ inch (3 mm) thick and cut into rounds. Make an incision right across half the rounds (these form wings). Bake 10 minutes in moderately hot oven, 375°F (190°C) Gas 5.

Mix filling. Spread biscuits with mixture. Place halves of cut biscuits, standing up to form wings.

VEGETABLES & SALADS
7

Cooking Roots

It is easy to overcook these and to send them sodden to table.
Intelligent cooks dish them at the right moment, send them to
table hot, and either dry, or finished and glazed in a little butter,
with the flavour in the dish instead of in the stock left in the
saucepan.

West Kent

Braising Root Vegetables

Fry them in dripping until lightly browned, then add enough
stock to half cover the vegetables, and a little seasoning. Cover
with a lid and cook gently till the vegetables are tender. Lift
them out on to a hot dish and continue to heat the liquid until
it is reduced and of a glazing consistency. Pour it over the
vegetables and garnish with parsley.

Cheshire

Purée of Vegetables

Potatoes, root vegetables or a mixture
1 oz butter or margarine (25 g) per lb
of purée (450 g)

Berkshire

Prepare the vegetables. Cook in boiling salted water until tender. Strain and pass through a fine wire sieve. Return to a clean saucepan and add butter or margarine. Dry over a gentle heat, shaking well.

Place on a hot dish, arranging neatly and smoothly to fit the shape of the dish.

Vegetable Curry

Sauce
1 oz dripping (25 g)
1 sliced onion
1 dessertspoon curry powder (20 ml)
1 chopped apple
1 oz flour (25 g)
Salt
¾ pint vegetable stock or milk and water
(400 ml)

Vegetables
1½–2 lb vegetables (¾–1 kg). A mixture of
cooked or raw vegetables including
a small tin of baked beans if liked
A little lemon juice
A good tablespoon sweet chutney
Boiled rice

Leicestershire and Rutland

Fry dripping, onion, curry powder and apple for 10 minutes without burning, add flour, some salt and the liquid, stir till boiling.

Put a mixture of cooked or raw vegetables into a casserole, add the sauce and cook in a moderate oven for 1–2 hours, 350°F (180°C) Gas 4.

Add a little lemon juice and a good tablespoonful sweet chutney before serving. Serve with boiled rice.

Serves 4.

Globe Artichokes

A great delicacy which you can grow yourself. 1 per person.

Pick them before they turn into handsome flowers. There are three parts to an artichoke; the leaves, the bottom of which you eat; the firm bottom part, which you eat; and the choke which obviously you do not eat.

To Prepare
Cut off the stalk part. Strip off the outer layer or two of coarse leaves. Cut off just the tips of all the leaves with scissors. Soak the artichokes upside down in salted water. All sorts of living creatures then drop out.

To Cook
Put them heads down in boiling salted water with some lemon juice in it for about 20–25 minutes. Drain.

To Serve Hot

Stand the artichoke up and remove the choke. This is easily done with a spoon. Serve on a hot dish with melted butter sauce or Hollandaise.

N.B. You pull off the leaves with your fingers and rather messily suck the succulent bit at the bottom. Then you eat the bottom or 'fond' with a knife and fork.

Hampshire

Jerusalem Artichokes

Artichokes can be treated like potatoes and boiled in their skins. A sharp cut through the outer layer and the tough part can be pulled away and the vegetable sent to table in the perfection of flavour.

They are good cut up raw and fried as chips.

West Kent

Asparagus

Scrape white end, tie in bundles. Cook in salted water for 20 minutes. Serve with melted butter.

Gloucestershire

Aubergines

Egg Plant

Remove hard stalk and bake in a casserole with a little milk and margarine for about 30 minutes.

Gloucestershire

Broad Beans (1)

If picked very young, both pods and beans can be used. Cook in salted water for approximately 10 minutes.

Gloucestershire

Broad Beans (2)

Gather while quite young. Shell and boil rapidly in a minimum of salted water until the inner shells begin to crack, about 25 minutes. Serve with parsley sauce.

Cumberland

Canadian Treacle Beans

8 oz butter beans (225 g)
8 oz fresh tomatoes (225 g) or 6 oz
  tinned tomatoes (170 g)
1 dessertspoon black treacle (25 g)
1 oz fat (25 g)
Salt and pepper to taste
Jacket potatoes
Cauliflower

Westmorland

Soak beans overnight, and then simmer gently until cooked (1½–2 hours).

Cook tomatoes and rub through a sieve, add treacle and fat and heat together, adding required amount of seasoning.

Strain beans, place in fireproof dish and pour over tomato mixture. Cover and bake in moderate oven, 375°F (190°C) Gas 5, for ¾–1 hour.

Serve with jacket potatoes and cauliflower.

Serves 4.

French and Scarlet Runner Beans

Cumberland

Gather while very young. Wash, remove the stalks and any strings which come away. Cut if desired, or cook whole. Boil rapidly until tender. Toss with butter and chopped parsley.

Guernsey Bean Jar

1 lb small dried beans (500 g)
1 pig trotter or piece of shin of beef
1 onion
Parsley and salt to taste
1 pint slightly thickened stock (600 ml)

Guernsey

Soak beans overnight, boil till tender, strain off water. Place all ingredients in stone jar or earthenware dish, add stock, cover down. Bake well in slow oven, 250°F (120°C) Gas ½, for 4–5 hours.

Note for Beginners

Small beans like haricot or small red beans usually take about 1 hour to boil until tender.

Beetroot

Beet is very seldom made the most of. Tiny beet look very smart when cooked and served in small moulds in a lemon or tarragon flavoured aspic.

Sliced raw beet, just covered with cold water, with a dessertspoon of butter, and boiled furiously for about 10 minutes, makes a good hot vegetable with beef.

A Hint to Prevent Bleeding
Dipping broken beetroot into dry flour before putting into the saucepan to boil will prevent bleeding and retain the colour.

West Kent

74

Baked Beetroot

Wash the beetroot. Wrap in greased paper or foil. Place on a baking tray and put into the middle of a moderate oven, 350°F (180°C) Gas 4. The cooking time varies, according to the size and the age of the beetroot, from 1–3 hours. To test for readiness, remove the greased paper and press the beetroot with the fingers, when the skin should come away easily. Baked beetroot may be served as for boiled beetroot.

Shropshire

Beetroot

Hot

Take even sized small beet. Wash and boil quickly until cooked. Skin whilst hot, put into a serving dish and cover with either a thin parsley sauce or oil and vinegar to which a little sugar has been added.

Shropshire

To Cook Beetroot

Devon Style

Wash and peel beetroot—RAW. Slice or cut into dice. Place in saucepan and just cover with water; add a little salt. Simmer until soft (about 20–30 minutes, according to age of beet).

Remove beet from juice with perforated spoon. To the hot juice add vinegar (about 3 tablespoons) and sugar to taste. Pour the juice back over the beet and allow to cool.

Devon

Polish Beetroot

Grate the beetroot. Melt the fat in a strong pan. First fry the onion, then add the beetroot, cover the pan and allow the beetroot to cook gently, shaking the pan occasionally to prevent sticking. If necessary, the vinegar may be added at this stage. Meanwhile, boil the potatoes. When both the vegetables are cooked, beat the potatoes with the beetroot. Add the seasoning and apple. Serve hot with grated cheese or grilled sausages and bacon, or cold, spoonfuls being wrapped in lettuce leaves.

Serves 6–8.

1 lb raw beetroot (500 g)
1½ oz fat (40 g)
1 chopped onion
2 tablespoons vinegar (30 ml or more), spiced if liked
1 lb peeled potatoes (500 g)
Seasoning
1 grated apple or 1 tablespoon apple chutney (30 ml)

Berkshire

Cabbage

To Cook

Savoy or 'drum head' cabbage
Pepper and salt
Knob of butter or margarine
Grated nutmeg

Optional
Tomato sauce
Croûtons of fried bread

West Kent

Shred cabbage finely, wash thoroughly and place in saucepan without drying. Add seasoning and fat, but no extra water. Simmer gently for about 15 minutes with the lid on; strain, make a sauce with the liquor and pour over the shreds. If liked, add pepper and a little grated nutmeg.

It can also be served with a little tomato sauce round the base and decorated with croûtons of fried bread or toast.

Bavarian Cabbage

1 large red cabbage
1 onion
1 cooking apple
3 oz butter (75 g)
Salt and pepper
1 dessertspoon sugar (10 ml)
¼ pint stock or water (150 ml)
A few caraway seeds
1 tablespoon flour (30 ml)
⅛ pint vinegar (75 ml)

Gloucestershire

Wash and quarter the cabbage and shred it finely lengthwise. Chop the onion finely, chop the apple. Melt butter in a thick saucepan, and fry the onion lightly. Add the cabbage, chopped apple, salt, pepper, sugar, stock and caraway seeds. Cover pan tightly and simmer very gently for 1 hour.

Sprinkle in the flour and stir. Add vinegar, stir and bring to the boil.

Serves 6–8.

Belgian Carrots

1 oz dripping (25 g)
1 lb diced carrots (450 g)
Pepper and salt
1 level tablespoon flour (15 ml)
1 teaspoon sugar for old carrots (5 ml)
Chopped parsley

Shropshire

Melt dripping in a saucepan. Put in carrots, pepper and salt. Sprinkle flour on top and just cover with boiling water. Cook over moderate heat for about 20 minutes or until tender. When cooking old carrots add a teaspoon of sugar. Garnish with chopped parsley.

Serves 4–5.

Carrots Vichy

2 lb young carrots (1 kg)
2 oz butter (50 g)
1 teaspoon sugar (10 ml)
Seasoning
Chopped parsley

Shropshire

Wash and scrape carrots. Put into a saucepan with butter, sugar and seasoning. Just cover with cold water and cook quickly until all the water is evaporated and the carrots are covered with the butter. Pile into a hot dish, sprinkle with parsley and serve.

Serves 6–8.

Glazed Carrots with Mint

Blanch the carrots in boiling salted water for 6–7 minutes. Strain and put them in a heavy pan with the butter; after 5 minutes gentle cooking, add the sugar; simmer gently. When the carrots are tender, season with salt and pepper and stir in the mint.

Thinly shredded older carrots may be used in the same way. Serves 4.

1 lb small new carrots (500 g)
2 oz butter (50 g)
1 tablespoon sugar (15 ml)
Salt and ground black pepper
1 tablespoon fresh, chopped mint (30 ml)

Berkshire

Celeriac
Baked

Peel the celeriac, cutting away hard parts, slice thickly and cook in a little water till tender with a pinch of salt. Drain and place in an ovenproof dish with the milk, butter, cheese, pepper and salt. Sprinkle with breadcrumbs and bake 20 minutes at about 375°F (190°C) Gas 5.

Serves 3.

1 root of celeriac
Salt and pepper
1 tablespoon milk (15 ml)
1 oz butter (25 g)
1 tablespoon grated cheese (30 ml)
Breadcrumbs

West Kent

Celery au Gratin

Cut the celery into thin slices, put in the saucepan with the water, butter, lemon juice and salt. Bring to the boil and cook gently for 35 minutes with lid on.

Drain the celery, keeping the liquor. Put celery in an ovenproof dish and keep hot, make the sauce, pour over and sprinkle on top the breadcrumbs and cheese, and brown under the grill.

Serves 4.

1 lb celery, prepared (450 g)
3 tablespoons water (45 ml)
1 oz butter (25 g)
Squeeze lemon juice
Salt and pepper
1 oz grated cheese (25 g)
Some breadcrumbs

Sauce
1 oz butter (25 g)
1 oz flour (25 g)
½ pint milk and vegetable liquor (300 ml)

Leicestershire and Rutland

Chestnuts and Brussels Sprouts

Peel, blanch and stew the chestnuts in stock very gently. Cook sprouts quickly in a little boiling water and drain well. Melt a large lump of butter in a stew pan and toss sprouts in this until they are thoroughly mixed in the butter. Drain chestnuts and pile them in the centre of a dish and arrange sprouts round them.

1 lb chestnuts (500 g)
Well-flavoured stock
1 lb Brussels sprouts (500 g)
A large lump of butter

Westmorland

Braised Chicory

8 oz chicory (250 g)
1 oz butter (25 g)
Salt
A few drops of lemon juice
Pepper
A little white stock or water

Shropshire

Wash and separate chicory. Lightly butter a fireproof dish. Put in chicory, other ingredients and remainder of butter. Cover closely and bake in a moderate oven, 350°F (180°C) Gas 4, for 30–40 minutes.

Celery or sea-kale can be cooked by the same method.

Courgettes
Tiny Young Marrows Will Do

1 lb courgettes (500 g)
2–3 oz butter (50–75 g)
1 teaspoon lemon juice (5 ml)
2 or 3 tablespoons mixed fresh herbs
   (30–50 ml), say, chives, basil and
   parsley
Black pepper

Hampshire

Courgettes are easy to grow and the more you pick the more will come along.

Wash and trim the ends of the courgettes. Cook in boiling salted water for 2–3 minutes. Drain and put in a fireproof dish. Melt the butter and lemon juice in a pan and pour over the courgettes. Sprinkle with herbs and a twist or two of the black pepper mill.

Cook at 325°F (160°C) Gas 3 for 30–35 minutes.
Serves 4.

Cucumbers
To Cook

West Kent

Slice them thickly; add pepper and salt, and some thinly sliced onions, a little stock and a nut of butter. Simmer slowly, and thicken with a little flour and grated nutmeg.

Another way—fry them with sliced onions till brown in a little butter, cover with a little good gravy and simmer till tender for about 20 minutes.

Leeks
To Clean

West Kent
78

Leeks are not difficult to free from grit if they are placed green ends down in a deep jug full of water. Most of the sand and earth then falls out, and after they have been split, they are cleaned very quickly. (This plan works well with dirty celery.)

Leeks à la Greque

Trim the leeks carefully, removing the outer tough leaves. Slit the top into a sort of fringe and wash very well under a running tap. They are great vegetables for having little bits of sand and grit hidden in their leaves. Get it all washed out.

Cut the leeks into 1 inch (2½ cm) slices. Put into a saucepan with the water, oil, tomato purée and sugar. Season with salt and freshly ground black pepper, cook for 5 minutes with the lid on. Add the rice, cook for another 5–10 minutes. The liquid should be almost absorbed by the rice, but the rice should not be soft and mushy. Leave in the pan with the lid off for another 4 minutes. Add lemon juice. Taste and check the seasoning. Serve chilled, with the olives and lemon slices on the top.

Serves 4.

3 or 4 medium leeks
½ pint water (300 ml)
¼ pint olive oil (150 ml)
1 tablespoon tomato purée (30 ml)
2 or 3 sugar knobs
Salt and freshly ground black pepper
2 oz long grain rice (50 g)
Lemon juice and lemon slices
12 black olives

Hampshire

Stewed Leeks

Wash, trim and stew the leeks until tender in just enough milk and water to cover them. Drain the leeks thoroughly and make up the liquid to a full ½ pint (300 ml). Melt the margarine, add the flour and stir for a minute until well blended. Draw the pan from the heat and add the liquid gradually, beating well to remove lumps. Return the pan to the heat, add seasoning and cook for a minute or two. Add the beaten yolk of egg to the sauce and pour the whole over the leeks, serve very hot with the crisp fried rashers of bacon as garnish.

Serves 4.

8 leeks
Milk and water
1 oz margarine (25 g)
1 oz flour (25 g)
Pepper and salt
1 yolk of egg
Small rashers of bacon

Oxfordshire

Beurre Noisette

For an old marrow cooked in the usual way.

Melt the butter, add the other ingredients. Combine with a spoon for a few seconds and pour while boiling over the cooked marrow.

Serves 4.

2 oz butter (50 g)
2 tablespoons herb vinegar (30 ml)
2 tablespoons chopped fresh herbs (30 ml)
Pepper and salt

Hampshire

Easy Cheesy Marrow

Cut marrow unpeeled in half, scoop out centre and pile up with crumbled cheese. Put in fireproof dish (no need to grease or add water). Scatter over browned breadcrumbs. Bake in a fairly hot oven, 375°F (190°C) Gas 5, about 1 hour.

Serves 4.

1 small marrow, young enough for seeds to be barely formed inside
8 oz moist crumbled Lancashire or Cheshire cheese (200 g)
Browned breadcrumbs

Westmorland

Stewed Marrow

1 small marrow
1 small onion
1 oz butter or margarine (25 g)
Pepper and salt

Leicestershire and Rutland

Peel the marrow and onion. Cut the marrow into small thick squares, remove seeds. Chop the onion finely. Put the fat and pepper and salt in a saucepan, when melted add the onion. Shake over the fire, add the marrow and let it cook until it pulps, stirring occasionally to prevent burning.

Arrange in a vegetable dish and serve hot.

Serves 4.

Vegetable Marrow Hongroise

1 medium marrow ($\frac{3}{4}$–1 kg)
1 oz butter (25 g)
1 tablespoon finely chopped onion (30 ml)
1 tablespoon vinegar (15 ml)
A pinch of dill seed finely crushed or chopped dill leaves
Salt and pepper
1 teaspoon paprika pepper (5–10 ml)
1 teaspoon sugar (5 ml)
1 teaspoon (heaped) flour (15 ml)

Oxfordshire

Peel marrow, cut in two, scoop out seeds, cut into slivers. Heat three-quarters of the butter in a large stew pan or frying pan, add marrow. Cook over moderate heat, shaking the pan frequently and turning over the marrow with a fish slice. When soft and melting lift out with the slice. Put onion into the pan, cook until soft, return marrow to the pan with vinegar, dill, seasoning and sugar, cook for a few minutes. Work remaining butter into the flour, add, and when melted reboil. Turn into a hot serving dish.

Serves 4.

Creamed Onions with Cauliflower

1 lb onions (450 g)
1 sage leaf
1 tablespoon flour (30 ml)
4 tablespoons milk (60 ml)
2–3 tablespoons grated cheese (30–45 ml)
Salt and pepper
1 good-sized cauliflower

Westmorland

Peel the onions and cook with the sage leaf in salted water until tender (20 minutes or more). Drain the onions but keep the water. Rub onions through a sieve. Mix the flour with some milk, add about 6 tablespoons (100 ml) of onion liquid. Stir into the onion purée and cook over low heat until it thickens. Stir in the grated cheese and season with pepper and salt. Put the cooked cauliflower in a deep dish and pour over onion cream and serve hot.

Serves 4–6.

Stuffed Onions

4 even-sized onions
2 oz grated cheese (50 g)
2 oz white breadcrumbs (50 g)
$\frac{1}{4}$ teaspoon dry mustard (2$\frac{1}{2}$ ml)
Salt and pepper
Little margarine
Chopped parsley
White sauce, tomato sauce or gravy

Boil the onions for 20–30 minutes according to size, after removing the papery outside skins. Do not allow to become too soft.

Combine the grated cheese, breadcrumbs and mustard in a basin. When the onions are cooked, scoop out the centre portion with a small spoon and add to the rest of the ingredients. Season to taste.

Fill the cavities in the onions with the stuffing mixture, place in a greased fireproof dish, dot the tops with margarine and bake in a hot oven, 425°F (220°C) Gas 7, for about ½ hour, until tender.

Sprinkle the top of each onion with parsley and serve with a good white sauce, a tomato sauce or gravy.

Alternative Stuffing
Minced bacon, breadcrumbs and finely chopped sage.

Derbyshire

Baked Parsnips

These are delicious if after washing and trimming they are baked round the joint. They will take about an hour. Should your joint be very small, partly boil the parsnips for about 20 minutes and finish off around the joint.

Northamptonshire and Soke of Peterborough

Cheesed Parsnips

Wash and peel parsnips. Cut into chunks and cook in salted boiling water until just done. Drain well.

Roll chunks in grated cheese. Pack in a fireproof dish and put under the grill or in the top of hot oven for about 10 minutes until the cheese is browned.

Parsnips
Grated cheese

Note for Beginners

The parsnips will take from 10 to 15 minutes to boil. Grate the cheese finely and allow about 3–4 oz (75–100 g) per pound (½ kg) of parsnips.

As a main dish this will serve 2–3; as a vegetable 4.

Shropshire

Flemish Peas

Start the carefully scraped tiny new potatoes cooking in boiling salted water, in which there is a small onion and the parsley. After a few minutes add the peas. Cook until both peas and potatoes are ready. Strain and serve together piled up on a hot dish and pour melted butter over them.

Serves 4–6.

About 15–20 very small new
   potatoes (500 g)
Salt
1 small onion
2 or 3 sprigs parsley
1 lb green peas, rather older (500 g)
3 oz butter (75 g)

Hampshire

81

Pease Pudding

8 oz yellow split peas (250 g)
1 pint water or stock (600 ml)
Salt and pepper
Knob of butter
1 dessertspoon top of milk (20 ml)

Pease Pudding has been served for generations in County Durham, generally with ham as the main dish at feasts and celebrations.

Put peas and water into casserole (or saucepan), cover and simmer until soft and water is absorbed, 1–1½ hours. Beat until creamy, add seasoning to taste, butter and milk and beat well. Turn into mould.

Can be eaten hot or cold with ham.

Serves 4–6.

Durham

Potatoes

The full flavour and nourishment of potatoes can only be tasted if they are boiled in their skins, baked or, as a second best, steamed.

As a general rule, fresh boiled potatoes are desirable for every kind of 'made-up' potato dish. Even potato salad should be of potatoes which are boiled in their skins, peeled and seasoned lightly with oil or a little melted bacon fat and lemon or vinegar while they are warm.

West Kent

Potatoes

Austrian

Potatoes
Dripping
Finely chopped onion
Salt

Steam potatoes in their skins and peel while still hot, cut into small pieces. Prepare a frying pan with dripping and finely chopped onion.

Let the onion get a golden brown in the dripping, then add the potatoes, salt and fry until a light brown crust forms on the bottom of the pan.

Dish up and serve hot. Do not use cold potatoes for this, as they must be hot and mealy.

Leicestershire and Rutland

Duchesse Potatoes

Sieve the potatoes. Melt the fat in a pan, add the potatoes and when warm add the beaten egg, about a tablespoon of creamy milk and seasoning to taste. Turn out on to a floured board and divide into small squares. Place these on a greased baking tin, brush over with beaten egg or milk and brown in a hot oven. If preferred, the mixture can be piped through a forcing bag, using a rosette nozzle. Glaze as above. Temperature 450°F (230°C) Gas 8.

Serves 4.

1 lb hot cooked potatoes (500 g)
1 oz margarine (25 g)
1 egg
'Top of milk'
Salt and pepper
Beaten egg or milk to glaze

Cheshire

Potato Croquettes

Boil potatoes and dry off well. Push through wire sieve into warm bowl or pan. Beat in yolk, butter and enough hot milk to make a fairly firm paste, add seasoning and herbs as desired.

Divide into small even-sized pieces on a slightly floured board and leave to cool. Form into cutlet or ball shapes, brush over with beaten egg and roll in the crumbs. Fry in shallow or deep fat.

Serves 4.

1 lb potatoes (500 g)
1 or 2 egg yolks
½ oz butter (15 g)
Hot milk
Salt and pepper
Chopped herbs
Dry white breadcrumbs

Cheshire

Roast Potatoes

Parboil potatoes, drain. Half fill frying pan with fat, heat, and put in potatoes. Cover with a lid and cook slowly for about ¾–1 hour, until crisp.

These can be done in a covered tin in a hot oven.

Note for Beginners

This is a very good way of cooking roast potatoes when the oven is not in use. To parboil the potatoes put them in boiling water and cook gently for 10–15 minutes according to size. Drain well before adding to the fat.

Use a foil lid if no other is available; this is important to keep the fat from splashing. Turn the potatoes over once during cooking, to brown both sides. Use about the same amount of heat as you would to keep a pan simmering.

Cheshire

Salsify and Scorzonera

Delicious vegetables, with a flavour like oysters.

Scrape salsify and cook like carrots.

Boil scorzonera in its skin and when tender the black skin peels off easily.

Cooked salsify and scorzonera are both delicious dipped in batter and fried.

West Kent

Spinach

Wash the spinach well, shake and put into a pan without further water. Put lid on and cook gently till tender, about 10 minutes, stirring frequently. When ready, drain well, chop finely or rub through a sieve. Serve very hot with butter and seasoning.

Cheshire

Spinach-Beet and Seakale-Beet

The green part of spinach-beet and seakale-beet cooks up well as greens. The ribs can be chopped and served with it, but, if they are cooked by themselves like celery and served with a little fresh or melted butter, they make an excellent dish, which travellers will remember meeting abroad under the name of Côte de Blette.

West Kent

Spinach

Creamed

2 lb spinach (1 kg)
2 oz butter (50 g)
½ gill cream (75 ml)
Salt and pepper

Pick all the stalks off the spinach and wash well in several waters. Put in a saucepan with a lid on and boil until thoroughly tender, about 20 minutes. Put through a wire sieve, put back in the saucepan with butter, cream and seasoning, heat thoroughly and serve in a hot dish.

Serves 4.

Leicestershire and Rutland

Swede Turnip

Prepare turnip by peeling thickly and cutting in pieces. Wash. Boil in salted water until soft. Drain. Squeeze water carefully out of turnip. Mash well or squeeze through the potato ricer. Season with pepper and stir in 2–3 tablespoons cream or a knob of butter. Reheat. Time to cook 20–30 minutes.

Cumberland

Sweet Corn

To Cook
Put into boiling salted water and cook for 12–15 minutes. Drain.

To Remove Corn from Cob
Use a sharp pointed knife and slit down the middle of each row of grain. Remove from the top half and then turn round and remove from the bottom half.

Berkshire

Sweet Peppers

Remove a slice from the stalk end and scoop out seeds and veins. Parboil the hollowed peppers in boiling water for 15 minutes. Drain well.

Fill with a stuffing and finish off in a moderate oven, 375°F (190°C) Gas 5, for another 15 minutes. Put a little water in the baking tin while cooking or brush over the surface with melted butter.

Many varieties of stuffings may be used, for instance, Risotto is a good stuffing.

Berkshire

Stuffed Peppers

Slice a lid from each pepper and scoop out every seed and the core. Wash and parboil in salted water for 5 minutes. Drain and cut in half lengthwise.

Melt butter in saucepan and lightly fry onion and mushrooms until onion is clear. Add tomatoes, ham and seasoning and cook for a further 3 minutes. Add egg yolk and soaked breadcrumbs.

Pile the mixture into the prepared peppers, and bake in a moderate oven, 350°F (180°C) Gas 4, until tender, about 20 minutes. Serve with tomato sauce.

3 or 4 peppers

Stuffing
2 oz butter (50 g)
2 chopped onions
2 mushrooms, peeled and chopped
2 medium-sized skinned and chopped
   tomatoes
4–6 oz lean ham (125–175 g), chopped
Seasoning
Chopped parsley
1 egg yolk
2 oz white breadcrumbs (50 g),
   soaked in a little milk
Tomato sauce to serve with it

Gloucestershire

Baked Tomatoes

Cut a cross in each tomato. Put a small teaspoonful of fresh chopped herbs into each cut, with a pat of butter on top. Bake at 425°F (220°C) Gas 7 until cooked—20 minutes or so. Serve at once as a garnish or as a separate vegetable.

For each person:
2 tomatoes
2 small teaspoons fresh chopped herbs
A pat of butter

Hampshire

Salads

A Salad for the Hot Days

Green or red cabbage
French dressing

Any of the following:
Chopped onion or chives
Shredded raw carrot
Diced tomato and cucumber
Chopped parsley
Diced orange and apple
Raisins
Coarsely chopped walnuts
Sliced radishes
Stoned and halved grapes

For serving
Lettuce or sprigs of watercress

Lincolnshire

Mix finely shredded cabbage with French dressing. Add any of the other ingredients. Pile on to a bed of lettuce or sprigs of watercress.

Bean and Pea Salad

½ pint very good parsley sauce, well
   seasoned (300 ml)
½ pint cooked broad beans (300 ml)
½ pint cooked green peas (300 ml)
Lettuce
Cucumber
Beetroot
Spring onion
Radishes
Mustard and cress

West Kent

Add cooked vegetables to the sauce and leave until quite cold.

Line a salad bowl with lettuce leaves and thin slices of cucumber and beetroot and shake in a little finely shredded spring onion. Pour in the bean and pea mixture and garnish with radishes and small bunches of mustard and cress.

Serves 4.

Cabbage or Brussels Sprouts Salad

¼ firm green cabbage or savoy heart or
   12 firm sprouts
2 oz walnuts (50 g)
1 sour dessert apple
1 celery heart
1 sliced onion
Salad dressing
2 tomatoes

Westmorland

Prepare the cabbage or sprouts and shred very finely. Chop the nuts, apple and celery, chop the onion very finely and add these to the cabbage. Blend lightly with salad dressing and pile in a salad bowl. Garnish with small sections of tomatoes.

Serves 4.

Cream Cheese and Celery Salad

Chop celery and mix with cream cheese. Trim watercress and arrange on dish. Pile cream cheese and celery on top and sprinkle with paprika. Sultanas and chopped apple may be added.
  Serves 4.

3 sticks celery
8 oz cream cheese (200 g)
1 bunch watercress
Paprika
Sultanas and chopped apple (if desired)

Durham

Cream Salad

Finely chop lettuce and onions. Mix with cream, sugar, salt and vinegar. Serve with new potatoes and cold beef.
  Serves 4.

1 lettuce
1 bunch spring onions or chives
¼ pint thick cream (150 ml)
1 teaspoon sugar
Salt and vinegar to taste

Yorkshire

Kidney Bean Salad

Slice the beans and cook in the usual way. Drain and leave until cold.
  Fry bacon, finely chopped, until slightly browned.
  Dress the beans with some cream or milk, a little vinegar, salt and pepper, and chopped onion and parsley. Then mix in the fried bacon.
  Serves 4.

1 lb kidney beans (500 g)
A small cube (2½ cm) of fat bacon
Cream or milk
A little vinegar
Salt and pepper
Chopped onion
Parsley

Herefordshire

Marinaded Beetroot

Mix the marinade until the sugar is dissolved. Cut the cooked beetroot into small cubes and place in a bowl. Pour over it the marinade, and leave if possible overnight.
  Serves 2–4.

3 tablespoons best vinegar (wine if
  possible)
1 tablespoon water
2 teaspoons caster sugar
4 cloves (cut in halves)
1 clove garlic (cut in half)
1 medium sized beetroot

Herefordshire

Midinette

Cut equal quantities of the ingredients into strips and mix together. Dress with mayonnaise diluted with vinaigrette (French dressing).

Sour apples
Cold chicken
Celery
Cheese
Mayonnaise
Vinaigrette

Leicestershire and Rutland

Minted Potato Salad

1 lb new potatoes (500 g)
1 tablespoon finely chopped mint
  leaves (30 ml)
1 level tablespoon caster sugar (15 ml)
1 tablespoon vinegar, or more (15 ml)
1 head of lettuce washed and dried
1 hard boiled egg

Westmorland

Boil potatoes in skins until tender, skin quickly and cut into neat slices whilst hot. Put mint, sugar and vinegar in a small bowl and allow to stand for at least an hour. Line a salad bowl with lettuce leaves, lay in it potato slices in layers, sprinkling mint, sugar and vinegar over each layer. Decorate with hard boiled egg.
  Serves 4.

Orange Salad

2 oranges
2 tablespoons chopped apple (60 ml)
2 tablespoons chopped pineapple or
  celery (60 ml)
1 tablespoon nuts (30 ml)
Mayonnaise
Lettuce

Yorkshire

Halve oranges and remove pulp with care. Add chopped orange to apple, celery and nuts and bind with mayonnaise. Line the orange skins with lettuce and pile in the mixture or place the mixture on the lettuce leaves.
  Serves 4.

Orange Salad for Roast Duck

2 thin skinned oranges
2 onions of equal size to oranges
2 oz granulated sugar (50 g)

Cumberland

Wash oranges and slice thinly—skins and all, removing any pips.
  Peel and slice onions thinly.
  Place alternate layers of orange and onion in a basin with sugar sprinkled between layers. Cover basin and leave in a cold place overnight so that the juices will be extracted and the flavours mingle.
  Serves 4.

Potato Salad

1 lb potatoes (500 g)
A little chopped onion
¼ pint salad cream (150 ml) or 5 oz
  carton (142 ml) yogurt with a dash
  of Worcester sauce
Mayonnaise (optional)
Chopped parsley (optional)

Yorkshire

Boil potatoes gently in salted water until just cooked. Drain and dry over a low heat. Cut potatoes into dice, add onion. Add dressing and flavouring whilst potatoes are still hot. Leave in cool place until dressing is absorbed. Then add more dressing or mayonnaise; can be garnished with chopped parsley.
  Serves 4.

Tomato Salad

Slice tomatoes thinly and arrange in a serving dish. Slice very thinly a few onion rings and arrange on top. Sprinkle with French dressing or a little lemon juice, sugar and parsley. Leave to stand 1 hour before serving.

Tomatoes
Onion
French dressing or lemon juice
Sugar
Parsley

Yorkshire

Rice and Mushrooms

Chop the mushrooms when cold and squeeze some lemon juice over them. Add the rice, season with salt, cayenne and ketchup.

1 part mushrooms (cooked in butter)
Lemon juice
2 parts rice (cooked)
Salt
Cayenne
Tomato ketchup

Note for Beginners

For a salad for 4 use approximately 200 g of cooked rice (100 g raw) and 100 g of mushrooms, fried in 15 g of butter.

Leicestershire and Rutland

Winter Salad (1)

Mix the ingredients, sprinkle with sugar and dress.

A very pleasant winter salad can be made of:
Well sliced Brussels sprouts
Grated carrots
Small amounts of swede and turnip, grated
A sprinkling of sugar
French dressing

Herefordshire

Winter Salad (2)

Mix beetroot, celery and cauliflower. Add some green stuff and serve with French salad dressing.

Small cubes of cooked beetroot
Chopped celery
Chopped curd of uncooked cauliflower
Green stuff
French dressing

West Kent

Salad Dressings

A Simple Dressing
Without Vinegar

2 parts olive oil
1 part honey
1 part lemon juice (or orange juice)

West Kent

Blend well in a cream-making machine or with an egg-beater.

Canadian Mayonnaise

2 oz margarine (50 g)
2 oz flour or cornflour (50 g)
¾ pint water (400 ml)
2 egg yolks
1 teaspoon lemon juice (5 ml)
2 tablespoons vinegar (30 ml)
½ teaspoon dry mustard (5 ml)
1 teaspoon salt (15 ml)
Shake of cayenne pepper
3 tablespoons salad oil (45 ml)

Yorkshire

Make a sauce by melting margarine, working in the flour. Add water and cook until thick. In a basin put egg yolks, lemon juice, vinegar, mustard, salt and pepper. Pour oil over. DO NOT STIR. Pour sauce over all whilst still hot. Beat immediately using egg whisk. If too thick add more water or vinegar.

Cream Dressing

½ teaspoon dry mustard (5 ml)
Pinch of salt
1 tablespoon sugar (15 ml)
2 tablespoons vinegar (30 ml)
¼ pint thin cream (150 ml)

Gloucestershire

Mix mustard, salt and sugar together with vinegar, and add the cream slowly.
  Serves 8.

French Dressing

3 parts oil
1 part wine vinegar
Crushed garlic (optional)
Mustard
Salt and freshly ground black pepper
Chopped herbs etc. as wished

Westmorland

Mix seasoning, and if used, garlic with oil, add vinegar and lastly herbs. Shake or stir until emulsified.

Hurry-Up-Mayonnaise

Put egg yolk into a deep bowl. Heat the other ingredients (except oil) in a small pan. When quite hot, add to yolk of egg and beat with a rotary egg-beater. Add oil generously and quickly. The mayonnaise will thicken almost immediately.

1 egg yolk
2 tablespoons vinegar (30 ml)
½ teaspoon salt (2½ ml)
½ teaspoon sugar (2½ ml)
¼ teaspoon pepper (1 ml)
Little paprika
1 teaspoon prepared mustard (5 ml)
Salad oil—¼ pint approximately (150 ml)

Yorkshire

Russian Salad Dressing

Mix all together.

1 tablespoon mayonnaise (30 ml)
1 tablespoon Heinz tomato sauce (15 ml)
1 tablespoon cream (15 ml)
½ teaspoon Worcester sauce (2½ ml)

Northamptonshire and
Soke of Peterborough

Salad Dressing

Cooked

Mix mustard, sugar, egg and seasoning in a saucepan—then add, stirring all the time, the oil, vinegar and milk, cook slowly stirring all the time until it thickens. This will keep for a long time. Makes about ¼ pint (150 ml).

1 dessertspoon mustard (15 ml)
1 dessertspoon caster sugar (15 ml)
1 egg
Salt and pepper
2 tablespoons salad oil (30 ml)
2 tablespoons vinegar (30 ml)
4 tablespoons milk (60 ml)

Oxfordshire

Summer Cream Dressing

Half whip the cream and mix with seasoning and lemon juice. Beat up egg white and fold into cream mixture.
   Serves 4.

3 tablespoons cream or evaporated milk (75 ml)
Pinch of cayenne pepper
¼ teaspoon sugar (1 ml)
Pinch of salt
2 teaspoons lemon juice (10 ml)
1 egg white

Oxfordshire

Thousand Island Dressing

½ pint mayonnaise (300 ml)
2 tablespoons tomato sauce (30 ml)
1 very small onion, finely chopped
2 chopped hard boiled eggs
1 tablespoon finely chopped sweet
   pickles (30 ml)
2 tablespoons sliced stuffed olives (60 ml)
1 tablespoon chopped parsley (30 ml)
1 tablespoon chilli vinegar (15 ml)

Mix all together, adding the vinegar last.

Hampshire

Yogurt Salad Dressings

Yogurt and Mint
Add fresh chopped mint and a little honey to yogurt.

Yogurt and Orange
Add the juice of a sweet orange to yogurt.

Lincolnshire

HERBS & FLAVOURINGS
8

Herbs and Their Uses

Compiled from information in books from Cheshire, Leicestershire and Rutland, West Kent and Yorkshire.

Angelica

The stems may be candied in May or June, and also small pieces of the stem may be stewed with rhubarb and the leaves, chopped, can improve salads.

Alecost

Use in salads, gives a faint flavour of mint. Useful in bread sauce.

Balm, Lemon

Useful in forcemeat, fish sauces and summer drinks; and for making wine.

Basil

With a clove-like flavour, is used to flavour soup, especially turtle and tomato soups; for herb cheeses; calves' liver; in salads; sprinkled on fish.

Bay (Leaves Fresh or Dried)

Leaves in a bouquet garni and to flavour soups, stews, sauces; with herrings; also to flavour custards and milk puddings.

Bergamot

Sparingly in salads and summer drinks.

Borage

In claret cup and other drinks.

Capers

Bottled in vinegar or use bottled nasturtium seeds. In sauces, salads, sandwich spreads.

Caraway

Use the seeds for flavouring cakes, breads, sweets, cabbage and other vegetables. The leaves may be used in salads.

Celery Seed

In soups, stews, sauces, gravies and savoury dishes, when celery is out of season.

Chervil

As a garnish and in salads, sauces, soused fish, soups, egg and cheese dishes.

Chives

Used fresh from the garden. In salads, egg dishes, rissoles, soups, stews, cheese sandwiches; and any dish needing onion flavour. Infuse chives in a light cider vinegar and strain off after ten days. The flavoured vinegar is excellent for salads and egg dishes.

Coriander

Seeds used for flavouring sweets and curries. Use leaves for flavouring soups and stews.

Dandelion

Flowers for wine, leaves for salads, and root for dandelion coffee.

Dill

Young leaves used for flavouring. Cucumber salad welcomes this in small quantities with lemon juice instead of vinegar.
      Soak seeds in vinegar for a few days to make dill vinegar.

Fennel

For sauces used with fish, in salads and pickles. A small shoot added to a bottle of nasturtium capers improves them. The seeds can be used for fennel tea or dusted over buns or rolls. They have an aniseed flavour.

Garlic

Each bulb is made up of many 'cloves'. Should be used very sparingly. Very small amounts in savoury dishes, quarter or half a small clove is sufficient to flavour a soup or stew for four.

Horehound

Excellent candy may be made with this.

Horseradish

Fresh root or bottled grated. The grated root of this may be made into a sauce or cream to be eaten with roast beef; may also be added to white sauce and served hot with fish. Excellent mixed with apple sauce; also in sandwich spreads and savoury dishes.

Lovage

With a celery flavour, used very sparingly in soups, stews and stuffings.

Marjoram

Dried or fresh. In sauces, stews, soups, rissoles, forcemeats and in a bouquet garni. Sprinkled over roast pork is a tasty addition and white fish is improved by small amounts of marjoram added as flavouring. Marjoram and onion when used together will each bring out the flavour of the other.

Mint

Fresh or dried. In sauces, with vegetables during cooking, in meat tarts, in stuffings for lamb; and in salads and sandwich fillings. In juleps and tea. With peas, potatoes, lamb, made into jelly, sprinkled in salad, the leaves also may be crystallized for cake decorations; also for mint pasties and syrups and with onion instead of sage for stuffing; also chopped with sugar for sandwiches.

Nasturtium

Leaves chopped in salads or with egg sandwiches; and the seeds pickled and used as capers.

Parsley

Fresh or dried (fresh is better). In all savoury dishes; to make parsley butter.

Rosemary

Chopped and sprinkled on mutton or lamb before roasting and finely ground for dusting fish before frying and can be added to flavour pickles; also in veal stuffing.

Sage

Fresh or dried. In savoury dishes and stuffings but especially with duck, pork and goose; for flavouring cheeses; also with baked beans and bacon; in salads.

Savory

For flavouring broad beans; in stuffings.

Sorrel

Leaves in salads.

Tarragon

A leaf or two in salads and cold sauces; vinegar.

Thyme

Fresh or dried. In stuffings, soups, sauces and savoury dishes. Lemon thyme is super-excellent for stuffings. In salads, cheeses, bouquet garni and *fines herbes*.

Bouquet Garni

Soups and stews are improved by adding a bay leaf, piece of parsley, thyme and marjoram, tied up in a piece of clean muslin and taken out before serving.

OR

Bouquet garni consists of sprigs of thyme, marjoram, parsley, basil, balm and a bay leaf, tied together in a bunch to flavour meat dishes, and taken out before serving.

OR

2 stalks celery, 1 sprig of thyme, 1 bay leaf, 1 sprig of marjoram.

Fines Herbes

A mixture of chopped fresh parsley, chervil and chives for omelettes and other egg dishes.

OR

Parsley, chives, chervil and tarragon.

Seasonings and Flavourings and Their Uses

Compiled from information in books from Cheshire and West Kent.

Cayenne Pepper

In savoury dishes. It is much stronger than ordinary pepper.

Chillies

These are very hot and are used sparingly in sauces, pickles, stews and savoury rice dishes.

Cinnamon

Ground or stick In cakes, puddings, sauces, stews and savoury dishes. Is great with raspberries.
Stick Simmer with fruits for compotes, and use for extra flavour with canned fruits. Use when pickling beetroot.
Ground Sprinkle on whipped cream for lemon, chocolate, butterscotch banana-cream or apple pie. On baked custards, junkets, melon or a cup of cocoa for novelty. To top breakfast cereals, pears, prunes or peaches. On your breakfast orange or grapefruit. Mixed with cottage cheese. On anything chocolate. Perks up cranberry sauce; adds character to apple sauce.

Cloves

Whole Add to soups, braised meats, dried fruits during cooking. Improves tomato soup or sauce. Peps up prunes and apples. Stick them into the pears you pickle.
Ground On sliced grapefruit, oranges or pineapple. In grapefruit cocktail, apple or peach pie, or chocolate pudding. In potato soups, meat stews and vegetable broths.

Curry Powder

A blend of spices. Add to baked beans, lamb or beef stew, hamburgers, gravy for roast chicken, stuffed eggs, French dressing or mayonnaise, savoury butters for sandwiches, creamed onions, buttered cabbage or string beans.

Curry adds piquancy to made-up fish dishes, or serve fish in an apple, raisin and curry sauce.

Essence

A great variety of flavours can be achieved by using different essences in puddings and cakes. Try vanilla in coffee and chocolate flavoured foods; almond essence in custard to serve with plums; lemon essence with apple.

Ginger

Crystallized Sliced in cakes, puddings and stewed fruits.
Ground Adds new interest to pot roast, apple sauce, creamed chicken, fish dishes and sauces. Sprinkle a bit on peaches, pears, apricots, melons.
Whole pickling (root) In sweet and savoury dishes but is removed before serving.

Lemon

Fresh fruit, dried peel or juice In fish dishes, stuffings, stews, sauces, cakes and puddings.
Rind For many sweet dishes, fish, sauces and cakes.

Mace

Blade or whole Try a piece in milk soups, white stews, rabbit fricassée and chicken pie, chicken soup, shrimp sauce. Mashed, hashed and creamed potatoes taste excellent with it.
Powdered or ground Use in pound cakes, cherry pie, chocolate puddings, fruit jellies. Sprinkle some on bottled or canned cherries, peaches, pears and apricots. Add to pickled damsons. Add to spinach, stuffings, stews and fish stock.

Mustard

Whole seed Generally only used in pickles and chutneys.
Ground Used in all savoury dishes.

Nutmeg

Complements vegetables—boiled cabbage, Brussels sprouts, mushrooms, asparagus, cauliflower and especially spinach. Makes delicious spinach or nettle soup, split pea soup, dumplings for chicken stew, hard sauce. Milk puddings, junkets and jellies. Use with fruits —fruit salads, sliced bananas, rhubarb pie and fruit cakes, Christmas cakes. With stewed rhubarb and sauce for cauliflower.

Orange

Rind or juice of fresh oranges or dried rind In savoury dishes, cakes, pies, puddings and sauces.

Paprika

Ground red pepper (less pungent than cayenne). For sprinkling on dishes to add colour and for flavouring. Used to make goulash.

Pepper

Whole peppercorns or ground. In all savoury dishes. Home ground pepper has the best flavour.

Salt

Cooking In all savoury dishes. A little in all sweet dishes, cakes, etc. improves the flavour.

Sugar

In all sweet dishes. A little in savoury dishes brings out the other flavours.

Vinegar

Malt, tarragon, chilli, garlic, wine, elderflower, etc. A little added to stews, sauces, or other savoury dishes often improves the flavour. Vinegar helps to make meat more tender.

The Drying of Herbs

When drying herbs, the aim is to preserve the natural colour as nearly as possible whilst retaining the full flavour and aroma.

Herbs just tied into bunches and left to dry soon lose their fresh colour, and naturally, they attract dust. The fine flavour is lost and the finished product is faded and insipid.

To dry herbs satisfactorily, pick them when free from dew or rain, before the full heat of the day, and before they come into flower.

Pick the leaves from the stalks of the larger varieties and tie the smaller ones into sprays.

Lay on shallow trays in thin layers so that the moisture can escape during drying. Do not pack tightly as the trapped moisture will darken the colour of the herbs and detract from the true flavour.

Leave in a cool oven, 110–130°F (45–55°C), until quite dry, or ideally, leave in the airing cupboard or on a rack over the stove until dry. Oven drying takes more care than the other methods and invites singeing should the oven temperature increase suddenly.

Parsley is the one exception to the above methods. Place in a hot oven, 400°F (200°C) Gas 6, for 1 minute then finish off in a cool oven or in the airing cupboard.

When the herbs are dry, roll them down with a rolling pin and pick out any stalks. Rub large leaved herbs through a wire sieve.

Store all herbs in tins or small jars and keep them in a cool dry place.

Herbs may also be put into deep freeze. Wash, drain and dry, taking care not to bruise. Either lay sprigs of herb flat and wrap in tin foil, or chop ready for use and pack into small plastic containers. To use, either thaw out or grate into the dish they are to flavour.

Yorkshire

A Mixed Seasoning for Stews and Soups

Dry thoroughly and put through a sieve. Put in airtight bottle or tin. Always ready. Use sparingly.

1 oz pepper (25 g)
½ oz powdered cloves, mace, ginger (15 g)
1 teaspoon powdered mixed herbs (10 ml)
1 oz powdered salt (25 g)

West Kent

Burnet or Cucumber Vinegar

Fill a wide mouthed jar with fresh green leaves of burnet and cover them with vinegar. Let them steep for 10 days; if you wish a very strong essence, strain the vinegar, put it on some fresh leaves and let them steep 14 days more.

The flavour of burnet resembles cucumber so exactly, that when infused in vinegar the nicest palate would pronounce it to be cucumber.

Cheese of the Seven Herbs

4 oz grated cheese (125 g)
2 tablespoons thick cream (30 ml)
3 tablespoons sherry or cider (45 ml)
2 level tablespoons herbs consisting of a
  mixture of finely chopped parsley,
  sage, thyme, tarragon, chives,
  chervil and winter savory (30 ml)
Seasoning to taste

Put all ingredients into a double saucepan and stir over a very gentle heat until the mixture is creamy and a pale green in colour. Whilst still warm, put into small pots and use when cold.

Lincolnshire

Mint Pastry

Chopped mint
Brown sugar
Currants
Pastry

Take equal parts fresh finely chopped mint, brown sugar and currants. Mix well and pound together to a soft, thick consistency. Spread between thin layers of pastry and cook until golden.

Note for Beginners

Make these with short pastry using 6 oz flour (150 g) and allowing about 2 oz each (50 g) of currants and sugar with 3 level tablespoons finely chopped mint (45 ml). Bake at 425°F (220°C) Gas 7, for about 20 minutes.

Lincolnshire

Mint Tea

1 teaspoon dried mint (10 ml)
½ pint boiling water (250 ml)
Squeeze of lemon juice
Sugar to taste

Pour the boiling water on to the dried mint, infuse 4 minutes, strain and add lemon juice and sugar.
  Excellent hot for colds and refreshing as a cold drink.

West Kent

Mint Vinegar

Put into a wide-mouthed bottle enough fresh young mint leaves to fill it loosely. Fill up with good vinegar, and infuse for 2 or 3 weeks. Pour off clear into another bottle, and cork down for use.

Fresh young mint leaves
Good vinegar

West Kent

Omelette with Herbs

Make omelette in usual way, but add chopped parsley and chives to egg mixture and water. Serve with sprigs of fresh parsley.
    Serves 2–3.

6 eggs
Salt and pepper
1 tablespoon chopped fresh parsley (30 ml)
1 tablespoon chopped chives (30 ml)
1 teaspoon water (5 ml)
1 oz butter (25 g)
4 sprigs fresh parsley

Yorkshire

Rosemary Cream

Beat the egg yolks and add to the milk in which a sprig of bruised rosemary has been infused, stir until the mixture thickens. Put in the sugar, stir until dissolved, then strain through a sieve to remove rosemary. Dissolve the gelatine in 1 tablespoon water (30 ml) and add to the custard. Whip the cream slightly and stir it lightly into the custard. Pour into prepared mould.
    Serves 4–6.

1 pint milk (500 ml)
1 sprig rosemary
2 egg yolks
1½ oz caster sugar (40 g)
½ oz gelatine (15 g)
¼ pint cream (150 ml)

Cambridgeshire

Rosemary Sugar

Clean and dry sprigs of rosemary. Place in a screw-topped jar, and fill up with sugar (caster). Shake well and leave 24 hours. Shake again, and leave for a week.
    The flavoured sugar is unusual, and good with any milk sweet.
    Lavender sugar can be made in the same way.

West Kent

Tarragon Vinegar

This is a very agreeable addition to soups, salad sauces and to mix mustard.

Fill a wide mouthed bottle with fresh gathered tarragon leaves.

(They should be gathered on a dry day between Midsummer and Michaelmas, just before the plant flowers.) Pick the leaves off the stalks and dry them a little before the fire; cover them with the best vinegar, let them steep for 14 days, and then strain through a flannel jelly bag and pour into bottles; cork them carefully and keep them in a dry place.

To Preserve Capers

Nasturtium Seeds

Nasturtium seeds
Salted water
Spiced vinegar

Wash nasturtium seeds in cold water and soak overnight in cold salted water. Cover with cold spiced vinegar. Seal and keep for 12 months before using.

Spiced Vinegar
1 quart vinegar (1¼ l)
2 oz salt (50 g)
A dozen peppercorns
A small piece of horseradish
2 cloves
3 or 4 tarragon leaves

Mix together.

SAUCES & STUFFINGS
9

Savoury Sauces

A Superior Sauce—Béchamel

Quick Method

Scald the milk, pour over vegetables and spices. Cover and leave to infuse for 30 minutes, then strain. Melt the butter, add the flour and cook without browning, add the flavoured milk and simmer, stirring all the time. Strain, add salt to taste and cream. Reheat before using, if necessary.

This sauce can be flavoured and coloured as desired.

Serves 4.

½ pint milk (300 ml)
Slice of carrot and turnip
2 inches celery (5 cm)
1 small onion stuck with cloves
1 blade mace
6 white peppercorns
1 oz butter (25 g)
1 oz flour (25 g)
Salt
1 tablespoon cream (15 ml)

Berkshire

Sauce Mornay

½ pint Béchamel sauce (300 ml)
1–1½ oz grated cheese (25–40 g)
  (Gruyère or Parmesan)
Pepper and salt
1 small teaspoon French mustard (5 ml)
Cream or the top of the milk

Berkshire

Beat the cheese thoroughly into the hot sauce off the fire. Add seasonings.

The cheese thickens the sauce considerably, and extra liquid may have to be added. The amount of flour in the basic sauce may be reduced to ½ oz to ½ pint of milk (15 g to 300 ml).

Reheat the sauce, taking care not to boil it or the sauce will curdle.

Use for eggs, vegetables, gratins, fish, spaghetti and gnocchi.
Serves 4.

Barbecue Sauce

1 oz butter (25 g)
1 small chopped onion
4 tablespoons tomato sauce (60 ml)
2 tablespoons vinegar (30 ml)
2 dessertspoons chutney (30 ml)
1 teaspoon made mustard (10 ml)
1 level teaspoon sugar (5 ml)
1 tablespoon Worcester sauce (15 ml)

Yorkshire

Melt butter. Add onion, sauté. Mix remainder of ingredients in saucepan and bring to boil.

Alternative Uses

1   This sauce can be used with lamb chops that have been cooked for 6–10 minutes. Remove chops. Drain fat, pour sauce over and cook 30–40 minutes in slow oven.
2   Alternatively place slices of cold cooked lamb into an oven-proof dish and gently warm through—one way of using the remains of the Sunday joint.
Serves 4.

Bitter Sweet Sauce

1 level teaspoon mustard (5 ml)
2 tablespoons vinegar (30 ml)
4 oz Demerara or soft brown sugar
  (100 g)
6 or 8 cloves
4 tablespoons liquor from boiled ham
  (60 ml)

Berkshire

To serve with boiled ham.

In a small saucepan blend the mustard and vinegar. Add the sugar and cloves. Set in a warm place to melt.

When the ham is cooked, add 4 tablespoons of the liquor in which it has been boiled. Stir well, heat thoroughly, strain, and serve with the ham.
Serves 4.

Cranberry Sauce

⅛ pint water (75 ml)
2 oz sugar (50 g)
8 oz cranberries (250 g)

Yorkshire

Heat water and sugar until sugar dissolves, bring to boil, add the washed and drained cranberries. Simmer for 7–10 minutes until tender. Sieve and test for sweetness. Serve with turkey or capon.
Serves 4–6.

Cumberland Sauce

Chop the shallots very finely, parboil for 2 minutes and drain. Peel and cut finely the orange and lemon. Cover with water and boil for 5 minutes. Drain well.

Place the shallots with the peel in a bowl and add the juice of the orange and half that of the lemon. Add ginger, cayenne and the jelly (melted) and the port. Mix well.

Suitable for cold meat or venison.

Serves 6.

3 shallots
1 orange
1 lemon
Pinch of powdered ginger
Pinch of cayenne pepper
6 level tablespoons red currant jelly (90 ml)
5 tablespoons port (75 ml)

Cumberland

Curry Sauce

Soak coconut in boiling stock for 15 minutes. Strain. Melt butter in pan, fry chopped onion, then chopped apple until soft. Add curry powder, fry 1 minute. Add flour, mix well. Remove from heat, stir in stock, stir over heat until boiling, add chutney and sultanas. Cover, but stir occasionally and cook for 30 minutes. Add lemon juice, add salt.

Any cold meats or vegetables may be added, and if served with boiled rice, makes a substantial meal.

Serves 4.

1 dessertspoon coconut (20 ml)
½ pint stock (300 ml)
1 oz butter (25 g)
1 medium onion
1 medium apple
4 level teaspoons curry powder (20 ml)
1 oz flour (25 g)
1 dessertspoon chutney (20 ml)
1 dessertspoon sultanas (20 ml)
1 dessertspoon lemon juice (10 ml)
Salt to taste

Yorkshire

Dutch Sauce

Melt butter, stir in flour, add water or stock and boil for 2 minutes. Remove from heat, cool and stir in oil, capers, salt, cayenne and vinegar. If added before the sauce has cooled, the oil etc. will float on the top. Stir in the yolks gradually, beat over the heat until the sauce thickens, but do not boil. If necessary, thin with a little more stock or water.

Serves 4.

½ oz butter (15 g)
½ oz flour (15 g)
¼ pint chicken stock or cold water (150 ml)
2 tablespoons salad oil (30 ml)
1 tablespoon chopped capers (15–30 ml)
¼ teaspoon salt (1 ml)
Cayenne pepper
1 tablespoon tarragon vinegar (15 ml)
2 egg yolks

Surrey

Espagnole Sauce

2 oz ham or bacon (50 g)
2 oz butter or dripping (50 g)
1 onion
1 small carrot
1 shallot
2 oz mushrooms (50 g)
2 oz flour (50 g)
1 pint brown stock (600 ml)
¼ pint tomato pulp (150 ml)
⅛ pint sherry (75 ml)
Pepper and salt

Cheshire

Cut up the ham or bacon and sauté in the butter or dripping. Slice the vegetables and fry them until beginning to brown. Add the flour and fry all slowly till a rich brown colour. Add the stock and bring to boiling point. Simmer for about 2 hours. Add the tomato pulp when the sauce is half cooked. Pass through a very fine strainer or a tammy cloth. Add the sherry. Re-heat the sauce and season.
    Serves 4–6.

Hollandaise Sauce

2 tablespoons water (30 ml)
2 egg yolks
2 teaspoons white vinegar (10 ml)
2 oz butter (50 g)
Squeeze of lemon juice
Salt and pepper

Westmorland

Put water, egg yolks and vinegar into the top of a double boiler. Stir till thick. Remove top pan to side of stove, stir in butter bit by bit, then lemon juice, salt and pepper to taste.
    Serve with fish, meat loaf, asparagus or cauliflower.
    Serves 2–4.

Horseradish Sauce That Will Keep

Horseradish
Vinegar
Salt

Leicestershire and Rutland

Grate the horseradish and bottle with a small quantity of vinegar and a little salt. This will keep for 6 months and can be used with roast beef.

Horseradish Sauce Cold

1 oz grated horseradish (25 g)
1 gill cream (125 ml)
A little pepper, salt, mustard, vinegar
  and caster sugar

Leicestershire and Rutland

Whisk the cream lightly and add the horseradish and seasonings.
    Serves 4.

Horseradish and Cucumber Cream

Beat all ingredients into cream taking care not to overbeat. Serve with cold chicken or game, cold fish, etc.
Serves 4.

¼ pint lightly whipped cream (150 ml)
1 tablespoon grated horseradish (30 ml)
2 tablespoons finely chopped cucumber (60 ml) (remove skin and pips)
A very small piece of onion very finely chopped
Pepper and salt
1 dessertspoon tarragon vinegar (10 ml)

Westmorland

Hot Beetroot Sauce

Dice beetroot. Peel and finely chop onion and apple. Put onion and apple in a saucepan with dripping and allow to cook and glaze without browning. Add diced beetroot, and keep stirring using a wooden spoon. Make a sauce with cornflour, water, vinegar and sugar. Add sauce just before serving. Serve with pork chops, ham or gammon.
Serves 4.

1 lb cooked beetroot (450 g)
1 medium onion
1 large green apple
Dripping size of a walnut
1 level tablespoon cornflour (15 ml)
3 tablespoons water (45 ml)
3 tablespoons vinegar (45 ml)
1 teaspoon brown sugar (10 ml)
Seasoning

Durham

Lord Welby's Sauce

A delicious substitute for horseradish sauce.

Mix all ingredients together and serve in a sauce boat. The parsnip, being sweet, requires no sugar.

The story of this recipe is that Lord Welby used to dine frequently at Christ Church College and on one occasion there was no horseradish sauce. The cook made a substitute sauce with parsnip and Lord Welby said that it was the best horseradish sauce he had ever tasted!
Serves 4.

2 tablespoons cream (30 ml)
1 tablespoon mustard (30 ml)
1 tablespoon vinegar (15 ml)
1 tablespoon grated parsnip (60 ml)
A little salt

Yorkshire

Mint Sauce That Will Keep

Boil vinegar and sugar together. Withdraw from heat and add chopped mint. Bottle when cold and seal.
When required for use, add more vinegar, as the sauce should be very thick when made.

1 teacupful finely chopped mint (150 ml)
6 oz white sugar (150 g)
½ pint vinegar (250 ml)

Leicestershire and Rutland

The Perfect Mint Sauce

Fresh mint leaves
Caster sugar
Boiling water
Lemon juice or wine vinegar

West Kent

Pound down the leaves, preferably with pestle and mortar. Cover with caster sugar to take up all juice. Add just a little boiling water as will dissolve the sugar. Sharpen with strained lemon juice, home-made wine vinegar, or shop vinegar if you must.

Sauce Indienne

3 oz butter (75 g)
1 heaped tablespoon plain flour (25 g)
1 teaspoon curry powder (10 ml)
½ pint milk (300 ml)
¼ pint cream (150 ml)
Salt

Berkshire

A very favourite sauce with the French. Can be used with fish, hard or soft boiled eggs, and is particularly good with chicken. Plain boiled rice should be served with the chicken, eggs or fish.

Make your sauce in the ordinary way and be sure to cook your curry powder dry with the flour—very important. If you do not want to use cream, use more milk.

This sauce is excellent cold in the summer—then put a tablespoon of aspic in the sauce, as it gives a more glazed look. Enough for 4 people.

Sweet-Sour Sauce

Chinese

A little oil for cooking
1 clove garlic
The finely chopped tops of 1 or 2 spring
  onions if available
1–1¼ teacups malt vinegar (170–200 ml)
½ teacup brown sugar (75 g)
1 dessertspoon chopped preserved
  ginger (20 ml) (or ginger marmalade)
1 dessertspoon chopped Chinese sweet
  pickles (20 ml)
3–4 drops soya (Chinese) sauce
1 dessertspoon cornflour (20 ml)

Devon

Heat a very little cooking oil in a heavy frying pan and cook the crushed clove of garlic and the onion tops for a few seconds. Next add the vinegar and sugar.

When the sugar is melted add the chopped ginger and sweet pickles and the soya sauce.

Thicken with cornflour mixed with a little water. Stir for a minute or two and then serve.

Serves 4.

Tomato Sauce

Melt the butter in a saucepan. Add the finely chopped onion and cook for a few minutes, but do not allow to brown.

Add the tomatoes cut in halves, the sweet basil, sugar and

seasoning. Cover with lid and simmer until the vegetables are quite cooked and pulpy.

Next rub the whole through a fine sieve. Return to the pan and thicken with a little plain flour. Cook for a moment or two and serve.

This makes approximately ½ pint (250 ml) of sauce.

With the addition of a little good stock it can be served as soup.

Serves 4.

½ oz butter (15 g)
1 medium sized onion
1 lb tomatoes (500 g) (tinned tomatoes can be used)
1 teaspoon dried sweet basil (5 ml)
1 teaspoon sugar (5 ml)
Pepper and salt to taste
A little plain flour

Devon

Sweet Sauces

Clotted Cream

Use new milk and strain at once as soon as milked into shallow pans. Let it stand for 24 hours in winter and 12 hours in summer. Then put the pan on the stove, or, better still, into a steamer containing water, and let it slowly heat until the cream begins to show a raised ring round the edge. When sufficiently cooked place in a cool dairy and leave for 12 or 24 hours. Great care must be taken in moving the pans so that the cream is not broken, both in putting on the fire and taking off. When required, skim off the cream in layers into a glass dish for the table, taking care to have a good 'crust' on the top. Clotted cream is best done over a stick fire.

Cornwall

Devonshire Clotted Cream

Put fresh milk into a wide bowl and leave to stand for approximately 12 hours in summer and 24 hours in winter.

Stand the bowl over a pan of water and heat this *very slowly* so that the water never boils.

Leave until the surface of the milk has formed a thick crust.

Stand in a cool place until next day, then carefully skim the scalded cream from the top of the milk.

Devon

Cornflour or Arrowroot Sauce

Sweet White Sauce

Mix cornflour or arrowroot with some milk, heat remainder with lemon rind. Stir on to cornflour or arrowroot, return to pan and boil for 5 minutes, remove lemon rind and add sugar.

Serves 4.

1 teaspoon cornflour or arrowroot (10 ml)
½ pint milk (250 ml)
Strip of lemon rind
1 dessertspoon caster sugar (10 ml)

Herefordshire

Custard Sauce

Economical

½ teaspoon cornflour (5 ml)
½ pint milk (300 ml)
1 egg
1 dessertspoon sugar (10 ml)
Pinch of salt
Flavouring if desired

Cheshire

Blend cornflour with a little of the milk. Add beaten egg, sugar, salt and the rest of the milk. Put into a pan and cook thoroughly, stirring all the time until it thickens. Cook another 5 minutes without allowing it to boil. Flavour if liked.
    Serves 4.

Custard Sauce

Rich

1 pint milk (600 ml)
Lemon rind
3 eggs or 5 yolks
Sugar to taste
Flavouring

Cheshire

Heat milk (boil in summer) with lemon rind. Beat eggs and sugar together. Pour milk over eggs, stirring at same time. Strain into pan and stir over gentle heat until custard thickens. Remove instantly. Serve hot or cold.
    Serves 8.

Jam and Marmalade Sauce

1 gill water (150 ml)
1½ oz loaf sugar (40 g)
1 tablespoon jam or marmalade (30 ml)
Few drops lemon juice for jam sauces
    and cochineal to improve colour
    when red jam is used

Herefordshire

Boil water and sugar for 3–4 minutes, stir in jam or marmalade, bring to boiling point and strain if jam is used.
    Serves 2–3.

Melba Sauce

Raspberries
Water
Sugar

Yorkshire

This can be made at the end of the raspberry season. Stew the raspberries with very little water. Sieve and sweeten. Ready to serve.
    To store, cool, pour into cartons, seal, label and freeze.

110

Rum Butter

Melt butter, add sugar and nutmeg. Pour in rum, mix well until it starts to thicken. Pour into an attractive old china bowl and leave to set.

Serves 8 or more.

1 lb butter (450 g)
1½ lb soft brown sugar (700 g)
2 teaspoons grated nutmeg (10 ml)
1 wineglass rum (100 ml)

Cumberland

Stuffings

Apple and Prune Stuffing

Bind all together. Good for pork.

12 prunes soaked, stoned and chopped
2 oz cashew nuts chopped (50 g)
2 oz melted butter (50 g)
1 egg, beaten
2 large apples cored, peeled and rough chopped
6 oz breadcrumbs (175 g)
Grated rind and juice of lemon
Seasonings

Hampshire

Chestnut Stuffing

Make a split in both ends of the nuts and boil them in water for 10 minutes, then skin. Put them into a pan with stock or milk to cover and simmer gently until tender. Mash or sieve the nuts.

Chop ham and add with other ingredients to the chestnuts. Bind with the beaten egg.

Use to stuff turkey, chicken, etc.

1 lb chestnuts (500 g)
½ pint stock or milk (300 ml)
2 oz ham or bacon (50 g)
4 oz breadcrumbs (100 g)
1 teaspoon chopped parsley (10 ml)
A little grated lemon rind
1 teaspoon sugar (10 ml)
Seasoning
1 oz margarine, melted (25 g)
1 egg

Northumberland

Forcemeat *Veal*

8 tablespoons breadcrumbs (250 ml)
1 tablespoon chopped parsley (30 ml)
2 tablespoons shredded suet (60 ml)
2 teaspoons chopped bacon (20 ml)
½ teaspoon chopped onion (5 ml)
1 teaspoon powdered herbs (10 ml)
Grated rind of lemon
Dash of pepper
½ teaspoon salt (5 ml)
1 egg
Little milk
(the bacon and onion may be omitted)

Yorkshire

Mix all the ingredients together thoroughly and bind with the beaten egg and a little milk.

Orange Stuffing

¼ pint orange pulp (150 ml)
4 oz breadcrumbs (100 g)
½ teaspoon grated lemon rind (5 ml)
½ oz butter (15 g), melted
3 tablespoons orange juice (45 ml)
The grated rind of an orange
2 teaspoons chopped mint (15 ml)
Salt

Hampshire

Four or five oranges will be needed. Combine all ingredients and use for duck really, but it is a delicious stuffing for turkey.

Raisin and Nut Stuffing

6 oz fresh breadcrumbs (150 g)
2–3 oz chopped stoned raisins (50–75 g)
2–3 oz chopped nuts (50–75 g)
2 oz melted butter (50 g), not oiled
1 heaped tablespoon chopped parsley
   (45 ml)
1 egg, beaten
Seasoning if liked

Berkshire

A good stuffing for vegetables.

Mix all the ingredients together.

Sage and Onion Stuffing

3 large onions
6 tablespoons breadcrumbs (200 ml)
1 dessertspoon chopped parsley (20 ml)
Dash of pepper
Small half teaspoon salt (2½ ml)
2 oz butter or margarine (50 g)

Yorkshire

Boil the onions for 5 minutes. Add to the other ingredients after chopping finely. Add the melted fat and mix well together.

Sweet Corn Stuffing

Melt the butter in a saucepan, add the chopped onion and cook over gentle heat until beginning to soften. Stir in the salt, pepper and sweet corn and cook for 2–3 minutes. Remove from the heat, add the lemon rind and juice, the parsley and beaten egg. Mix thoroughly and fill loosely into the bird.

Sufficient to stuff a 3–4 lb (1½ kg) bird.

1 oz butter (25 g)
1 small onion, finely chopped
Salt and pepper
½ can sweet corn kernels, drained
   (5 oz or 140 g)
Finely grated rind of ½ a lemon
Squeeze lemon juice
1 tablespoon chopped parsley (30 ml)
1 egg

Surrey

To Serve With a Fowl

Grate the suet and add to the other ingredients finely chopped. Bind together with beaten egg.

2 oz suet (50 g)
4 oz breadcrumbs (100 g)
1 small onion, chopped finely
1 tablespoon chopped parsley (30 ml)
1 teaspoon chopped mint (10 ml)
½ teaspoon chopped thyme (2½ ml)
4 nasturtium leaves, chopped
Salt and pepper
1 egg

Yorkshire

Unusual Stuffing for Turkey

Mix all together. This quantity is sufficient to stuff the crop of the bird.

4 oz fresh breadcrumbs (100 g)
4 oz diced apple (100 g)
2 oz chopped onion (50 g)
1 oz raisins (25 g)
1 oz melted margarine (25 g)
Pepper and salt

Pembrokeshire

HOT PUDDINGS
10

Apple and Almond Pancakes

Pancakes
4 oz plain flour (100 g)
1 egg
Pinch salt
½ pint milk (250 ml)

Filling
1 lb cooking apples (500 g)
Juice 1 lemon
2 oz butter (50 g)
2 oz caster sugar (50 g)
½ teaspoon cinnamon (5 ml)
1 oz ground almonds (25 g)
1 oz sultanas (25 g)
2 oz flaked or nibbed almonds (50 g)
Icing sugar

Yorkshire

Peel, core and slice apples, toss in lemon juice. Melt butter in pan, add sugar and stir in apples, juice and cinnamon. Cook gently, stirring occasionally until soft. Stir in ground almonds and sultanas.

Cook pancakes—spread filling along centres, roll up and arrange in an ovenproof dish. Sprinkle almonds on top—reheat in oven and dredge with icing sugar before serving.

Serves 4.

Apple Crisp

Peel, core and slice apples and stew with 2 tablespoons sugar until soft.

Sieve baking powder and ground rice together, add coconut.

Cream margarine and caster sugar until light, adding almond essence slowly.

Beat egg and add alternately with dry ingredients to the creamed mixture.

Grease a shallow fireproof dish and spread the jam over the bottom.

Place stewed apples over the jam then cover the apples with the creamed mixture.

Bake in a fairly hot oven, 400°F (200°C) Gas 6, for 15–20 minutes or until top is crisp.

Serves 4.

1 lb Bramley or other cooking apples (500 g)
2 tablespoons sugar (50 g)
1 oz ground rice (25 g)
1 level teaspoon baking powder (5 ml)
2 oz desiccated coconut (50 g)
2 oz margarine (50 g)
2 oz caster sugar (50 g)
½ teaspoon almond essence (2½ ml)
1 egg
2 tablespoons jam (60 ml)

Devon

Apple Flan

Line a greased flan tin with short pastry. Into this put grated apple, raisins, sprinkled sugar and a little powdered cinnamon in layers, finishing with apple. Pour over this a few tablespoons of (melted) golden syrup. Put a few knobs of butter on top, and bake for about 20 minutes at 425°F (220°C) Gas 7.

(My own invention and well liked.)

Short pastry
Grated apple
Raisins
Sugar
Cinnamon
Golden syrup, melted
A few knobs of butter

Devon

Apple Soufflé

Peel, core and slice apples, cook with sugar and a little water if necessary. When tender add butter, cinnamon and beaten yolks. Whisk whites stiffly and fold into apple mixture. Turn into well buttered soufflé dish, sprinkle with almonds. Place in oven 375–400°F (190–200°C) Gas 5–6, for about 30 minutes. Serve with whipped cream.

Serves 4.

2 medium apples (¾ lb or 350 g)
2 oz caster sugar (50 g)
1 oz butter (25 g)
Pinch cinnamon
2 egg yolks
3 egg whites
1 oz chopped almonds (25 g)
Whipped cream
1½ pint soufflé dish (1 l)

Durham

Apple Streusel

Make pastry and line a 7–8 inch (18–20 cm) flan ring. Peel, core and slice apples, toss in lemon juice and arrange in pastry shell. Sprinkle with sugar and spices. For topping mix together flour,

Pastry
6 oz flour (150 g)
3 oz lard (75 g)
Water to mix.

115

Filling
1 lb cooking apples (450 g)
Slice of lemon
1 oz sugar (25 g)
¼ level teaspoon cinnamon (1 ml)
¼ level teaspoon nutmeg or allspice (1 ml)

Topping
3 oz sifted plain flour (75 g)
3 oz brown sugar (75 g)
Grated rind of lemon
6 tablespoons softened butter or
   margarine (75 g)

Yorkshire

sugar and lemon rind. Cut up softened butter or margarine into mixture using pastry blender or two knives until crumbly. Sprinkle mixture over apples.

Bake in hot oven 450°F (230°C) Gas 8, for 15 minutes. Reduce to 350°F (180°C) Gas 4, and cook for 20 minutes.

Serves 6.

Note: Pastry shell can be omitted and sweet made in a pie-dish.

Baked Lemon Whip

6 oz caster sugar (175 g)
1 level tablespoon plain flour (15 ml)
Good pinch of salt
2 eggs
Rind and juice of 1 large or 2 small
   lemons
¼ pint milk (150 ml)
1 oz butter (25 g)
Light sprinkling of caster sugar

Yorkshire

Sift sugar, flour and salt together, beat in egg yolks, lemon juice and rind and milk. Melt butter and stir in mixture. Beat egg whites then fold into mixture.

Pour into a dish and stand in baking tin with hot water half-way up. Bake at 375°F (190°C) Gas 5, for 30–40 minutes. Sprinkle top with caster sugar.

Serves 3–4.

Blackcurrant Flan

4 oz plain flour (125 g)
¾ dessertspoon cinnamon (10 ml)
2½ oz butter or margarine (70 g)
¾ oz ground almonds (20 g)
¾ oz caster sugar (20 g)
1 teaspoon lemon juice (5 ml)
1 tablespoon beaten egg (15 ml)
12 oz blackcurrants (350 g)
3 oz sugar (75 g)

Cumberland

Sieve the flour and cinnamon, rub in the margarine, mix in ground almonds and sugar.

Sprinkle with the lemon juice, beat in the egg to a firm paste. Reserve ¼ of the paste to form a lattice topping on the flan. Roll the remaining paste and line a 7 inch (18 cm) flan ring (preferably fluted).

Prepare the blackcurrants, half fill the case with the fruit, sprinkle on the sugar, fill the case with the remaining fruit. With the trimmings and reserved paste, cut strips ⅓ inch (1 cm) wide and arrange in a lattice pattern on the top. Brush the lattice with water and sprinkle with caster sugar to produce a glaze.

Bake at 400°F (200°C) Gas 6, for approximately 20–25 minutes.

Serves 4.

Bread Pudding de luxe

Grease the pie-dish. Put milk into a saucepan and bring to the boil, then add lard and stir until melted. Crumble bread into greased dish and add fruit and sugar. Beat egg and salt and add to boiled milk and melted lard. Pour over bread and mix well together.

Bake in oven 400°F (200°C) Gas 6, for 30 minutes.

Serves 4.

½ pint milk (300 ml)
2 oz lard (50 g)
4 oz bread (100 g) (not crust)
2 oz currants (50 g)
2 oz sultanas (50 g)
2 oz raisins (50 g)
2 oz moist brown sugar (50 g)
1 egg
Pinch of salt

Berkshire

Caramelled Rice

Cook rice in milk with vanilla and sugar, very slowly, for 1–1½ hours. Stir in peel and cherries while hot. When cool, fold in cream.

Put in a dish, and sprinkle with brown sugar and crisp under grill for 1 minute. Serve with cream or ice-cream.

3 oz rice (75 g)
1 pint milk (600 ml)
Vanilla essence
2 oz sugar (50 g)
2 oz candied lemon peel (50 g)
1 oz glacé cherries (25 g)
½ gill thin cream or evaporated milk (75 ml)
2–3 oz brown sugar (50–75 g)

Note for Beginners

The best way of cooking the rice is in a double boiler, cooking until the rice is soft and the mixture creamy.

It makes enough for 4, more if served with ice-cream.

Northumberland

Cheese Surprise

Make pastry and line an 8 inch (20 cm) flan ring. Bake in a moderate oven, 375°F (190°C) Gas 5.

Mix cheese, egg yolks, sugar, rind and milk or cream together thoroughly. Add the stiffly beaten egg whites and pour into the already cooked pastry case. Bake for 15–20 minutes at 350°F (180°C) Gas 4.

Decorate with more orange rind cut into strips.

Serves 4–6.

Cooked pastry flan made with 4 oz flour (100 g) and 2 oz butter (50 g)
6 oz cream cheese (150 g)
2 eggs
4 tablespoons sugar (100 g)
Grated rind of ½ orange
¼ pint cream or top of milk (125 ml)
Little orange rind to decorate

Cumberland

Coconut Apple Pudding

Peel and stew the apples in the water until tender, and beat with a wooden spoon until smooth. Stir in the coconut, sugar, breadcrumbs, lemon rind, butter and beaten egg. Mix all together thoroughly and turn into a greased fireproof dish.

Bake in a moderate oven, 350°F (180°C) Gas 4, until set, about 25 minutes. Lower the heat if the pudding shows any tendency to boil.

Serves 4.

1 lb cooking apples (500 g)
½ pint water (250 ml)
2 tablespoons desiccated coconut (40 g)
2 tablespoons sugar (50 g)
1 oz breadcrumbs (25 g)
Grated rind of 1 lemon
1 oz butter or margarine (25 g)
1 egg

Isle of Ely

Coffee and Walnut Pudding

2 oz butter (50 g)
2 oz sugar (50 g)
2 eggs
2 oz plain flour (50 g)
1 oz ground rice (25 g)
2 oz chopped walnuts (50 g)
1 dessertspoon coffee essence (10 ml)
Vanilla flavouring
1 teaspoon baking powder (10 ml)

Northumberland

Cream butter and sugar, add beaten egg and flour gradually. Add ground rice and walnuts, coffee and vanilla essence and baking powder. Mix well and put into a greased basin, 1 pint size (600 ml), and steam for 1½ hours. Serve with hot custard.

Serves 4.

Cornish Burnt Cream

Baked custard
Clotted cream
Citron peel
Caster sugar

Cornwall

Put a layer of baked custard in the bottom of a pie-dish, then a layer of clotted cream, then more layers of custard and cream until the dish is full. Slice some citron very thin and put on top. Sprinkle with caster sugar and lightly brown.

Devonshire Omelet

3 large cooking apples
2 tablespoons caster sugar (50 g or more)
½ oz fresh butter (15 g)
Powdered cinnamon
2 tablespoons powdered macaroons (50 g)
2 eggs
Caster sugar for sprinkling

Devon

Peel, core, slice and cook the apples in a pan with 3 tablespoons of water, and the sugar, until it is a soft pulp. Add the butter and mix thoroughly, also the powdered cinnamon, macaroons and the beaten yolks.

Whisk the whites to a stiff froth and stir lightly into the other ingredients.

Thickly butter a 1 pint (600 ml) fireproof dish and pour in the mixture. Dredge the surface with caster sugar, and place the dish in a hot oven, 400°F (200°C) Gas 6, for about 20 minutes until it is puffed up and brown.

Serves 4.

Elizabeth Raffald's Apple Pudding

18th Century

Short crust pastry
4 oz stewed apples (100 g)
4 oz butter (100 g)
3–4 oz soft brown sugar (75–100 g)
3 eggs
Grated rind of 1 lemon

Yorkshire

Line a 7 inch (18 cm) flan tin with pastry and bake blind.

Cream the butter and add to the warm stewed apple. Beat well. Beat the eggs and add to the apple mixture with the sugar and lemon rind. Fill pastry case and bake in a moderate oven for about 30 minutes, 375°F (190°C) Gas 5.

Serves 4.

Grenadier's Pudding

Mix well and steam in a ¾ pint (425 ml) greased basin for 2 hours. Serve with custard sauce.

Serves 4.

4 oz breadcrumbs (100 g)
3 oz red jam (75 g) (any variety)
½ teaspoon bicarbonate of soda (2½ ml)
2 oz sugar (50 g)
2 oz butter (50 g), melted
1 well beaten egg

Northumberland

Isle of Wight Pudding

Roll out pastry to a rectangle. Spread with golden syrup and sprinkle with cleaned dried fruit. Roll up into a neat roll leaving ends unsealed. Put into pie-dish and pour milk over the roll to glaze and until the milk is about half-way up the side of the roll. Bake for ¾–1 hour in a moderate oven, 375°F (190°C) Gas 5. Serve hot.

Serves 4.

4 oz pastry (short or flaky) (100 g flour)
2 tablespoons golden syrup (50 g)
3 oz dried fruit (75 g)
½ pint milk (approx.) (250 ml)

Oxfordshire

King George First's Christmas Pudding

Mix the dry ingredients. Moisten with eggs beaten to a froth, and the milk, lemon juice and brandy mixed. Stand for at least 12 hours in a cool place, then turn into buttered moulds. Boil for 8 hours at first, then for 2 hours before serving.

This quantity makes three puddings of about 3 lb each (1½ kg).

Note for Beginners

For the dried plums use large plump prunes. For just one large pudding make a third of the recipe. Cook it in the same way as any ordinary steamed pudding, making sure it does not boil dry during the long cooking.

1½ lb finely shredded suet (700 g)
1 lb dried plums (450 g), stoned and halved
1 lb mixed peel (450 g) cut in long strips
1 lb small raisins (450 g)
1 lb sultanas (450 g)
1 lb currants (450 g)
1 lb sifted flour (450 g)
1 lb sugar (450 g)
1 lb brown breadcrumbs (450 g)
1 heaped teaspoon mixed spice (15 ml)
½ nutmeg, grated
2 teaspoons salt (10 ml)
1 lb eggs (450 g), weighed in their shells
½ pint new milk (300 ml)
Juice of one lemon
A very large wineglass of brandy (170 ml)

Berkshire

Marmalade Pudding

4 oz flour (100 g)
4 oz Demerara sugar (100 g)
4 oz breadcrumbs (100 g)
4 oz suet (100 g)
Pinch of salt
6 oz marmalade (175 g)
1 egg
About ¼ pint milk (150 ml)
½ teaspoon bicarbonate of soda (2½ ml)

*Northamptonshire and
Soke of Peterborough*

Mix thoroughly the flour, sugar, breadcrumbs, suet and salt, add marmalade and mix together with beaten egg and milk. Dissolve bicarbonate of soda in a little milk and mix well with the batter. Pour into a well greased mould coated with brown sugar, 1½–2 pint size (1 l), cover with greased paper and steam 2 hours. Turn out and serve with marmalade sauce or white sauce.
    Serves 6.

Pineapple Upside-down Pudding

1 oz margarine (25 g)
2 oz brown sugar (50 g)
1 tin pineapple rings (4–6 rings)
Cherries
4 oz cake crumbs (100 g)
2 oz ground almonds (50 g)
4 tablespoons milk (60 ml)
2 oz butter (50 g)
2 oz caster sugar (50 g)
2 eggs

Cheshire

Melt the margarine and brown sugar in the bottom of a cake tin, place the pineapple rings over the surface, placing a cherry in the centre of each. Place the cake crumbs, ground almonds, into basin, pour on milk and add some small pieces of pineapple. Cream the butter and caster sugar and beat in yolks of eggs. Add the crumb mixture and fold in the stiffly whisked egg whites. Put on top of pineapple and bake in moderate oven. Turn out on to a hot dish with the pineapple uppermost.
    Serves 4–6.

Note for Beginners

Use either a round tin large enough to take 4 rings of pineapple or a larger oblong tin to take 6 rings. In the latter case the cake mixture will be thinner and cooking time a little less. Bake at 375°F (190°C) Gas 5, for 30–45 minutes.

Pumpkin Pie

Pumpkin
Brown sugar
Currants
Grated nutmeg
A little lemon juice
Shortcrust pastry
Cream or custard

Devon

Cut one pumpkin into small cubes. Cover with water and simmer until tender. Strain and put into pie-dish. Add brown sugar, currants, grated nutmeg and a little lemon juice. Cover with shortcrust pastry and bake in a moderate oven, 400°F (200°C) Gas 6, for 30–45 minutes.
    Serve with cream or custard.

Rhubarb and Banana Tart

Prepare rhubarb and cut in pieces, peel and chop bananas, put in a pie-dish (600 ml) with water and sugar to taste. Cover with pastry and bake in oven as for any fruit pie, about 40 minutes at 425°F (220°C) Gas 7.
Serves 4.

Shortcrust pastry (150 g flour)
1 lb young rhubarb (500 g)
3 large or 4 medium bananas
Water (2 tablespoons)
Sugar to taste (50 g)

Isle of Ely

Rhubarb Charlotte

Toss the crumbs in the melted butter, shaking the pan as they absorb it evenly. Spread a thin layer of these over the bottom of a buttered 2 pint (1 l) ovenproof dish. Cover with rhubarb cut into 1 inch (2½ cm) lengths. Mix together the sugar and spices and the grated orange rind. Sprinkle some of this over the rhubarb. Repeat the layers until the dish is full, ending with a layer of crumbs.

Heat the syrup with the fruit juices and 2 tablespoons water. When melted pour over the charlotte. Cover with a piece of greaseproof paper and bake in the centre of oven 400°F (200°C) Gas 6, for 20–30 minutes, depending on the age and thickness of the rhubarb, then uncover and cook for a further 10 minutes approximately until the top is golden and crisp. Serve with thin cream.
Serves 4.

6 oz white breadcrumbs (150 g)
2 oz melted butter (50 g)
1 lb rhubarb (450 g)
2 oz brown sugar (50 g)
½ teaspoon ground ginger (5 ml)
¼ teaspoon cinnamon (2½ ml)
¼ teaspoon grated nutmeg (2½ ml)
Grated rind of 1 orange
2 tablespoons golden syrup (30 ml)
1 dessertspoon orange juice (10 ml)
1 dessertspoon lemon juice (10 ml)
Thin cream

Derbyshire

Rochester Pudding

Cream butter and sugar until light and fluffy, add yolks of eggs, beat well. Stir in the flour, then fold in the stiffly beaten whites of eggs.

Grease a basin, 1¾ pint size (1 l), put in golden syrup (and a little lemon juice if liked), put the mixture on top. Cover and steam for 2 hours.
Serves 4–6.

4 oz butter or margarine (100 g)
4 oz sugar (100 g)
2 eggs
4 oz self-raising flour (100 g)
4 oz golden syrup (100 g)
A little lemon juice (optional)

Gloucestershire

Saxon Pudding

1½ oz butter (40 g)
1 oz toasted split almonds (25 g)
4 sponge cakes
2 oz ratafias (50 g)
3 eggs
1 oz sugar (25 g)
½ pint milk (250 ml)
¼ pint cream (150 ml)
3 tablespoons sherry (45 ml)

Shropshire

Butter a 1½ pint (850 ml) basin, spread with the almonds. Slice sponge cakes and fill basin in layers with ratafias. Beat eggs, add sugar, milk, cream and sherry. Pour over the sponge cake. Let soak. Steam for ½ hour. Serve hot or cold.

Serves 4.

Tipsy Strawberry Meringue

1 lb strawberries (500 g)
1 tablespoon brandy (15 ml)
3 egg whites
6 oz caster sugar (175 g)

Isle of Ely and Pembrokeshire

Wash and hull strawberries, if large cut in half and place in attractive ovenproof dish. Pour brandy over strawberries. Whisk the egg whites until stiff. Whisk in half the sugar lightly, the other half of the sugar is then folded in with a metal spoon. Cover the fruit with the meringue mixture, and cook in centre of pre-heated oven until lightly browned, about 10–15 minutes, 400°F (200°C) Gas 6. Can be served hot or cold.

Serves 4–6.

Treacle George

A little butter
Short pastry
Golden syrup
Fine white breadcrumbs
Lemon juice
Clotted cream

Devon

Butter a pie-dish and line the bottom with thin short pastry. Spread with a good layer of golden syrup and fine white breadcrumbs. Add a sprinkle of lemon juice.

Fill up the dish with layers of pastry, syrup and crumbs, sprinkling each layer with a few drops of lemon juice. Bake in a fairly quick oven, 400°F (200°C) Gas 6, for ¾ hour. Serve hot or cold with clotted cream.

COLD SWEETS
II

Apple Soufflé

Boil the milk with the lemon rind and strain on the egg yolks which have been worked with the sugar.

Add the gelatine and thicken over the fire without boiling.

Strain, and when cool fold in lightly the stiffly whipped egg whites, apple purée and two-thirds of the cream.

Put into small dishes and decorate with the rest of the cream when quite cold.

Serves 4–6.

¾ pint milk (400 ml)
The rind of 1 lemon
2 eggs
2 oz sugar (50 g)
1 dessertspoon gelatine (15 g)
4 tablespoons apple pureé (250 ml)
2–3 tablespoons cream (30–45 ml), whipped

Devon

Breadcrumb Mousse

Put the egg yolks in a basin with the sugar and add the gelatine dissolved in a little water. Beat over a pan of boiling water until the mixture is thick and creamy. Remove from the heat and add the breadcrumbs. Allow to cool a little and then add the whipped cream and sherry. When almost cold add the beaten whites of the eggs and pour into a mould to set. Serve with clear fruit juice.

Serves 4–6.

2 eggs
2 oz caster sugar (50 g)
¼ oz powdered gelatine (10 ml)
2 heaped tablespoons wholemeal breadcrumbs (30 g)
1 gill cream (150 ml), whipped
Little sherry (15 ml)
Clear fruit juice

Yorkshire

Caramel D'Orange

1 lb loaf sugar (400 g)
½ pint water (250 ml)
1 pint cream (500 ml)
6 oranges
Ginger snaps

Make a caramel with the sugar and water and pour it on to an oiled baking sheet, leaving it to cool.

Whip your cream, peel and quarter the oranges, and pound the caramel very fine in a mortar. Arrange in layers in a glass dish, and serve with ginger snaps.

Serves 6.

Note for Beginners

To make the caramel heat and stir sugar and water until the sugar dissolves, then boil rapidly until it turns a deep amber colour.

An alternative method for crushing the cold caramel is to break it into small pieces and process it in the electric blender.

Northamptonshire and Soke of Peterborough

Chestnut Cream

1 lb chestnuts (500 g)
Grated chocolate
Whipped cream
Sweet oranges

Boil the chestnuts, skin and pass through a wire sieve. Mix a liberal supply of grated chocolate with the chestnuts. Put into a glass dish and spread over a thin layer of whipped cream.

Cover the surface with little divisions of carefully peeled sweet oranges and overlay them neatly.

Just before serving sprinkle over with a little grated chocolate not to be made wet with the cream.

Serves 4.

Note for Beginners

To boil chestnuts:
Wash, cut a slit in the rounded sides of the shells, cover with water and boil for about 30 minutes. Drain and peel off shell and skin.

Northamptonshire and Soke of Peterborough

Chocorum Cold Dessert

6 oz plain chocolate (175 g)
4 eggs, separated
2 tablespoons rum (30 ml)
¼ pint double cream (150 ml), whipped
1 oz chopped nuts (25 g)

Melt the chocolate in a basin over a pan of hot water, then cool slightly. Beat the egg yolks into the chocolate then add the rum. Whisk egg whites stiff and carefully fold into chocolate mixture. Divide between individual glasses (6), chill and decorate with cream and nuts.

Serves 6.

Yorkshire

Coffee Ice-cream

Dissolve the sugar in the water in a thickish pan. Bring to the boil and boil fast for 5 minutes. Cool slightly. Pour on to the beaten egg yolks in a thin stream beating all the time. Put the bowl over hot water and beat until thick. When cold fold in the whipped cream and the coffee dissolved in the water. Freeze. Beat when just beginning to set and refreeze.

Serves 6–8, about 2 pints ($1\frac{1}{4}$ l).

6 oz caster sugar (175 g)
$\frac{1}{4}$ pint water (150 ml)
5 egg yolks
$\frac{1}{2}$ pint cream (300 ml)
$1\frac{1}{2}$ level tablespoons instant coffee (25 ml)
2 teaspoons water (10 ml)

Hampshire

Cold Chocolate Soufflé

Separate eggs. Whisk yolks and sugar over hot water until thick and pale. Dissolve the chocolate in the milk and the gelatine in a little hot water; add both strained to the yolks, the lemon juice and vanilla. When nearly set, add whipped cream and lastly the stiffly beaten egg whites.

Serves 6.

3 eggs
2 oz caster sugar (50 g)
2 oz Chocolate Meunier (50 g)
$\frac{1}{2}$ gill milk (75 ml)
$\frac{1}{2}$ oz gelatine (15 g)
Juice of 1 lemon
$\frac{1}{2}$ pint cream (300 ml)
Vanilla essence

Note for Beginners

Warm the milk gently to dissolve the chocolate. Use about 3 tablespoons hot water to dissolve the gelatine. Be careful not to let the chocolate mixture set before adding cream and egg whites or the soufflé will be lumpy instead of smooth. Pour it into a large soufflé dish or individual dishes and leave in a cold place to set.

Berkshire

Custard Jelly

Warm the milk, add the beaten egg yolks and sugar and flavouring. Stir over gentle heat until creamy. Pour into a basin.

Dissolve the gelatine in the water and add to the contents of the basin.

Lastly stir in the stiffly beaten egg whites. Pour into a wetted 2 pint (1 l) mould and leave until set. Turn out.

Serves 4.

1 pint milk (500 ml)
2 eggs
2 tablespoons sugar (50 g)
Few drops vanilla essence or other
    flavouring
$\frac{1}{2}$ oz powdered gelatine (15 g)
1 tablespoon water (30 ml)

Leicestershire and Rutland

Fruit and Hazelnut Galette

Brown the nuts in the oven at 350°F (180°C) Gas 4 until husks can be rubbed off (approx. 7–8 minutes when nuts should be a deep golden brown). Reserve a few nuts for decoration and pass the remainder through a mincer or work until fine in a blender.

3 oz shelled hazelnuts (75 g)
3 oz butter (75 g)
2 rounded tablespoons caster sugar (50 g)
$4\frac{1}{2}$ oz flour (100 g)
Pinch of salt

125

Filling
Fresh or tinned fruit
½ pint double cream (300 ml)
Icing sugar (for dusting)
1 oz sugar (25 g) if fresh fruit is used

Soften butter, add sugar and beat together until light and fluffy.

Sift flour and salt and stir into mixture with the prepared nuts. Chill for at least 30 minutes.

Divide pastry into three and place each piece on a lightly floured baking sheet. Roll or pat into very thin rounds approximately 7 inches (18 cm) in diameter. Bake for about 10 minutes in the oven at 375°F (190°C) Gas 5.

When cooked cut one round into six individual portions, cool on a rack.

Whisk cream until thick. If fresh fruit is used sprinkle on the 1 oz (25 g) sugar.

To finish, sandwich the layers together with cream and fruit alternately, placing the cut portions on top. Dust with icing sugar. Pipe a rosette of cream on each portion and decorate by placing a whole hazelnut on each rosette.

The cooked pastry rounds will freeze well if carefully packed into a container.

Serves 6.

Derbyshire

Fruit Flan

Shortcrust pastry
2 oz butter (50 g)
2 oz sugar (50 g)
1 egg
2 oz ground almonds (50 g)
2 oz chopped walnuts (50 g)
2 oz glacé cherries (50 g)
2 oz sultanas (50 g)

Northumberland

Line a 7 inch (18 cm) cake tin or flan ring with the pastry. Beat the sugar and butter to a cream, add the beaten egg, mix in the ground almonds, then the other ingredients. Bake in a moderate oven, 325°F (160°C) Gas 3, for ½ hour or till brown on top.

Serves 4.

Fruit Sorbet

1 egg
4 oz golden syrup (100 g)
Juice of 1 orange
Juice of 1 lemon
1 banana
1½ gills cold water (200 ml)

Durham

Beat egg until frothy, then whisk in syrup. Add the orange and lemon juice and the smoothly mashed banana. Stir in water. Turn into refrigerator tray, freezing until firm and beat up well when half frozen.

Serves 4.

Ginger Mould

Dissolve the gelatine in the hot water, add it to the milk, sugar, butter and well beaten egg yolks. Stir over heat in a double saucepan until thick, but do not boil. Add ground ginger and, when nearly set, fold in stiffly beaten egg whites and lemon juice. Pour into a wetted mould, 1¼–1½ pint size (700–850 ml) and leave to set. When set turn out and serve with preserved ginger and syrup.

Serves 4.

½ oz gelatine (15 g)
2–3 tablespoons hot water (30–45 ml)
½ pint milk (300 ml)
2 oz caster sugar (50 g)
3 oz butter (75 g)
2 eggs
½ teaspoon ground ginger (5 ml or more)
Juice of 1 lemon
Preserved ginger and syrup

Herefordshire

Gooseberry Velvet

Cook 1 lb gooseberries (450 g) with ½ pint water (300 ml) and 3 oz sugar (75 g). Pass through a very fine sieve or muslin—make up to 1 pint (600 ml) with water. Sprinkle gelatine over the warm liquid—stir until dissolved. Tint to a delicate green. Cool, then pour into 6 sundae glasses—leave to set.

Cook the remaining gooseberries in 2 tablespoons water (30 ml) and 4 oz sugar (100 g) until fruit is soft. Sieve and leave to cool.

Make the custard—leave to cool, covered to prevent skin forming.

Lightly whip the cream.

Fold the custard into the gooseberry purée, add colouring to colour of jelly—fold in whipped cream. Pour on to the jelly in the glasses. Leave to set.

Decorate with crystallized ginger, poached whole berries and grated chocolate.

Serves 4–6.

2 lb gooseberries (1 kg)
7 oz sugar (200 g), or to taste
Approximately ½ pint water (300 ml)
½ oz gelatine (15 g)
Green colouring
¼ pint double cream (150 ml)
Crystallized ginger
Grated chocolate
Poached whole berries for garnish

Custard
¼ pint milk (150 ml)
3 level teaspoons custard powder (15 ml)
3 level teaspoons sugar (15 ml)

Cumberland

Honey Cream

Dissolve the jelly in ¾ pint (400 ml) hot water, add lemon juice. Allow to cool.

When starting to set, whisk until light and frothy, add finely grated lemon rind, honey and cream. Blend thoroughly, pour into mould and allow to set.

Serves 4.

Lemon jelly
Juice of 1 lemon
Grated rind of ½ lemon
2 tablespoons honey (30 ml)
¼ pint cream (150 ml), whipped

Cumberland

127

Ice-cream

2 egg whites
★¼ pint prepared evaporated milk (140 ml)
4 level tablespoons icing sugar (about
 1½ oz or 40 g)
1 teaspoon vanilla essence (5 ml)

Whip egg whites until very stiff. Whip milk lightly, adding the sugar and vanilla essence. Gradually whip egg whites into milk. Pour into ice drawer and freeze. (The mixture is sufficient to fill about two trays.)

★ *To prepare evaporated milk* Place unopened tin of milk in saucepan of cold water. Bring to the boil and boil for 15 minutes. Leave to cool and when cold store in refrigerator until next day. It is then ready for use. Several cans may be prepared at the same time and stored indefinitely in the refrigerator.
 Serves 6–8.

Yorkshire

Lemon Cream

Homburg Crème

2 eggs
4 oz sugar (100 g)
1 lemon

Beat yolks with sugar. Add lemon juice and finely grated rind. Heat over boiling water till thickened, stirring constantly. When cold add stiffly beaten egg whites. Serve at once.
 Serves 3.

Note for Beginners

The egg yolk mixture can be cooked in advance and this and the unbeaten egg whites stored in a cold place. Whip the whites and combine the two just before the meal is to be served.

Cumberland

Lemon Ginger Crunch

2 bananas
2 oz ginger biscuits (crushed) (50 g)
5 oz cream (150 ml)
Two 5 oz cartons lemon yogurt (142 ml
 each)
Garnish: 4 thin slices lemon

Peel and slice bananas into the bases of 4 or 5 sundae glasses. Sprinkle on half the ginger crumbs.
 Whip cream until thick, reserving a little for decoration, fold the rest into the lemon yogurt. Spoon the lemon cream over the ginger crumbs, and cover the cream with the remaining crumbs.
 Top with the reserved cream and decorate with the lemon slices. Chill well before serving.
 This recipe was also tested using pineapple yogurt; it was delicious.
 Serves 4.

Derbyshire

Martinique Egg

Place on a slice of pineapple a round coffee ice-cream and cap with half a peach. Arrange whipped cream or whipped evaporated milk all round to resemble fried egg. Pour over a little rum and serve cold.

Pineapple slices
Coffee ice-cream
Peach halves
Whipped cream or whipped
   evaporated milk
Rum

Oxfordshire

Orange Cream

Beat yolk and sugar. Add juice. Heat over boiling water till thickened. Dissolve gelatine in $\frac{1}{4}$ pint boiling water in which the rind has been soaking. Add to mixture and when it has cooled fold in stiffly beaten whites. Put into dish or individual glasses and allow to set.

   Serves 3.

2 eggs
2 oz sugar (50 g)
1 orange
$\frac{1}{8}$ oz gelatine (7$\frac{1}{2}$ ml)
$\frac{1}{4}$ pint water (150 ml)

Cumberland

Orange Jelly Soufflé

Soak the gelatine in the orange juice for a short time, then add the sugar and heat very gently in a saucepan (do not boil). Remove from the stove and pour gently over the beaten yolks of eggs. Stir well and leave to cool. Add the stiffly beaten egg whites and fold them into the soufflé. Leave to set and put whipped cream, flavoured with a little sherry, on top. Decorate with slices of blanched almonds.

   A small tin of mandarin oranges added to the soufflé makes a delicious flavour.

   Serves 6–8.

1 tablespoon powdered gelatine (15 g)
1 pint orange juice (600 ml) (canned or
   fresh)
2 tablespoons sugar (50 g)
3 eggs
Whipped cream
Sherry
Blanched almonds
A small tin of mandarin oranges
   (optional)

Oxfordshire

Quick Ice-cream

Whip the cream. Separate egg and whisk yolk and white separately. Fold all together with sugar and vanilla.

   Pour into trays and freeze till firm. No stirring is needed.

   Flavourings can be varied by using a little fresh fruit purée instead of vanilla.

   It makes sufficient for 4–6.

$\frac{1}{4}$ pint cream (150 ml)
1 large egg
2 oz caster sugar (50 g)
Vanilla essence

Cumberland

Stone Cream

Gelatine to set 1 pint (600 ml)
2 or 3 laurel leaves
1 pint milk (600 ml)
3 eggs (yolks only)
1 oz caster sugar (25 g)
A little apricot jam
A few almonds if liked
Cream

Oxfordshire

Dissolve the gelatine in hot, not boiling water (about 4 tablespoons). Tear laurel leaves in half and simmer in milk for a few minutes. Remove leaves from milk. Pour on to eggs—add sugar and return to saucepan. Stir until it coats the spoon—do not boil—allow to cool, add gelatine—put jam at bottom of glass bowl and strain contents of saucepan over. Allow to set and serve with cream. Decorate with split almonds.

Serves 4.

Strawberry Ice-cream

½ pint cream (300 ml)
2 oz icing sugar (50 g)
8 oz strawberries (225 g) or a tin of
    strawberries, puréed
2 egg whites

Hampshire

Whip the cream lightly and fold in the sieved icing sugar and the strawberry purée. Whisk the egg whites stiffly and fold into the mixture. Put in containers in the ice box compartment and freeze until solid. Bring out and beat until it is smooth and creamy. Return until needed. About another 2 hours to freeze again.

If you brush the container out with glycerine it will prevent the ice-cream from sticking.

Serves 4.

Note for Beginners

If using canned strawberries you will need enough drained strawberries to give about ¼ pint (150 ml) of purée.

Strawberry Mousse

1 lb can of strawberries (454 g)
1 pkt strawberry jelly
2 egg whites
½ pint double cream (300 ml)

Cumberland

Drain strawberries and make juice up to ½ pint (300 ml) with water. Heat liquid and pour over the jelly, allow to become cold but not set.

Whisk egg whites—whisk cream and reserve some for decoration. Fold cream into jelly mixture, followed by egg whites and strawberries—reserve 4 for decoration. Pour mixture into a glass dish—allow to set.

Decorate with piped cream and strawberries.

Serves 6–8.

Surprise Roll

Dip biscuits one by one in sherry, upend and coat with whipped cream. Place coated biscuits together forming a long roll on the plate, cover with more whipped cream and then with grated chocolate.

Place the sweet in the refrigerator overnight so that it sets firmly before serving.

Serves 4.

1 pkt Maryland cookies or biscuits with chopped chocolate (about 6 oz or 170 g)
Sweet sherry
$\frac{1}{3}$ pint cream (to be whipped) (200 ml)
Grated plain chocolate

Cumberland

Syllabub

Finely grate rind of lemon, squeeze juice. Put rind, juice, sherry, sugar and brandy in bowl and stir until sugar is dissolved. Pour in cream and whisk until thick. Spoon into individual glasses, leave in cool place. Can be made one day in advance.

Serves 6.

1 large lemon
$\frac{1}{4}$ pint medium sweet sherry (150 ml)
2 oz caster sugar (50 g)
2 tablespoons brandy (30 ml)
$\frac{1}{2}$ pint double cream (300 ml)

Shropshire

FRUIT
12

Apple Hedgehog

4 lb apples, weighed after paring and
    coring (2 kg)
3 lb sugar (1½ kg)
Lemon juice if liked

Westmorland

Very useful for windfalls. Can be stored for several months.
Ready to turn out and serve.

Place prepared apples in a preserving pan with enough water
to prevent burning. When cooked, beat to a smooth pulp,
return to pan and add sugar and lemon juice. Stir over gentle
heat until sugar is dissolved, then boil for 30 minutes. Place in
small moulds, cover and tie down.
    To serve, turn out and decorate with whipped cream and
chopped nuts or with custard sauce.

Honey Apples

4 oz chopped walnuts (100 g)
1 oz raisins (25 g)
2 tablespoons honey (30 ml)

Mix together half the chopped walnuts, raisins, honey and
breadcrumbs, fill apples with the mixture. Bake until apples
are tender, at 350°F (180°C) Gas 4, for 45 minutes.

Prepare the glaze, heat together in a saucepan jam, water and lemon juice. Bring to the boil and keep on the heat for 3 minutes. Remove from heat and pass through sieve. Brush cooked apples with the glaze and coat sides with remaining walnuts. Decorate with angelica and cherries.

Serve hot with custard sweetened with honey.

Honey may be used instead of jam for glaze.

1 oz fine breadcrumbs (25 g)
4 large apples, washed and cored

To Glaze
2 tablespoons apricot jam (60 ml)
2 tablespoons water (30 ml)
Little lemon juice

Decoration
Angelica
Cherries

Yorkshire

Portuguese Apples

Peel and core some apples, stand them on some paper in a baking tin, fill centres with raspberry jam, bake till the apples are quite tender. Pour custard sauce over and serve when cold.

Apples
Raspberry jam
Egg custard sauce ($\frac{1}{2}$ pint or 300 ml for 2–3 apples)

Note for Beginners

A piece of foil can be used instead of paper. When cooked transfer apples to serving dish before pouring the custard over them.

Baking temperature can be from 350–400°F (180–200°C) Gas 4–6, time about 40 minutes depending on temperature and size of apple.

*Northamptonshire and
Soke of Peterborough*

Stuffed Baked Apple

Remove the centre of the apple with a corer and make a cut round the middle. Put the apple in a heatproof dish and fill the hole with any of the suggested fillings. Place a small piece of butter or margarine on the apple and pour two tablespoons water round it.

Bake in a moderately hot oven about 45 minutes until the fruit is quite tender, 375–400°F (190–200°C) Gas 5–6.

1 large cooking apple

Alternative Fillings
Demerara sugar and crystallized ginger
Chopped dates with lemon juice
Stoned raisins or sultanas
Marmalade or mincemeat

Derbyshire

Apricot Ambrosia

Choose the finest dried apricots and soak for at least an hour in just enough water to cover them. Cook slowly with an orange finely shredded (rind and pulp) until most of the water is absorbed. Rub through a fine sieve, add a little honey and a few spoonfuls of any good orange liqueur. The mixture should be a thick purée but not solid.

1 lb dried apricots (450 g)
1 orange
Honey
Orange liqueur
Lemon skins
Blanched almonds

133

Scoop out the pulp of lemons and make cups of the half rinds, cutting the edges into scallops. Fill these shells with the ambrosia and sprinkle with finely cut almonds.
Serves 6–8.

Apricots in Port Wine

Dried apricots
Inexpensive port wine
Large jar with well-fitted lid

Pembrokeshire

Fill the jar with chopped dried apricots, pressing well down. Fill jar to brim with port wine and cover tightly. Top up with port wine from time to time, keeping at least 6 months.
Serve with ice-cream or Christmas pudding.

Baked Bananas in Raisin Sauce

2 oz seedless raisins (50 g)
1½ oz honey (40 g)
Juice of 1 large lemon
1½ level teaspoons cornflour (7½ ml)
  blended in a little cold water
6 bananas
1 oz butter (25 g)
Thick cream

Cambridgeshire

Simmer raisins in ½ pint (300 ml) cold water for 10 minutes. Strain and save the liquid. Stir in the honey, lemon juice and the blended cornflour. Cook together until the mixture thickens. Return the raisins to the sauce.

Halve the peeled bananas lengthwise and lay in a 2 pint (1 l) fireproof dish in which the butter has been melted. Pour over the hot sauce and cook at 375°F (190°C) Gas 5 for 25 minutes.

Serve hot or cold with thick cream.
Serves 4–6.

Banana Bake

1 banana
1 tablespoon rum (15 ml), optional
1 tablespoon cream (15 ml), whipped
  (optional)

Derbyshire

Place a banana in its skin on the shelf of the oven at about 350°F (180°C) Gas 4 until the skin turns black, about 20 minutes. Open out on to the serving dish.

This tastes quite delicious on its own, and the addition of the rum and whipped cream turn it into a party dish.

Banana Sweet

1 banana
1 oz chocolate (25 g)
Whipped cream
Glacé cherries

Berkshire

Allow these quantities for each person. Slice bananas into a shallow dish or individual dishes. Cover thickly with grated chocolate. Decorate with whipped cream and/or glacé cherries.

Blackberry and Banana

Put the blackberries in a basin, sprinkle with caster sugar, leave a few hours and press several times.

Peel the bananas, cut into 4 or 8 pieces each, lengthwise. Put a layer of blackberries into a dish, then one sliced banana. Repeat with blackberries and second sliced banana.

Serves 4–6.

1 lb blackberries (500 g)
Caster sugar
2 bananas

West Kent

Blackberry Apples

Scoop out cores without breaking the apples. Mash the blackberries with the sugar and fill apple centres. Place the stuffed apples on a baking tin and pour round golden syrup mixed with an equal quantity of water. Bake in a slow oven, baste frequently with the syrup.

6 large cooking apples
4 oz blackberries (125 g)
Sugar to taste
3 tablespoons golden syrup (45 ml)

Note for Beginners

For baking apples in a slow oven use a temperature of 325°F (160°C) Gas 3 and allow an hour or more depending on the size and variety of apple. Test the centres with a fork to see when they are soft.

West Kent

Cherries Stewed without Water

Place the cherries in a double boiler with the sugar and lemon juice. Cook until tender. The rich juice produced makes a very colourful dish.

1 lb ripe dark cherries (500 g), stoned
4 tablespoons demerara sugar (100 g)
Juice of 1 lemon

West Kent

Iced Currants

Select fine clusters of red, white or black currants. Well beat the egg whites and mix with the water. Take the currants, a cluster at a time, and dip them in. Drain for a moment, then roll or shake them in the caster sugar. Let them dry on clean kitchen paper, when the sugar will crystallize round each currant, giving a very pretty effect.

All fresh fruit may be prepared in this way and attractively arranged on one dish makes an excellent summer dessert.

Currants
2 egg whites
$\frac{1}{4}$ pint water (150 ml)
Caster sugar

Devon

Cream, Mixed Fresh Fruit

½ teacup white currants (85 ml)
1 teacup red currants (170 ml)
½ teacup Kentish cherries (85 ml)
1 lb loaf sugar (400 g)
1 teacup raspberries (170 ml)
1 teacup strawberries (170 ml)
1 pint cream (600 ml)

West Kent

Boil currants and cherries for 10 minutes quickly with sugar, skim often, add raspberries and strawberries, simmer 2 minutes longer. Press through a sieve.

Stir in the cream and whisk quickly until it thickens. Serve in glasses.

Make 2 hours before serving. Keep in a very cool place or refrigerate.

Serves 6.

Fresh Fruit Jelly

½ oz powdered gelatine (15 g)
½ pint fruit syrup (300 ml)
½ pint water (300 ml)
Juice of ½ lemon

Leicestershire and Rutland

Dissolve the gelatine in 2 or 3 tablespoons of water, heated very gently. Mix the syrup, water and lemon juice together, and add the dissolved gelatine. Stir thoroughly and pour into a wet mould, 1½ pint (1 l).

Serves 4.

Fresh Fruit Salad

Lincolnshire

Make an hour or two before serving. Prepare any fruit, sprinkling well with caster sugar. For a special occasion add wine, cider or ginger ale. A dash or two of angostura bitters develops the flavour of the fruit.

If bananas or pears are included add a tablespoon of lemon juice. Sprig of mint and frosted grapes at the end add a party air.

Quick Fruit Salad

1 Cox's orange pippin apple
1 large orange
2 level tablespoons sugar (30 ml)

Derbyshire

136

Scrub the apple and peel the orange. Remove any pith left on the orange. Slice it down in rings, then cut roughly into cubes. Place it in a basin.

Cut apples into quarters, peel each quarter and remove the core. Cut into slices and then into cubes again. Put in the basin.

Sprinkle with sugar and leave to mature for at least 1½ hours.

Serves 2–3.

Filled Melon

Scoop out inside of melon with a ball scoop. Mix the fruit and ginger together with a small amount of syrup. Put all inside the melon case and pour over cointreau or brandy.

1 melon
Apples, pears (cut small)
Grapes (pipped)
Ginger (stem or crystallized)
Apricots
Sugar syrup
2 tablespoons cointreau or brandy

Pembrokeshire

Peaches in Wine

Melt sugar in water and simmer for a few minutes. Skin the peaches by dipping them in boiling water like tomatoes. Simmer them in the syrup for 4 minutes. Remove.

Slice the peaches into goblets, pour in just enough Sauterne to cover and put a very large blob of soured cream on the top of that. Serve with the langues de chat.

4 oz caster sugar (100 g)
½ pint water (250 ml)
6 peaches
Sauterne
Soured cream
Plain chocolate 'langues de chat'

Hampshire

Pears Baked in Syrup

Make a thick syrup of brown sugar and water. Peel, halve and core the pears. Place in a baking dish with ½ inch (1 cm) of syrup. Bake slowly, and baste often until the pears are cooked and coated with a thin layer of brown syrup.

Brown sugar
Water
Pears

Note for Beginners

To make a thick syrup dissolve about 4 oz sugar (100 g) in ½ pint water (300 ml). Cook the pears at about 325°F (160°C) Gas 3; time depending on the type of pears used, average about 1 hour.

West Kent

Pear Hedgehogs

Peel and core some pears, cook in a little water (plus some red wine) until soft. Sweeten, add rind of lemon too.

When cooked stuff the stalk end of fruit with sliced almonds. Fill the cavity with a spoon of Devonshire cream and decorate with a few more almonds.

Pears
Red wine
Sugar
Rind of lemon
Almonds
Devonshire cream

Isle of Ely

Pears in Red Wine

5 oz lump sugar (125 g) (Gives a crystal
  clear liquid)
¼ pint water (150 ml)
¼ pint red wine (150 ml)
Strip of lemon rind
Small piece of cinnamon stick
5–6 ripe dessert pears
1 teaspoon arrowroot (10 ml)
1 oz almonds (25 g) (shredded and
  browned)
Whipped cream (optional)

To make syrup—dissolve sugar, water, wine and flavourings slowly in a pan, bring to the boil, boil 1 minute.

Keeping stalks on pears, remove peel and the 'eye' from each base and place in the prepared syrup.

Poach pears in the pan, covered, until tender, allow 20–30 minutes to prevent them discolouring around the cores. Remove pears and strain syrup.

Mix the arrowroot with a little water before adding to syrup and stir until boiling, cook until the liquid is clear.

Arrange pears in a serving dish, spoon over the wine sauce and finish by scattering the browned and shredded almonds on top. Serve cold, hand round a bowl of whipped cream separately.

To shred and brown almonds
Blanch, skin and split, cut each lengthways in fine pieces and brown quickly in the oven at 350°F (180°C) Gas 4.

Cumberland

Prunes with a Difference

Prunes
Tea
1 tablespoon golden syrup (25 g) to 1 lb
  prunes (450 g)

Wash the prunes and cover them with a solution of half water and half tea (poured from the teapot after tea is over). Leave the prunes to soak in the usual way.

Place in the oven in a fireproof dish. Add syrup about ½ hour before prunes are cooked.

Note for Beginners

If modern soft prunes are soaked overnight they will only need ½ hour in the oven after they have come to simmering point, so add the syrup at the beginning of the cooking time. Cook at 350°F (180°C) Gas 4.

Yorkshire

New Twist

Prunes

4–8 oz prunes (100–200 g)
1 pint packet black currant jelly (500 ml)

Stew prunes in the usual way, then dissolve a black currant jelly in a little hot water and make up to 1 pint (500–600 ml) with the prune juice.

Leave jelly until the point of setting, then gently drop the prunes into it, and leave till jelly is firm.

Yorkshire

138

Poached Quinces

Quinces are worth looking for. They have a delicious flavour and scent.

Peel the fruit and leave whole—with their stalks still on. Stand upright in a fireproof dish containing the water. Pour honey over each quince and put cloves in the dish. Cover tightly and cook in a very slow oven, 275°F (140°C) Gas 1, for 2 or even 3 hours. Serve cold with mountains of whipped cream.

Quinces
½ gill water (75 ml)
1 tablespoon honey for each quince
 (15–20 ml)
1 or 2 cloves
Whipped cream

Hampshire

Dream Raspberries

Place the raspberries straight into a dish in which a little caster sugar has been sprinkled. Cover over with the rest of the sugar and pour the rum on top. Put in a cool place for an hour or two or longer. Serve with the cream whipped, sweetened slightly and flavoured with almond essence.

A plate of sponge cakes or sponge fingers makes a pleasant accompaniment.

Serves 4.

1 lb ripe raspberries (500 g)
4 oz caster sugar (100 g) (or more if
 desired)
1 dessertspoon rum (10 ml)
½ gill cream (75 ml)
Sugar
5 drops almond essence
Sponge cakes or sponge fingers

*Northamptonshire and
Soke of Peterborough*

Röde Gröde

A Scandinavian Cold Sweet (loosely translated means 'Red Gruel').

Summer Time
2 pints raspberries or raspberries and red currants (1¼ l)
A good ½ pint water (300 ml)

Boil together gently for an hour, then strain. Measure 1 pint (600 ml).

Winter Time
1 large tin (426 g) Scottish raspberries sieved and made up to 1 pint (600 ml)

To Thicken
1 oz cornflour (25 g)
A little extra sugar (about a heaped tablespoon)

Put measured pint of purée (600 ml) (less a little to blend cornflour) into saucepan and bring to boil. Add sugar and cornflour previously mixed to a smooth paste with a little of the cold purée. Continue to cook for a further 3 minutes. Pour into dish to set.

To Garnish
Whipped cream
Blanched almonds

Serve with whipped cream all over it and with blanched almonds standing up in the cream.
Serves 3–4.

Rhubarb Compote

1½ lb rhubarb (750 g)
3–4 tablespoons jam (175–250 g)
If raspberry jam is used warm it first
  and rub it through a sieve to remove
  pips.

Rhubarb invariably keeps whole without any attention.

Wipe rhubarb and cut it into short lengths. Spread a layer of jam in the bottom of a casserole. Cover thickly with rhubarb and add a little more jam. Fill up with rhubarb and finish with the rest of the jam. Cover and cook in a moderate oven for ½ hour, 350°F (180°C) Gas 4.
Serves 6.

Oxfordshire

Stewed Rhubarb

Rhubarb
Sugar
1 lemon

Cut rhubarb into 1 inch (2½ cm) lengths. Put into pan with water to cover. Cook until a fork will pierce (like potatoes). Drain well. Put rhubarb into dish, cover well with sugar and then add grated lemon rind and juice of a lemon. Leave to stand about an hour. This method is much better than stewing in the usual way.

Yorkshire

To Stew Rhubarb

1 lb rhubarb (500 g)
1 cup sugar (200 g), approximately

Cut up in 1 inch (2½ cm) pieces. Place in a fireproof dish (that has a cover). Add the sugar. Leave overnight. Then carefully cook in own juice, in a slow oven, 325°F (160°C) Gas 3, for about ¾ hour.

Devon

140

CAKES
13

Banbury Cakes

Cream the butter and sugar together until soft. Add the beaten egg and mix thoroughly. Add cake crumbs or ground almonds, mixed peel, currants and spice. Mix well together.

Roll out the pastry thinly. Cut into 5 inch (12 cm) rounds. Damp half-way round the edge of each round. Put 1 spoonful of filling in the centre of each round. Draw the edge up over the filling, taking care to put the damped edge on to the top of the other edge. Press lightly together. Form into an oval shape, turn over, flatten slightly with the hand or rolling pin, reshape into an oval. Glaze with a little milk. Sprinkle with sugar.

Put into a flat baking tin and bake in a hot oven for 20–25 minutes, 425°F (220°C) Gas 7. Cool on wire tray. Makes 10–12 cakes.

8 oz rough puff pastry (using 200 g flour)

Filling
1 oz butter (25 g)
2 oz brown sugar (50 g)
$\frac{1}{2}$ egg
1 oz cake crumbs or ground almonds (25 g)
2 oz mixed peel (50 g)
4 oz currants (100 g)
$\frac{1}{2}$ level teaspoon mixed spice (2$\frac{1}{2}$ ml)
Milk for brushing
Sugar to sprinkle on top

Oxfordshire

Barm Brack

4 oz cleaned currants (100 g)
1 oz chopped mixed peel (25 g)
4 oz cleaned sultanas (100 g)
4 oz soft brown sugar (100 g)
7½ fl. oz warm strained tea (200 ml)
8 oz self-raising flour (225 g)
1 large egg, beaten

Cumberland

Put fruit and sugar in a bowl, pour tea over and leave overnight.

Next day, line a 6 inch (15 cm) square tin with grease-proof paper and grease.

Add flour and egg to soaked fruit, mix well. Turn mixture into prepared tin and smooth over.

Bake in centre of oven, 350°F (180°C) Gas 4, for 1 hour, then reduce heat to 300°F (150°C) Gas 2 for a further ¾ hour.

Cut next day. Excellent eaten with butter.

Belgian Chocolate Cake

8 oz plain chocolate (200 g)
8 oz margarine (200 g)
2 eggs
2 level dessertspoons sugar (20 ml)
8 oz Marie biscuits (200 g)
½ oz chopped walnuts (15 g)
Vanilla or almond essence or 1 teaspoon
   liquid coffee (5 ml)
Plus a drop of brandy
More nuts for decoration

Cambridgeshire

Grease and line 7 inch (18 cm) cake tin with a detachable base.

Melt chocolate over heat.

Melt margarine in pan. Beat eggs well; add sugar and pour in margarine very slowly, stirring all the time. Add melted chocolate and beat well. Fold in broken biscuits (about ¼ inch (6 mm) size). Add nuts and flavouring and brandy.

Transfer mixture to cake tin. Decorate with nuts or ½ walnuts. Cover with paper and set aside to set. One hour is required in a fridge or up to 6 hours otherwise. Remove from tin by pushing up base.

Border Tart

Traditional Recipe

Pastry
5 oz plain flour (125 g)
1 oz lard (25 g)
1½ oz margarine (40 g)
Pinch of salt
Cold water to mix

Filling
2 oz margarine (50 g)
2 oz caster sugar (50 g)
1 egg
2 oz currants (50 g)
1 oz cut peel (25 g)
1 oz ground almonds or chopped nuts
   (25 g)
Few drops almond essence

Icing
3 oz icing sugar (75 g)
2 teaspoons lemon juice (10 ml)

Northumberland

Make the pastry and line a 7 inch (18 cm) plate or sandwich tin.

Beat margarine and sugar to a cream. Beat the egg and add to the mixture. Add the dried fruit, almonds and essence. Put the mixture into the pastry case, and smooth the top. Roll out the pastry trimmings, cut into strips, and cover the mixture in a trellis pattern. Bake at 400°F (200°C) Gas 6 for 15 minutes, then reduce to 350°F (180°C) Gas 4 for a further 15 minutes.

Ice top of the tart while warm, adding a few drops of water to make the icing thin.

Buttery Dick

Line a Swiss roll tin with shortcrust pastry. Prick with a fork.

Cream margarine and sugar, add egg, ground rice and currants. Spread evenly over pastry.

Bake in a moderate oven, 375°F (190°C) Gas 5, until golden brown, about 30 minutes. Cut in pieces.

Shortcrust pastry (using 100 g flour)
4 oz margarine (100 g)
4 oz sugar or soft brown (100 g)
1 egg
1 oz ground rice (25 g)
4 oz currants (100 g)

Cumberland

Cheese Cake (1)

Mix biscuit crumbs and sugar into melted margarine. Press into the base of an 8 inch (20 cm) flan ring. Sieve cottage cheese and mix with cream cheese. Add sugar and vanilla essence. Beat eggs and add to cheese mixture, beating well until smooth. Pour on to biscuit base, cook for 20 minutes, 375°F (190°C) Gas 5. Remove from oven and increase to 450°F (230°C) Gas 8. Mix topping and pour over cheese cake, bake at new heat for exactly 5 minutes. Leave overnight in cool place. The topping is optional.

Biscuit Base
4 oz crushed digestive biscuits (100 g)
2 oz melted margarine (50 g)
1 level tablespoon sugar (15 ml)

Cheese Mixture
8 oz cottage cheese (200 g)
4 oz philadelphia or cream cheese (100 g)
2 oz caster sugar (50 g)
2 eggs
3 drops vanilla essence

Topping
$\frac{1}{4}$ pint cream (150 ml)
1 teaspoon lemon juice (5 ml)

Yorkshire

Cheese Cake (2)

Make up the pastry and mould an 8 inch (20 cm) flan ring. Keep trimmings for decorating the top.

Prepare the mixture for filling as follows. Mix the margarine and sugar, add the beaten egg, cheese, peel, currants and grated lemon rind, add vanilla essence, mix thoroughly and fill prepared flan ring. Decorate the flan with pastry strips and brush with beaten egg. Bake for 30–35 minutes at 350°F (180°C) Gas 4 or until lightly browned and filling set.

A variation of the basic recipe is to place sliced drained mandarin oranges on the top of the cooked cheese cake just before serving.

Pastry
8 oz flour (200 g)
4 oz butter (100 g)
1$\frac{1}{2}$ oz sugar (40 g)
Pinch of salt
1 egg
Milk and water

Filling
2 oz margarine (50 g)
1 oz caster sugar (25 g)
10 oz curd cheese (275 g)
1 egg
1 oz currants (25 g)
1 oz chopped peel (25 g)
Lemon rind
Vanilla essence
Egg for brushing

Yorkshire

Chocolate Orange Drizzle Cake

6 oz margarine (175 g)
6 oz caster sugar (175 g)
3 eggs
6 oz self-raising flour (175 g)
2 tablespoons milk or juice of 1 orange
    (30 ml)
Finely grated rind of 2 oranges

Orange Syrup
Strained juice of 2 oranges
4 oz sugar (100 g)
    OR
Juice of 1 orange and 2 oz sugar (50 g) if
    juice of 1 orange is used in cake mixture

Chocolate Topping
4 oz block plain chocolate (125 g)
½ oz butter (15 g)

Cambridgeshire

Set oven to 350°F (180°C) Gas 4. Grease 2 lb (1 kg) loaf tin and line with greased greaseproof paper.

Cream margarine and sugar until light and fluffy. Beat in eggs one at a time. Fold in sifted flour and add milk or orange juice with last tablespoon of flour. Add orange rind. Put cake mixture in tin and cook 1 hour. Turn cooked cake out to cool and when nearly cold make slits in top of cake and drizzle orange syrup across top. To make syrup mix orange juice with sugar.

Break the chocolate into small pieces in bowl with butter and allow to melt over steaming water. Mix well and use immediately.

Christmas Cake

6 oz butter (175 g)
6 oz brown sugar (175 g)
5 eggs
2 oz chopped nuts (50 g)
2 oz ground almonds (50 g)
2–4 oz glacé cherries (50–100 g)
½ grated nutmeg
1 teaspoon ginger (10 ml)
1 teaspoon mixed spice (10 ml)
Grated rind of orange and lemon
Vanilla essence
About 2 lb fruit (900 g) — currants,
    sultanas, and raisins
2 oz candied peel (50 g)
8 oz self-raising flour (225 g)
Egg cup brandy, sherry or rum (30 ml)
1 tablespoon black treacle if liked (25 g)

Almond Paste
12 oz ground almonds (350 g)
12 oz caster sugar (350 g) (or ½ caster,
    ½ icing sugar)
1 egg
Juice of 1 orange and 1 lemon,
    approximately
2 teaspoons brandy or sherry (10 ml)

Line a 7–8 inch (18–20 cm) tin with double greaseproof paper.

Cream butter and sugar together. Beat eggs lightly with fork. Add small quantities to the butter and sugar. Beat thoroughly. Add black treacle if liked with last of egg. Beat thoroughly. Add chopped nuts and beat again. Add ground almonds and glacé cherries. Again beat. Add spice, orange and lemon rind, also vanilla and fruit. Give a final beating and then fold in flour using a metal spoon. Add sherry to make a nice dropping consistency. Put mixture in tin and level. Brush top with a little milk or sherry.

Cook at 300°F (150°C) Gas 2 for 2 hours, 275°F (140°C) Gas 1 for 1 hour, 250°F (120°C) Gas ½ for 1 hour. Allow cake to cool in tin.

Almond Paste
Mix almonds and sugar together. Mix to a soft dough with liquids. Well cover cake all over (first brushing cake with melted jelly).

White Icing
Beat together egg whites, lemon juice and glycerine. Add sifted icing sugar gradually. Beat thoroughly all the time. The icing should be stiff but not too stiff for fancy icing. It should retain its shape while beating.

Quantities for a 9–10 inch tin (24–26 cm)
10 oz butter (285 g)
10 oz brown sugar (285 g)
6–8 eggs
4 oz ground almonds (100 g)
About 3 lb fruit (1½ kg)
12 oz self-raising flour (350 g)
Continue as for 8 inch tin (20 cm)

Add ½ hour cooking time to each of the lower temperatures, making 5 hours in all.

Cambridgeshire

White Icing
3–4 egg whites
2 teaspoons lemon juice (10 ml)
1 teaspoon glycerine (5 ml)
2 lb icing sugar (900 g)

Christmas Cake

About 80 Years Old

Beat the butter and sugar to a cream, then add the eggs, beating well between each one. Mix all the dry ingredients together and mix well into the butter, sugar and eggs.

Line a 7½ inch (19 cm) tin with paper, put the mixture into the tin and bake in a moderate oven for 3 hours, 275–300°F (140–150°C) Gas 1–2.

This cake is better for keeping a week or two.

After it is baked and cooled down, make a hole with a knitting needle and put in the brandy and it will keep for months in an airtight tin.

8 oz butter (225 g)
8 oz brown sugar (225 g)
5 eggs
4 oz almonds (100 g)
8 oz cherries (225 g)
4 oz currants (100 g)
8 oz sultanas (225 g)
4 oz candied peel (100 g)
12 oz flour (350 g)
¼ oz baking powder (10 ml)
½ wineglass brandy (75 ml)

Cheshire

Coffee Almond Cake

Line and butter a 6 inch (15 cm) cake tin.

Cream butter and sugar, beat in eggs and a little flour. Fold in sifted flour and ground almonds, add coffee essence and 1 tablespoon sherry. Place in tin and sprinkle with chopped almonds and place in centre of moderate oven, 325°F (160°C) Gas 3. Bake for 1½ hours.

Leave cake in tin for 15 minutes, then turn out and cool on a wire tray.

When cold pour rest of sherry over cake, when it has soaked through, wrap cake in greaseproof paper and place in tin. It can be made a week before using and will keep.

4 oz butter or margarine (100 g)
4 oz caster sugar (100 g)
2 eggs
5 oz self-raising flour (125 g)
2 oz ground almonds (50 g)
2 tablespoons liquid coffee essence (30 ml)
3 tablespoons sherry (45 ml)
½ oz finely chopped almonds (15 g)

Cambridgeshire

Cornish Heavy Cake

2 lb flour (900 g)
8 oz lard (225 g)
12 oz fruit and peel (350 g)
6 oz sugar (175 g)
½ teaspoon salt (2½ ml)
1 pint milk (600 ml) (more if required)
Spice if desired
8 oz butter (225 g)
Egg for brushing

Cornwall

Rub in lard as for pastry, add fruit, sugar, salt, mix with milk (not too light). Roll out fairly long. Flake small pieces of butter over the top two-thirds of the pastry. Fold the bottom third upwards and the top third down on it. Give it a half turn and roll out, repeat this. Form into circle or square ½ in (1 cm) thick. Lightly mark in squares with a knife, brush with egg. Bake about ½ hour in a hot oven, 425°F (220°C) Gas 7.

Makes about 48 squares. Recipe can be divided by 2 or 4.

Gingerbread

Family

10 oz self-raising flour (275 g)
1 level teaspoon salt (5 ml)
1½ level teaspoons ground ginger
    (7½ ml)
2 level teaspoons cinnamon (10 ml)
½ level teaspoon nutmeg (2½ ml)
8 oz Demerara sugar (225 g)
6 oz fat (175 g) (lard and margarine,
    mixed)
8 oz treacle (225 g)
2 eggs
¼ pint milk (150 ml)
3 oz chopped raisins (75 g)
2 oz chopped walnuts (50 g) (optional)
Sifted icing sugar to sprinkle on top

Gloucestershire

Grease an oblong tin measuring approximately 9½ × 7½ inches (23 × 19 cm) and line the bottom.

Sift together flour, salt and spices, and mix in the Demerara sugar. Melt fat and treacle together, stir into dry ingredients with the beaten eggs and beat until the mixture is quite smooth. Mix in the milk, raisins and walnuts if used, and turn the batter into the prepared tin.

Bake for 1–1½ hours at 350°F (180°C) Gas 4. Sprinkle top with icing sugar.

Hot Durham Parkin

Traditional Recipe

8 oz plain flour (200 g)
Pinch of salt
2 level teaspoons ground ginger (10 ml)
1 level teaspoon mixed spice (5 ml)
2 level teaspoons bicarbonate of soda
    (10 ml)
4 oz medium oatmeal (100 g)
4 oz dripping (100 g)
4 oz treacle (100 g)
6 oz soft brown sugar (150 g)
¼ pint milk (125 ml)

Durham

Grease and line a 7 × 10½ inch (18 × 26 cm) tin.

Sift flour, salt, ground ginger, mixed spice and bicarbonate of soda in a bowl. Mix in oatmeal.

Place dripping, treacle and brown sugar in large pan and heat gently until melted. Stir in milk and dry ingredients. Blend well. Pour into prepared tin and bake in moderate oven, 350°F (180°C) Gas 4, for about 30–45 minutes, until firm. When cold cut into 15 pieces.

Maids of Honour

Line 12 small tins with pastry, saving a little for decoration. Put a little raspberry jam in each pastry case.

Whip up the white of egg and add ground almonds, caster sugar and ground rice which have previously been mixed together. Fold in gently and place a teaspoonful of the mixture on top of each case.

Cut the remaining pastry into thin strips and place a cross on each one.

Bake in a moderate oven, 350–375°F (180–190°C) Gas 4–5, for 15–20 minutes.

4 oz short pastry (using 100 g flour)
Raspberry jam
White of an egg
2 oz ground almonds (50 g)
4 oz caster sugar (100 g)
1 oz ground rice (25 g)

Cheshire

Manse Cake

Boil all except the soda, flour and egg together for 3 minutes and when cold add the soda and flour. If the egg is used, add it before the flour. Put in a lined 7–8 inch (18–20 cm) tin and bake in a moderate oven, 350°F (180°C) Gas 4, for 1½ hours.

It is better kept for a few days before cutting.

1 breakfast cup sugar (200 g)
1 breakfast cup cold water (250 ml)
1½ breakfast cups raisins, currants or sultanas (250 g)
1 tablespoon treacle (50 g)
4 oz lard or butter (100 g)
½ teaspoon cinnamon or ground ginger (5 ml)
½ teaspoon allspice (5 ml)
A pinch of salt
1 teaspoon bicarbonate of soda (5 ml) dissolved in a little warm water
2 cups flour (250 g)
1 egg (optional)

Note for Beginners

This recipe can be started the day before and the boiled ingredients left overnight to cool; or prepare in the morning for an afternoon baking.

Devon

Marmalade Gingerbread

Sieve flour with spices. Melt syrup and margarine together gently. Pour into dry ingredients. Stir in marmalade, hot water and well beaten egg. Mix well and pour into a greased 8 inch square (20 cm) cake tin.

Bake for approximately 50 minutes at 325°F (160°C) Gas 3.

8 oz self-raising flour (225 g)
1 level teaspoon cinnamon (5 ml)
2 level teaspoons ground ginger (10 ml)
6 oz golden syrup (175 g)
3 oz margarine (75 g)
8 oz thick orange marmalade (225 g)
2 tablespoons hot water (30 ml)
1 egg

Cumberland

Mocha Gâteau

4 oz margarine (100 g)
4 oz sugar (100 g)
4 oz plain flour (100 g)
2 oz ground rice (50 g)
1 level dessertspoon cocoa (10 ml)
1 oz drinking chocolate (25 g)
1 teaspoon baking powder (10 ml)
3 eggs
1 teaspoon coffee essence (5 ml)

Filling
2 tablespoons milk (30 ml)
2 tablespoons drinking chocolate (60 ml)
1 teaspoon coffee essence (5 ml)
3 oz margarine (75 g)
3 oz icing sugar (75 g)

Chocolate Coating (To be used if desired)
4 oz plain chocolate (125 g)
2 dessertspoons milk (20 ml)
½ teaspoon coffee essence (2½ ml)
2 or 3 drops salad oil

Durham

Beat margarine and sugar to a cream. Mix dry ingredients together. Add to creamed mixture alternately with well beaten eggs and coffee essence. Bake in an 8 inch (20 cm) greased cake tin, in moderate oven, 325°F (160°C) Gas 3, for about 45 minutes.

Filling
Stir milk, chocolate and coffee essence over a gentle heat until chocolate is melted. Leave to cool. Beat margarine, add sieved icing sugar and cooled chocolate mixture. Beat well. Split the cold cake and fill.

Chocolate Coating
Break chocolate, add milk, essence, and oil. Heat over pan of hot water until warm. Beat well, then pour over cake.

Old English Cider Cake

8 oz plain flour (225 g)
½ teaspoon ginger (5 ml)
½ teaspoon bicarbonate of soda (2½ ml)
Pinch of nutmeg
4 oz butter (100 g)
4 oz caster sugar (100 g)
2 eggs
¼ pint cider (150 ml)

Devon

Sift dry ingredients, except sugar. Cream butter and sugar until fluffy. Beat in eggs, stir in half dry ingredients. Add cider (previously whisked till frothy). Add rest of dry ingredients; beat well.

Cook in a well greased shallow tin, 8 × 6 inches (20 × 15 cm). Bake in centre of oven at 325°F (160°C) Gas 3 for 45 minutes.

Leave at least 1 day before cutting.

Oozie-woozie Tart

8 oz shortcrust pastry (200 g flour)
2 large tablespoons mincemeat (100 ml)
2 large cooking apples
2 tablespoons lemon curd (60 ml)

Lincolnshire

Line 8 inch (20 cm) pie plate with pastry, spread with mincemeat, peel, core and cut apples into thin slices and overlap to cover mincemeat, trickle the lemon curd over the apples.

Damp pastry edges and arrange lattice strips over top.

Bake near top of oven, 400°F (200°C) Gas 6, for 30 minutes.

Serve hot or cold for 4–6 people.

148

Orange Honey Cake

Cream fat and sugar and beat in the eggs gradually. Stir in the flour and baking powder with the warm honey and marmalade. Place in a greased 7 inch (18 cm) tin and bake in a slow oven for approximately 1–1¼ hours, 300°F (150°C) Gas 2.

3 oz fat (75 g)
3 oz sugar (75 g)
2 eggs
8 oz flour (225 g)
1 teaspoon baking powder (10 ml)
4 oz honey (100 g)
2 oz marmalade (50 g)

Yorkshire

Simnel Cake

Make almond paste by beating eggs with lemon juice and adding dry ingredients. Knead well but do not over handle.

Into large pan put all cake ingredients, except flour and bicarbonate of soda. Bring slowly to the boil, stirring occasionally. Simmer 3 minutes, remove from heat and cool to just warm. Sift flour and bicarbonate together and stir into cooled mixture and mix well.

Put half into prepared tin, about 8 inches (20 cm), and level. Roll one-third almond paste about ¼ inch (6 mm) thick and put on top of the cake mixture, cover with rest of mixture. Level out and bake in a cool oven, 300°F (150°C) Gas 2, for 1 hour and 275°F (140°C) Gas 1 for another 1–1¼ hours.

Sieve apricot jam into pan, add water and bring to boil. Remove from heat; when cake is cold, brush top with glaze and cover with remaining paste and brown under pre-heated grill.

This is traditional cake for Mothering Sunday, but can be Easter Cake by putting part of paste on top and decorating with the rest made into eggs, etc., and browned under grill.

Almond Paste
2 small eggs
1 tablespoon lemon juice (15 ml)
10 oz icing sugar (275 g)
10 oz caster sugar (275 g)
10 oz ground almonds (275 g)

Glaze
1 tablespoon apricot jam (30 ml)
1 tablespoon water (15 ml)

Cake
8 oz butter (225 g)
¼ pint water (150 ml)
6 oz sweetened condensed milk (150 g)
3 oz peel (75 g)
6 oz sultanas (150 g)
6 oz currants (150 g)
3 oz glacé cherries (75 g)
2 oz ground almonds (50 g)
2 oz chopped almonds (50 g)
Grated rind of 1 orange and 1 lemon
8 oz plain flour (225 g)
½ level teaspoon bicarbonate of soda (2½ ml)

Durham

Sly Cakes

Roll out some flaky pastry thin, cover half with currants and chopped peel to taste; fold over the remainder of pastry and lightly roll. Sprinkle top with sugar, then cut into various shapes and bake at 425°F (220°F) Gas 7 for 15–20 minutes.

Flaky pastry
Currants
Chopped peel
Sugar to sprinkle on top

Cornwall

Somerset Apple Cake

8 oz flour (200 g)
3–4 oz fat (75–100 g)
3–4 oz sugar (75–100 g) (according to apple used)
A little mixed spice if liked
1 lb cooking apples (450 g), chopped
A little milk or beaten egg
Sugar for sprinkling

Somerset

Rub fat into flour—add sugar and spice and chopped apples—mix with a little milk or beaten egg to make a stiff mixture.

Spread in a greased 8 inch (20 cm) pie plate or any fairly shallow dish or tin—bake till nicely brown in a fairly hot oven, 400–425°F (200–220°C) Gas 6–7. Serve hot sprinkled with sugar.

A very great winter tea time favourite in this family.

Yorkshire Parkin

3 oz margarine (75 g)
8 oz golden syrup (225 g)
1 tablespoon black treacle (25 g)
8 oz medium oatmeal (225 g)
4 oz plain flour (100 g) and
1 level teaspoon baking powder (5 ml)
  OR 4 oz self-raising flour
4 oz moist brown sugar (100 g)
1½ level teaspoons ground ginger (10 ml)
⅓ pint milk (200 ml)

Yorkshire

Melt the margarine in the syrup and treacle and add to the dry ingredients. Add the milk, pour the mixture into a lined 8 inch (20 cm) square baking tin.

Bake at 325°F (160°C) Gas 3 for 2 hours.

BISCUITS & COOKIES
14

Afternoon Tea Biscuits

Cream the butter or margarine and sugar together, beat in three parts of the egg with one tablespoon of flour, add the remainder of the flour, and if necessary, the remaining egg. Mix to a stiff paste, roll out to about $\frac{1}{4}$ inch (6 mm) thick, cut into rounds, bake in a moderate oven, 350°F (180°C) Gas 4, until a golden brown. Coat with jam while hot and stick two together. Decorate with the lemon icing.

Using a $2\frac{1}{2}$ inch (5 cm) cutter this makes 12 finished biscuits.

3 oz butter or margarine (75 g)
2 oz sugar (50 g)
1 small egg
6 oz flour (150 g)
Jam

Lemon Icing
4 oz icing sugar (100 g)
Juice of lemon to mix

*Northamptonshire and
Soke of Peterborough*

Almond Biscuits

Cream sugar and margarine with the hand, add flour and ground almonds. Make into a roll about $2\frac{1}{2}$ inches thick (5 cm) and cut into slices about $\frac{1}{4}$ inch thick (6 mm), or roll out and cut in rounds. Put a split almond on each biscuit. Bake in a moderate oven, 350°F (180°C) Gas 4, for about 20–25 minutes.

Makes about 30 biscuits.

4 oz caster sugar (100 g)
4 oz margarine (100 g)
4 oz plain flour (100 g)
4 oz ground almonds (100 g)
Split almonds

Gloucestershire

Almond Slices

6 oz self-raising flour (150 g)
3 oz butter (75 g)
2 teaspoons sugar (20 ml)
2 yolks of egg
Jam

Filling
2 egg whites
3 oz icing sugar (75 g)
2 oz ground almonds (50 g)
A few chopped almonds

Yorkshire

Rub butter into flour, mix in sugar, mix with beaten egg yolks. Roll out and line Swiss roll tin, spread with jam.

Filling
Beat egg whites stiff, add sugar and ground almonds, mix well. Spread over the jam and put a few chopped almonds on top. Bake in moderate oven, 350°F (180°C) Gas 4, for 25–30 minutes. Cut in slices.

Australian Jack

Short pastry using 6 oz (150 g) flour
Jam
8 oz butter or margarine (200 g)
3 tablespoons golden syrup (150 g)
8 oz Quaker oats (200 g)
½ teaspoon essence of almonds (2½ ml)

*Northamptonshire and
Soke of Peterborough*

Roll pastry into one thin sheet, put on a baking sheet, spread with jam. Cream butter and syrup, work in Quaker oats, and add flavouring essence. Spread this mixture over the jam, and fold over the edges of pastry. Bake ¾ hour in a hot oven, 375°F (190°C) Gas 5, cool and cut into fingers.

Makes about 30 fingers.

Brandy Snaps

2 oz butter or margarine (50 g)
2 oz sugar (50 g)
2 tablespoons golden syrup (50 g)
2 oz flour (50 g)
1 level teaspoon ground ginger (5 ml)
1 teaspoon brandy (5 ml)
¼ teaspoon grated lemon rind (1 ml)

These Brandy Snaps have been a traditional sweetmeat on sale at Hull Fair for many years.

Melt the fat, sugar and syrup in a pan. Remove from the heat and add the other ingredients and mix well.

Drop in teaspoons on a greased baking sheet at least 3 inches (8 cm) apart as they will spread in cooking.

Bake in a moderate oven, 350°F (180°C) Gas 4, for 7–10 minutes until golden brown.

Remove the baking sheet from the oven and allow to stand a moment on the stove top until the biscuits can be easily lifted from the sheet with a knife. Roll the biscuits round a wooden spoon handle and leave for a minute to set.

Note for Beginners

Bake these in relays, a few at a time; the mixture will not spoil with keeping. Use more than one wooden spoon handle if possible and roll the biscuits with the upper surface on the outside. Removal is easier if the trays have been floured as well as greased. If the last ones in a batch become too hard to roll, return to the oven for a minute.

Yorkshire

Canadian Shortbread

Cream butter and sugar, add other ingredients, knead well together. Divide into two and press into two 7 inch (18 cm) sandwich tins. Bake 15–20 minutes at 375°F (190°C) Gas 5. (Watch carefully as it soon burns.)

As soon as it is cooked mark the shortbread into triangles, using a small sharp knife. Leave in the tins to cool before turning out.

Each will cut into 8–12 triangles.

If polka dots are not available other similar tiny plain chocolate sweets may be used.

4 oz butter (100 g)
4 oz soft brown sugar (100 g)
6 oz plain flour (150 g)
1 oz broken walnuts (25 g)
1 oz polka dots (25 g)

Yorkshire

Cheese Biscuits

Rub all the ingredients together till they form a firm paste (add no liquid). Roll out thin and cut into shapes. Bake in a moderate oven, 350°F (180°C) Gas 4, till pale gold, about 10 minutes.

Makes about 24 biscuits, approximately 2 inch (5 cm) size.

2 oz grated cheese (50 g)
2 oz margarine (50 g)
2 oz plain flour (50 g)

Yorkshire

Chocolate Crisps

Rub well together, knead and work in the palms of your hands, 1 dessertspoonful at a time till a round flat cake is formed. Place well apart on a greased tin and bake slowly, 325°F (160°C) Gas 3, till crisp and *hard in centre*. This last is important.

Makes 24 crisps.

8 oz self-raising flour (200 g)
2 oz cocoa (50 g)
5 oz granulated sugar (125 g)
3 oz margarine (75 g)
2 oz lard (50 g)

Devon

Chocolate Petits Fours

Mix all dry ingredients together and bind with the beaten egg. Divide into 16 pieces, roll in balls and put an almond or cherry on top of each. Bake for 15 minutes at 375–400°F (190–200°C) Gas 5–6.

1 oz drinking chocolate (25 g)
4 oz sugar (100 g)
1 oz chopped walnuts (25 g)
3 oz ground almonds (75 g)
1 small egg
Almonds or cherries for decoration

Yorkshire

Coconut Macaroons

1 oz flour (25 g)
6 oz desiccated coconut (150 g)
6 oz sugar (150 g)
2 whites of eggs, beaten

Mix the flour, coconut and sugar together in a bowl. Bind with the whites of eggs, and place in rough heaps on a greased baking sheet lined with rice paper. Bake for 20 minutes at 325°F (160°C) Gas 3.

Makes about 16 macaroons.

Note for Beginners

As the size of egg whites varies, you may need to use some more to bind the ingredients. It should be a very stiff mixture which can be moulded into heaps using your hands.

Yorkshire

Coconut Shortbread

4 oz butter (100 g)
4 oz coconut (100 g)
4 oz rolled oats (100 g)
2 oz sugar (50 g)
1 teaspoon vanilla essence (5 ml)
Pinch of salt
1 teaspoon baking powder (10 ml)

Melt butter and mix into other ingredients. Press mixture down into a 7–8 inch (18–20 cm) flan tin. Bake in a slow oven, 300°F (150°C) Gas 2, about ¾ hour.

Cut when warm but leave in the tin until quite cold.

Cuts into 8–10 pieces.

Yorkshire

Date Flapjacks

4 oz stoned dates (125 g)
2 oz margarine (50 g)
2 oz moist brown sugar (50 g)
4 oz rolled oats (100 g)
Lemon juice

Put dates through a mincer. Cream margarine and sugar and work in rolled oats. Grease a small tin, about 5–6 inches (12–15 cm) square and press in smoothly half the mixture and spread with the dates. Sprinkle with a very little lemon juice, cover with the rest of the mixture. Bake in a moderate oven, 325°F (160°C) Gas 3, for about 40 minutes and cut in oblongs.

Shropshire

Fruit and Treacle Cookies

Sift the flour, salt and cinnamon into a bowl. Cream the margarine in another bowl until very soft. Add sugar and cream again until mixture is light and fluffy. Stir in the treacle, then the beaten egg thoroughly. Fold in the sifted flour, and then stir in the raisins and nuts. Put heaped teaspoonsful of the mixture on greased baking sheets and bake at 425°F (220°C) Gas 7 for 12–15 minutes.

Makes 24 cookies.

8 oz plain flour (200 g)
1 level teaspoon salt (5 ml)
2 level teaspoons cinnamon or mixed spice (10 ml)
4 oz margarine (100 g)
3 oz Demerara sugar (75 g)
1 tablespoon treacle (15 ml) (black if available or molasses)
1 beaten egg
4 oz seedless raisins or sultanas or currants (100 g)
2 oz chopped nuts (50 g)

Isle of Ely

Ginger Biscuits

Traditional Recipe

Put all ingredients except the flour into a pan. Bring to boiling point until golden brown. Add plain flour until it can be rolled out and cut into biscuits. Place on greased baking sheet, bake in a moderate oven, 350°F (180°C) Gas 4, for about 15 minutes.

This mixture absorbs approximately 1 lb flour (450 g).

When rolled about $\frac{1}{4}$ inch (6 mm) thick and cut with a $2\frac{1}{2}$ inch (1 cm) cutter it will make about 4 dozen biscuits.

4 oz lard (100 g)
8 oz sugar (200 g)
8 oz syrup (200 g)
1 dessertspoon ginger (20 ml)
1 dessertspoon bicarbonate of soda (10 ml)
Pinch of salt
Plain flour (approximately 1 lb or 450 g)

Durham

Ginger Crispies

Sieve flour, salt and ginger. Cream margarine and sugar, beat in egg, then chopped ginger. Fold in flour mixture. With floured hands pinch out pieces the size of a walnut, roll into a ball then roll in the cornflakes and lay on lightly greased tin, well apart. Bake 20 minutes at 350°F (180°C) Gas 4.

Makes about 18 crispies.

4 oz self-raising flour (125 g)
Pinch of salt
1 level teaspoon ground ginger (5 ml)
3 oz margarine (75 g)
3 oz caster sugar (75 g)
1 egg
1 oz crystallized ginger (25 g)
Cornflakes

Lincolnshire

Grasmere Shortbread

Traditional Recipe

4 oz butter or margarine (100 g)
4 oz brown sugar (100 g)
1 tablespoon golden syrup (15 ml)
8 oz flour (200 g)
½ dessertspoon ground ginger (10 ml)
Pinch of salt
½ teaspoon bicarbonate of soda (2½ ml)
½ teaspoon cream of tartar (2½ ml)

Westmorland

Cream fat and sugar, add syrup and then sifted dry ingredients. Put into greased Yorkshire pudding tin (about 6½ × 8½ inches (16 × 22 cm)). Spread evenly and press down lightly with the back of a spoon. Cook in a slow oven, 300–325°F (150–160°C) Gas 2–3, for 30–40 minutes. Leave in the tin to cool but mark in squares before cold.
   Makes 16–20 squares.

Hazelnut and Honey Biscuits

4 oz butter (100 g)
2½ oz caster sugar (70 g)
5 oz plain flour (125 g)
3 oz ground hazelnuts (75 g)

Filling
A little honey

Decoration
3 oz plain dessert chocolate (75 g)
1½ oz ground hazelnuts (40 g)

Northumberland

Cream butter and sugar, sift flour and stir into mixture with ground nuts. Knead into a ball, roll out thinly, and cut into rounds. Bake in a moderate oven for 12 minutes, 350°F (180°C) Gas 4. Cool on tray.
   Sandwich together with honey.
   Break up chocolate, and melt over a pan of hot water. When smooth roll edges of biscuits in the chocolate, then in ground nuts. If there is any chocolate left over put through an icing tube, and decorate tops of biscuits.
   With a 2½ inch (5 cm) cutter it makes 12–18 completed biscuits.

Hungarian Nut Cookies

4 oz margarine (100 g)
4 oz soft brown sugar (100 g)
5 oz plain flour (125 g)
2 oz walnuts (50 g)

Oxfordshire

Cream margarine and sugar together, add flour and lastly chopped nuts. Roll in pieces about 2 inches (5 cm) long, press flat with a fork. Bake in a moderate oven, 350°F (180°C) Gas 4, for about 15 minutes or until lightly browned. Leave them to set for a few minutes before removing from the trays.
   Makes about 30 cookies.

Melting Moments

4 oz butter or margarine (100 g)
1 oz icing sugar (25 g)
2 oz self-raising flour (50 g)
2 oz cornflour (50 g)
A little vanilla essence
Butter icing

Herefordshire

Beat butter and sugar to a cream, add other ingredients. Put into a forcing bag and force into about 24 rosettes. Bake until very pale brown, 350°F (180°C) Gas 4, for 10–12 minutes. Cool on the tray, then join in pairs with a little butter icing.

Nut Brownies

Whisk eggs well, add sugar, vanilla and whisk again till stiff. Add flour and baking powder and mix well. Add dates and nuts. Spread mixture evenly on small greased tin, 9 × 7 inches (23 × 18 cm). Bake in a moderate oven, 325°F (160°C) Gas 3, for 30–35 minutes.

While still hot cut into 16 fingers and roll in icing sugar.

2 eggs
6 oz soft brown sugar (150 g)
Few drops vanilla essence
4 oz brown flour (100 g) and
    1 teaspoon baking powder (10 ml)
    OR
4 oz self-raising brown flour (100 g)
5 oz chopped dates (125 g)
4 oz chopped walnuts or hazelnuts
    (100 g)
Icing sugar for dusting

Cumberland

Peanut Shortbread Biscuits

Roast the peanuts golden brown, rub to remove skins, and crush.

Cream the sugar and margarine, add the egg yolk and dry ingredients. Knead the dough well and leave for an hour. Roll out about $\frac{1}{4}$ inch (6 mm) thick and cut into shapes. Bake for 30 minutes in a slow oven, 275–300°F (140–150°C) Gas 1–2.

Makes 18 biscuits using a $2\frac{1}{2}$ inch (5 cm) cutter.

2 oz roasted peanuts (50 g), crushed
2 oz caster sugar (50 g)
4 oz margarine (100 g)
1 egg yolk
5 oz plain flour (150 g)
Pinch of salt

Northumberland

Shortbread

Cream butter and sugar by hand and gradually add flour. Roll out on a floured board into two round cakes about $\frac{1}{2}$ inch (1 cm) thick. Put on trays.

Mark each cake in triangles and bake at 325°F (160°C) Gas 4 for 35 minutes. Allow to cool a little before lifting the shortbread off the baking trays.

4 oz butter (100 g)
2 oz caster sugar (50 g)
5 oz flour (125 g)
3 oz rice flour (75 g)

Variations:

Pitchaithly Bannock
Add 1 tablespoon chopped peel and 1 tablespoon chopped almonds.

Huby Bannock
Add 1 tablespoon chopped preserved ginger and 1 tablespoon chopped almonds.

Yorkshire

Shortbread Creams

8 oz margarine (200 g)
3 oz icing sugar (75 g)
7 oz plain flour (175 g)
3 oz cornflour (75 g)
Butter cream or raspberry jam
Icing sugar for dusting

Cheshire

Beat the margarine and sugar to a soft cream. Sift the flour and cornflour and work it gradually into the creamed mixture. Using a vegetable star pipe, force in finger lengths on a greased baking tray or roll into balls and press with a fork. Bake for about 20 minutes at 350°F (180°C) Gas 4. When cool, sandwich with jam or cream and dust with icing sugar.

Makes about 24 completed creams.

Spiced Finnish Biscuits

1½ oz margarine (40 g)
1 oz sugar (25 g)
2 oz golden syrup (50 g)
3½ oz self-raising flour (100 g)
¼ teaspoon cinnamon (2½ ml)
½ teaspoon ginger (5 ml)
¼ teaspoon bicarbonate of soda (1 ml)
1 tablespoon water (15 ml)

Durham

Put margarine and sugar with syrup into a saucepan. Melt over gentle heat. Sieve dry ingredients into a bowl. Dissolve bicarbonate in water and add to the margarine, sugar and syrup. Pour into dry ingredients and mix. Leave in a bowl overnight or place in refrigerator until firm enough to use.

Roll out ⅛ inch (3 mm) thick and cut into shapes. Bake at 300°F (150°C) Gas 2 for 12–20 minutes. Using a 2 inch (5 cm) cutter it makes about 30 biscuits.

QUICK BREAD & SCONES
15

Quick Breads

Banana Loaf

Brush a 1 lb (½ kg) loaf tin with melted fat and line the base with greaseproof paper. Sift flour, bicarbonate of soda, baking powder and salt into a bowl. Rub lard and margarine in with tips of fingers. Add sugar and chopped walnuts. Skin and mash the bananas and add to the mixture to form a stiff dropping consistency. Turn the mixture into the prepared tin and bake in a moderately hot oven, 375°F (190°C) Gas 5, for ½ hour. Reduce heat to 325°F (160°C) Gas 3 for ¾ hour until loaf is well risen and firm in centre.

7 oz plain flour (200 g)
½ teaspoon bicarbonate of soda (2½ ml)
1 level teaspoon baking powder (5 ml)
Pinch of salt
1 oz lard (25 g)
1 oz margarine (25 g)
4 oz caster sugar (100 g)
3 oz chopped walnuts (75 g)
3 bananas—if small add 1 tablespoon milk (15 ml)

Durham

Borrowdale Tea Loaf

4 oz currants (100 g)
4 oz raisins (100 g)
1 oz mixed peel (25 g)
4 oz sugar (100 g), brown preferred
Water
8 oz self-raising flour (200 g)
1 egg

Durham

Put fruit and sugar in a basin and barely cover with water. Leave overnight.

Next day put flour into a basin and add beaten egg, fruit, sugar and water. Mix well. Put into greased 1 lb ($\frac{1}{2}$ kg) loaf tin and bake for 1–1$\frac{1}{4}$ hours at 350°F (180°C) Gas 4 (middle shelf of oven).

When cold cut into slices and spread with butter.

Date and Walnut Loaf

6 oz plain flour (175 g)
$\frac{1}{2}$ level teaspoon bicarbonate of soda (2$\frac{1}{2}$ ml)
2 teaspoons baking powder (15 ml)
1$\frac{1}{2}$ oz soft brown sugar (40 g)
4 oz dates (100 g), chopped
1$\frac{1}{2}$ oz shelled walnuts (40 g), chopped
1$\frac{1}{2}$ oz black treacle (40 g)
$\frac{3}{4}$ oz butter or margarine (20 g)
$\frac{1}{4}$ pint milk (150 ml)

Gloucestershire

Grease and line a 1 lb ($\frac{1}{2}$ kg) loaf tin with greaseproof paper. Sift flour and other dry ingredients. Mix in sugar, dates and walnuts.

Warm black treacle, butter and milk until melted. Stir into flour mixture and beat until the batter is smooth. Pour into tin.

Bake at 350°F (180°C) Gas 4 for 1–1$\frac{1}{2}$ hours.

This cuts into approximately 8 slices.

Farmhouse Loaf

8 oz self-raising flour (225 g)
6 oz mixed dried fruit (175 g)
2 oz chopped peel (50 g)
$\frac{1}{2}$ teaspoon mixed spice (5 ml)
3 oz soft brown sugar (75 g)
3 oz margarine (75 g)
3 oz golden syrup (75 g)
1 egg
4 tablespoons milk (60 ml)

Durham

Mix flour, fruit, peel and spice. Melt sugar, margarine and syrup and stir into dry ingredients with beaten egg and milk. Put in a greased 6 inch (15 cm) tin or a loaf tin.

Bake 1 hour 10 minutes at 325°F (160°C) Gas 3.

Lincolnshire Plum Bread

4 oz butter (100 g)
4 oz Demerara sugar (100 g)
2 eggs
1 tablespoon brandy (15 ml)
7 oz self-raising flour (200 g)

Cream butter and sugar together, beat in eggs and brandy, sift in the flour and salt, stir in the fruit.

Well grease a 1 lb ($\frac{1}{2}$ kg) loaf tin. Bake for 3 hours at 275°F (140°C) Gas 1.

Plum breads are best made about a week in advance of using. Keep in an airtight box.

Pinch of salt
4 oz sultanas (100 g)
2 oz cut peel (50 g), if liked
4 oz chopped prunes (100 g)
4 oz currants (100 g)

Lincolnshire

Luncheon Spice Loaf

Sift flour and spice together. Rub in fat, add all other ingredients, bicarbonate of soda and vinegar last and milk if needed. Bake in a greased 1 lb (½ kg) loaf tin in a moderate oven, 350°F (180°C) Gas 4, approximately 1¼ hours.

This is nice served with cheese.

8 oz plain flour (200 g)
1 teaspoon sweet spice, cinnamon or ginger (10 ml)
2 oz dripping (50 g)
2 oz margarine (50 g)
3 oz brown sugar (75 g)
3 oz currants (75 g)
1 level teaspoon bicarbonate of soda (5 ml)
1 dessertspoon vinegar (10 ml)
2–3 tablespoons milk (30–45 ml), if required

Oxfordshire

Malt Loaf

Grease and line a 2 lb (1 kg) loaf tin with greaseproof paper.

Sieve flour and bicarbonate of soda into a bowl, add dates and walnuts. Warm malt and syrup gently in the milk, add the lightly beaten egg to dry ingredients and also the milk mixture. Turn into the prepared tin.

Bake at 375°F (190°C) Gas 5 for about 1¼ hours, until loaf is well risen.

When cold, store in a tin for at least a day before cutting, then serve spread with butter.

8 oz plain flour (200 g)
1 level teaspoon bicarbonate of soda (5 ml)
2 oz chopped dates (50 g)
2 oz chopped walnuts (50 g)
½ pint milk (250 ml)
3 tablespoons golden syrup (45 ml)
3 tablespoons malt extract (45 ml)
1 egg

Durham

Mrs O'Flanagan's Brown Bread

Put the wholemeal flour in a bowl. Sift in the white flour and other dry ingredients. Mix to a stiffish dough with the milk. Turn on to a floured board and form into a compact shape.

Bake in a hot oven, 425°F (220°C) Gas 7, for exactly ¾ hour.

The proportions of brown to white flour may be altered to suit individual tastes. A very little extra milk is needed for an entire brown loaf.

10 oz plain wholemeal flour (300 g)
6 oz plain white flour (175 g)
1 teaspoon sugar (10 ml)
1 teaspoon salt (5–10 ml)
1 teaspoon bicarbonate of soda (5 ml)
1 teaspoon cream of tartar (10 ml)
½ pint and 1 tablespoon of sweet milk (300 ml)

Devon

Orange Tea Bread

6 oz self-raising flour (175 g)
½ level teaspoon salt (2½ ml)
3 oz caster sugar (75 g)
Grated rind of 1 medium orange
2 level tablespoons coarse cut
    marmalade (30 ml)
1 tablespoon cooking oil (15 ml)
1 egg, beaten
3 tablespoons milk (45 ml)

Derbyshire

Sift flour and salt into a bowl and add sugar and orange rind. Make a well in the middle and stir in the marmalade, oil, egg and milk. Mix well.

Put in a greased 1 lb (½ kg) loaf tin. Bake 40–45 minutes in an oven 350°F (180°C) Gas 4.

Allow to cool. Cut in slices and butter.

Scones

Alton Tea Cakes

6 oz flour (150 g)
3 oz sugar (75 g)
3 oz butter (75 g)
1 teaspoon baking powder (10 ml)
1 egg
A little milk (50 ml)

*Northamptonshire and
Soke of Peterborough*

Rub the butter into the flour and sugar, and add the baking powder. Beat the egg in a little milk and add to the other ingredients, making the mixture rather moist. Bake in two buttered shallow, 5 inch (12 cm), cake tins about 20 minutes at 375–400°F (190–200°C) Gas 5–6.

Cut and butter like ordinary tea cakes and serve very hot.

Apple Scones

6 oz flour (170 g)
1 teaspoon baking powder (10 ml)
2 oz lard (50 g)
1 oz sugar (25 g)
1 large cooking apple
1 egg
Milk if necessary

Sift flour and baking powder together, rub in lard, add sugar. Add the apple, finely chopped. Beat the egg and add to the dry ingredients to make a stiff elastic dough, using a very little milk if necessary. Turn the dough on to a board and divide into the number of scones required. Shape and flatten by hand, about an inch (2½ cm) thick and bake in a moderate oven, 400°F (200°C) Gas 6, for about ½ hour. Dredge with sugar and serve hot—buttered.

Note for Beginners

A large cooking apple weighs about ½ lb (225 g). If more convenient, self-raising flour may be substituted for the plain flour and baking powder. If the mixture is made into 6 large scones the baking time needs to be about ½ hour, for small ones a little less.

Yorkshire

Cheese Scones

Sieve flour, rub in butter and grated cheese. Beat up egg with a little milk, add to flour and mix to a soft dough. Turn out on to a floured board and roll out to ¾ inch (2 cm) thick, cut into rounds and place on greased baking sheet in a hot oven, 450°F (230°C) Gas 8, for about 10 minutes. Makes 8 scones using a 2½ inch (6 cm) cutter.

6 oz self-raising flour (175 g)
1 oz butter (25 g)
3 oz grated cheese (75 g)
1 egg
Milk to mix

Gloucestershire

Cheese and Bacon Scones

Sift flour, salt and mustard into bowl. Rub fat in gently. Stir in bacon and cheese. Mix to a soft dough with milk. Turn out on to a floured board. Roll into ½ inch (1 cm) thickness. Use 2–2½ inch cutter (5–7 cm) to cut into rounds. Put on a greased baking tray and bake towards top of hot oven, 425°F (220°C) Gas 7, for 10 minutes or until golden brown and cooked through. Serve with butter. Makes approximately 12 scones.

8 oz self-raising flour (225 g)
½ teaspoon salt (2½ ml)
½ level teaspoon dry mustard (2½ ml)
1½ oz margarine (40 g)
2 oz bacon (50 g) cooked and cut up finely
2 oz grated cheese (50 g)
Just under ¼ pint milk (just under 150 ml)

Yorkshire

Cornish Sandwiches

Rub the jam through a sieve, split the scones and remove part of the soft inside. Spread a little jam on each half of the scone, and a teaspoonful of thick cream on the lower half of each, press each scone together. These are best prepared only a short time before they are to be eaten.

2 spoonsful of damson, whortleberry
  or blackberry jam
2 spoonsful of clotted cream
8 or 9 little scones, very fresh, but cold

Cornwall

Fat Rascals

Rub margarine into flour and salt, add sugar and currants. Mix with milk. Roll out ½ inch (1 cm) thick. Cut into rounds with pastry cutter. Bake second shelf from top at 425°F (220°C) Gas 7 for 15–20 minutes. Makes 12 scones using a 2½ inch (5 cm) cutter.

8 oz self-raising flour (200 g)
Pinch of salt
4 oz margarine (100 g)
1 oz sugar (25 g)
2 oz currants (50 g)
7 tablespoons milk to mix (90 ml)

Yorkshire

Finger Scones

Put flour, baking powder, sugar and salt in basin and rub in butter. Moisten with beaten egg and milk enough to make a

8 oz flour (200 g)
1 teaspoon baking powder (10 ml)
1 tablespoon sugar (25 g)
Pinch of salt
2 oz butter or margarine (50 g)
1 egg
Milk
Caster sugar

Oxfordshire

soft dough. Divide into 24 pieces and shape into fingers. Dip in milk and roll in caster sugar.

Bake for 10–15 minutes in quick oven on greased sheet, 450°F (220°C) Gas 8.

Note for Beginners

Self-raising flour can be used instead of the flour and baking powder.

Girdle Cakes

8 oz plain flour (225 g)
2 oz lard (50 g)
2 oz margarine (50 g)
1 teaspoon baking powder (10 ml)
2 oz currants (50 g)
1 tablespoon sugar (25 g)
A little milk (100 ml)
Butter

Rub the lard and margarine into the flour, add other dry ingredients and mix well. Mix with sufficient cold milk to form a soft dough. Roll out, cut into small round cakes and bake on a hot girdle until golden brown on both sides.

Split open and butter whilst hot.

Note for Beginners

This mixture will make approximately 18 girdle cakes if rolled $\frac{1}{4}$ inch (6 mm) thick and a $2\frac{1}{2}$ inch (5 cm) cutter is used. Cooking time will be 8–10 minutes.

Instead of using a girdle the cakes can be cooked in an electric frying pan at about 375°F (190°C). Grease the pan lightly with lard or oil.

Northumberland and Durham

Light Splitters

8 oz self-raising flour (200 g)
A good pinch of salt
1 dessertspoon caster sugar (25 g)
4 oz lard (100 g)
Milk and water to mix (about 125 ml)

Northamptonshire and
Soke of Peterborough

Add the salt and sugar to the flour, rub in the lard lightly with tips of fingers, form a soft dough with milk and water, roll out about $\frac{1}{2}$ inch (1 cm) thick, cut in rounds with fluted cutter, brush over with a little milk and bake about 15 minutes in a moderate oven, 425°F (220°C) Gas 7. Makes 12 splitters using $2\frac{1}{2}$ inch (5 cm) cutter. Split through the centre, butter with salt butter and serve hot.

Sweet Scones

Add salt to flour. Rub in margarine, add sugar and sultanas. Mix together with beaten egg and milk. Cut into rounds ½ inch (1 cm) thick. Bake in hot oven, 450°F (230°C) Gas 8, for 7–10 minutes. Makes 12 scones, using 2½ inch (5 cm) cutter.

8 oz self-raising flour (200 g)
Pinch of salt
3 oz margarine (75 g)
3 oz sugar (75 g)
2 oz sultanas (50 g)
1 egg
1 dessertspoon milk (10 ml)

Durham

Welsh Cakes

Rub margarine into flour and sugar. Add fruit. Mix to a stiff paste with beaten egg and milk. Roll out, cut in rounds and put in frying pan. Cook till sides are done. Cooking time— 10 minutes.

If rolled about ¼ inch (6 mm) thick and cut with a 2½ inch (5 cm) cutter the mixture makes about 4 dozen cakes.

1 lb self-raising flour (450 g)
8 oz sugar (225 g)
8 oz margarine (225 g)
8 oz mixed fruit (225 g)
1–2 eggs
Milk to bind

Durham

YEAST COOKERY
16

Yeast Cookery

The breads, buns and cakes made by the use of yeast are a feature of local recipes and of the English tea table.

Notes on Yeast

Compressed Bakers' Yeast

When bought this should be pale fawn in colour, have a fresh smell and crumble easily. It will keep well if stored in a cool place and closely wrapped in waxed paper or in foil. All yeast is apt to dry out and discolour if exposed to the air. The length of keeping varies, but if the yeast is in good condition when bought and is carefully stored it should keep a week or two.

Dried Yeast

This is dehydrated and usually in the form of pellets. It is more concentrated than compressed yeast and is used in about half the quantity of fresh yeast normally referred to in recipes. It requires 'reconstituting' in a little warm water sweetened with sugar—$\frac{1}{2}$ oz sugar (15 g) to $\frac{1}{2}$ pint (300 ml) warm water—before use. It is generally somewhat slow in action. Dried yeast is usually a 'branded' product and any manufacturers' directions should be followed.

Berkshire

Method of Making a Plain Bread Dough

Mixing the Dough

Choose a strong plain flour which will have a high gluten content.

Add the yeast liquid all at once, using the fingers stretched open, until all the flour has been absorbed (add a little more liquid or flour at this stage if necessary). Work quickly including all the flour from the side of the bowl as well. The dough should feel firm but soft at this stage and the basin should be clean.

Kneading the Dough

This is necessary to strengthen the dough and get a good rise.

The dough may at first feel soft and sticky but do not add more flour. It will improve with further kneading. Kneading is a process in which the dough is pulled, stretched, squeezed and folded in a rhythmic manner. The fingers will be clean and the dough firm and elastic when ready.

If you have a mixer the kneading can be done at a low speed using the dough hook, until the mixture collects in one piece leaving the bowl quite clean.

Rising the Dough

All yeast doughs MUST be risen before baking.

The dough must be covered to prevent a hard skin from forming and to ensure the dough remains moist. Greasing the container will prevent the dough sticking.

Suggestions:
Large oiled polythene bag which can be loosely tied.
Plastic storage jar with a lid (large enough to allow for rising).
Casserole or saucepan with lid.
Cloth or tea towel.

How Long Will It Take?

The Temperature Will Affect the Time Taken
The rising time can be made to suit your convenience. Remember a long slow rising gives a stronger dough and a better result. Warm rising gives a weaker dough and it is inclined to become dry. When risen the dough is double its original volume.

Possible Rising Times:
1 hour in a warm kitchen or other warm place.
2 hours in a cooler room.
4–6 hours in a cool place.
12 hours in a refrigerator. Good for overnight rising if warm rolls are needed for breakfast.
Allow to come to room temperature before shaping, proving and baking.

Surplus dough can be stored about 2 days in a refrigerator or longer in a deep freeze
if well wrapped to prevent drying. Thaw before shaping, proving and baking.

Knocking Back the Dough

A process whereby the air bubbles the yeast has produced are 'knocked out'. The big bubbles
of gas would make large holes in the dough if baked and the action of the yeast will have
softened the dough, so kneading is again necessary to strengthen it.

The dough should regain its elasticity and firmness.

The mixer can be used for this process on a low speed.

Shaping

The dough is ready for shaping according to instructions or can be adapted for various
recipes by the addition of further ingredients.

Proving or Second Rising

The dough recovers and puffs up to twice its size as the yeast becomes active again and
'proves' itself. The dough must not be allowed to form a skin as a dry surface would impede
the rising. It is most important to cover lightly or use a greased polythene bag at this stage
or choose a warm and humid place.

Baking

Use a hot oven at first to kill the action of the yeast. This can be reduced later if necessary.

Common Faults in Bread	Causes
White pimples or spots on top of the loaf	Dough had a skin on it before being placed in the oven due to chilling or evaporation. A damp muslin or suitable covering for the dough will help to avoid this.
Coarse honeycomb texture	Too much liquid. Too little kneading.
A 'flying top' when the top breaks away from the rest of the loaf	The top crust baked hard before there is full expansion of dough due to under-proving or chilling—or dough too tight because not well worked.

Lack of volume, uneven texture	Under-proving and kneading or baking at too high a temperature.
Lack of volume, open texture and crumbly	Over-proving and weakening of gluten or baking at too low a temperature.
Smell of alcohol	Over-proving.

NATIONAL FEDERATION OF WOMEN'S INSTITUTES *Yeast Cookery*.

Note for Beginners

For richer doughs modifications of the method above for plain doughs are used and these are given in the individual recipes.

With buns and soft rolls, after the first rising, instructions often say 'knead lightly'. This means to knead only enough to shape the buns or rolls. If long kneading is given the dough must be allowed time to double its bulk again before baking; the usual procedure after 'light' kneading is to prove until the buns or rolls look light and puffy, about 20–30 minutes.

White Bread Dough

Four 1 lb ($\frac{1}{2}$ kg) Loaves

Put the yeast fresh or dried plus sugar in a pint jug or bowl and add to this $\frac{1}{2}$ pint (300 ml) warm water just slightly hotter than blood heat. Stir and then leave about 10 minutes to become frothy (rather like beer).

Sieve flour and salt and rub in the fat if used. Add yeast liquid all at once together with the remaining warm water and oil if this is used to make a firm dough. A little more flour or water can be added at this stage to adjust the consistency but beware of making the mixture too tight (dry).

Knead the dough and put to rise to double the bulk. Knock back and divide the dough into four pieces.

1 oz fresh yeast (25 g) or $\frac{1}{2}$ oz dried yeast (15 g) plus 1 teaspoon sugar
1$\frac{1}{2}$ pints warm water (900 ml)
3 lb strong plain flour (1$\frac{1}{2}$ kg)
1 oz cooking salt (25 g)
1 oz lard (25 g) or 2 tablespoons corn oil (30 ml)

Shaping
Tin loaf Flatten each piece and roll Swiss roll fashion to fit greased and floured 1 lb ($\frac{1}{2}$ kg) loaf tins. Place the crease underneath and push the ends well into the sides of the tin. Prove, and bake in a hot oven, 450°F (230°C) Gas 8, about $\frac{3}{4}$ hour.

When cooked it will sound hollow when tapped on the bottom.

Cob
Shape $\frac{1}{4}$ dough to a round ball and flatten slightly. Put on a floured baking sheet. Prove and bake.

Make half the recipe for ease in handling. For details of kneading and rising a dough, see page 167.

NATIONAL FEDERATION OF WOMEN'S INSTITUTES *Yeast Cookery*.

Wheatmeal Dough

Quickly Made

1½ oz fresh yeast (40 g) or ¾ oz dried yeast (20 g) plus 1 teaspoon sugar
1½ pints warm water (900 ml)
3 lb flour (1½ kg), a mixture of brown and white in any proportions
1 oz sugar (25 g)
1 oz salt (25 g)
1 oz lard (25 g) or 2 tablespoons corn oil (30 ml)

Put yeast, fresh, or dried plus sugar, into ½ pint (300 ml) of the measured warm water. Leave 5–10 minutes to become frothy. Sieve or mix the flour, salt and sugar and rub in the fat if used. Add the rest of the warm water to the yeast liquid together with the oil if preferred. Mix to a soft dough, leaving the basin clean and adding a little more flour or water if necessary. Knead for 10 minutes on a floured board.

Shape into a bap, cob, rolls, tin loaf or bake in earthenware flower-pots. When shaped the dough is covered and put to rise. Bake in the centre of a hot oven, 450°F (230°C) Gas 8, for about 40 minutes.

Note: For soft crust brush with oil before proving, for a crisp crust brush with salt and water and sprinkle with crushed wheat before baking.

Flower-pot loaves The pot must be well greased before use. It is advisable to grease and bake them empty several times.

Wheatmeal dough is strengthened by cooler rising and can be refrigerated in the same way as white dough, see page 168.

Variations
Add an egg to enrich the dough.

Use honey, treacle or brown sugar in place of the white sugar.

Add oats, barley flakes or cereal bran (2–3 oz (50–75 g) per pound (½ kg) of flour).

Using part of the dough, add a few caraway seeds, dried fruit and nuts.

Note for Beginners

This mixture makes two 2 lb (1 kg) loaves.

For ease in handling make half the recipe. If this is made into two small loaves they will take about 30 minutes to cook.

NATIONAL FEDERATION OF WOMEN'S INSTITUTES *Yeast Cookery*.

Wholemeal Bread

Put ½ pint (300 ml) measured water into a jug. Add fresh yeast or dried yeast and sugar to the water and leave 5–10 minutes to become frothy.

Mix flour and salt in a bowl. Rub in the lard. Add the yeast liquid to the flour with the corn oil if used, with sufficient warm water to make a soft but firm dough which clings together and leaves the bowl clean.

Add a little more water or flour if necessary. Knead on a lightly floured board. Cover and leave to rise until it doubles in size. Divide dough into two pieces.

Knead each piece again. Shape into loaves, cobs or rolls. Cover and put to rise.

Bake in the middle of a hot oven, 450°F (230°C) Gas 8, for 30–40 minutes. The loaves will shrink from the sides of the tin when baked. Makes two 2 lb (1 kg) loaves.

NATIONAL FEDERATION OF WOMEN'S INSTITUTES *Yeast Cookery.*

1½ pints warm water (110°F or 45°C) (900 ml)
2 oz yeast (50 g) or 2 level tablespoons dried yeast plus 2 teaspoons sugar
3 lb wholemeal flour (1½ kg)
2 level tablespoons salt (30 ml)
1 oz lard (25 g) or 2 tablespoons corn oil (30 ml)

Apricot and Walnut Bread

Mix flours, salt and sugar together in a bowl. Blend yeast in the water and add all at once to the dry ingredients. Mix to a clear, scone-like dough. Knead. Put bowl in greased polythene bag and leave in a warm place until dough doubles in volume.

Squeeze and work in all the other ingredients with one hand until the mixture is no longer streaky. Put into prepared 2 lb size tin (1 kg) (bottom lined and greased), and put inside polythene bag until the dough doubles in volume.

Put on the topping *before* baking.

Topping
Rub together the margarine, sugar and flour until it looks like coarse breadcrumbs. Sprinkle this over the dough, then sprinkle over crushed cornflakes.

Bake in centre of oven, 450°F (230°C) Gas 8, for 30–40 minutes.

8 oz plain brown flour (225 g)
8 oz plain white flour (225 g)
2 level teaspoons sugar (10 ml)
2 level teaspoons salt (10 ml)
½ oz fresh yeast (15 g) or 2 level teaspoons dried yeast (10 ml)
½ pint water (300 ml)
4 oz dried chopped apricots (100 g)
2 oz broken walnuts (50 g)

Topping
1 oz margarine (25 g)
1 oz sugar (25 g)
1½ oz flour (40 g)
Crushed cornflakes

Cumberland

Bara Brith

Traditional Welsh Recipe

Put the yeast or dried yeast and sugar into ¼ pint (150 ml) of the measured warm milk.

Sieve the flour in a warm basin. Rub in the fat. Add all dry

1½ oz yeast (40 g) or ½ oz dried yeast (15 g)
plus 1 teaspoon sugar
1 pint warm milk (500 ml)
3 lb flour (1·3 kg)
12 oz lard or butter or mixed fats (300 g)
12 oz brown sugar (300 g)
2 level teaspoons salt (10 ml)
1 lb stoned raisins (400 g)
2 lb mixed dried fruit (800 g)
4 oz peel (100 g)
½ teaspoon mixed spice (5 ml)
2–3 eggs

ingredients. Make a well in the centre, add eggs and remaining warm milk to yeast liquid and use to mix to a soft dough. Knead. Cover and leave in a warm place to rise for 1½ hours or until twice its original size.

Knead lightly on a floured board. Divide into four and put into greased tins (1 lb or ½ kg). Put to prove in a warm place for about 20 minutes.

Bake at 350°F (180°C) Gas 4 for 1½–2 hours.

When cold, slice as for bread and butter, thinly and butter well.

NATIONAL FEDERATION OF WOMEN'S INSTITUTES *Yeast Cookery*.

Bath Buns

8 oz flour (250 g)
3 oz lard (75 g)
½ oz yeast (15 g)
¼ pint milk (150 ml)
1 egg
3 oz caster sugar (75 g)
1½ oz chopped peel (40 g)
2 oz sultanas (50 g)
Egg for brushing
1 oz loaf sugar (25 g)

Somerset

Rub the lard into the flour, cream the yeast, add the milk and the egg. Beat well to a dough. Put to rise to double the size.

Beat in the sugar, chopped peel and sultanas.

Form into small buns and leave to rise. Brush over with egg and sprinkle with crushed loaf sugar.

Bake at 475°F (240°C) Gas 9 for 10 minutes. Makes 12 buns.

Bread Sticks

½ oz yeast (15 g) or ¼ oz dried yeast (10 ml)
plus ½ teaspoon sugar
½ pint warmed milk (300 ml)
1 lb flour (500 g)
1 teaspoon salt (10 ml)
1 oz butter (25 g)
Rock salt

Put the yeast or dried yeast and sugar into ¼ pint (150 ml) of the warmed milk and leave for 5 minutes. Sieve flour and salt into a warm bowl. Make a well in the flour and add the yeast liquid to the centre of the flour.

Stir a little flour in and leave to rise 20 minutes. Add remaining milk and melted butter, form into a dough and leave to rise for a further 10 minutes. Remove dough from bowl, roll into sticks the size and width of the little finger and about 8 inches long (20 cm). Prove on prepared baking sheet 20 minutes. Brush with milk, sprinkle with rock salt, bake in a moderate oven, 350°F (180°C) Gas 4. May need crisping in a cooler oven for 20 minutes or left in the oven with the door open and heat turned off. Store in tins for use. Makes 4 dozen sticks.

NATIONAL FEDERATION OF WOMEN'S INSTITUTES *Yeast Cookery*.

Chelsea Buns

Sieve flour and salt. Put to warm. Rub in the margarine. Cream yeast and sugar. Warm milk, add beaten egg and sugar, add to the creamed yeast and place in a well in the centre of the flour. Mix to a light dough. Knead until smooth and free from creases. Allow to rise until double in bulk. Re-knead lightly and then roll out to a square about $\frac{1}{2}$ inch (1 cm) thick. Brush all over with melted margarine. Spread with currants and dust thickly with the sugar. Roll up like a Swiss roll. Cut into $1\frac{1}{2}$ inch (3·75 cm) slices. Place cut side down on to a greased and warmed meat tin, 1 inch (2½ cm) apart. Prove until touching. Bake in a hot oven, 425°F (220°C) Gas 7, for 10 minutes or until risen and lightly browned, then reduce the heat to 375°F (190°C) Gas 5 for a further 10–20 minutes. Brush while hot with hot glaze or alternatively, reserve a little of the beaten egg, and brush with this *before* cooking. Makes 5–6 large buns.

8 oz flour (225 g)
1 level teaspoon salt (5 ml)
1 oz margarine (25 g)
$\frac{1}{2}$ oz yeast (15 g) plus 1 level teaspoon sugar (5 ml)
$\frac{1}{8}$ pint milk (75 ml)
1 egg plus 1 oz sugar (25 g)

Filling
Little melted margarine
1½ oz currants (40 g)
1½ oz sugar (40 g)

Glaze
1 tablespoon sugar (30 ml)
1 tablespoon water (15 ml)
OR
Beaten egg

Shropshire

Cornish Splits

Cream the yeast and sugar together until they are liquid, then add the milk; sieve the flour and salt into a basin. Melt the butter gently, add it and the milk etc., to the flour and mix all into a smooth dough. Knead thoroughly. Put the basin in a warm place, to let the dough rise for $\frac{3}{4}$ hour.

Then shape it in small round cakes and place them on a floured baking tin. Bake in a quick oven, 450°F (230°C) Gas 8, for 15–20 minutes.

Split and butter them. Serve very hot. Or may be left until cold, when split and butter them, or split and eat with cream, jam or treacle.

$\frac{1}{2}$ oz yeast (15 g)
$\frac{1}{2}$ oz caster sugar (15 g)
$\frac{1}{2}$ pint tepid milk (300 ml)
1 lb flour (500 g)
$\frac{1}{4}$ teaspoon salt (2½ ml)
1 oz butter (25 g)

Splits eaten with cream and treacle are known as 'thunder and lightning'.

Cornwall

Cumberland Tea Cakes

Sieve flour and salt together. Rub in fat, add sugar and currants. Disperse yeast in warm liquid. Add liquid to flour etc. and knead to a clear dough.

Put in a warm place to rise, until it doubles its volume. Scale into 3 oz (75 g) pieces. Mould round, place on greased sheet to prove.

Bake at 400–425°F (200–220°C) Gas 6–7 for 15 minutes. Cool slightly before brushing with butter.

This quantity makes 10 tea cakes.

1 lb plain flour (450 g)
1 teaspoon salt (5 ml)
2 oz lard (50 g)
1 oz margarine (25 g)
1 oz sugar (25 g)
1½ oz currants (40 g) (optional)
1 oz yeast (25 g)
$\frac{1}{2}$ pint liquid (300 ml), $\frac{1}{2}$ milk $\frac{1}{2}$ water, warm
Melted butter for brushing

Cumberland

Devonshire Splits

1 lb plain flour (500 g)
½ teaspoon salt
½ pint skimmed milk (300 ml)
½ oz yeast (15 g)
1 teaspoon caster sugar
2 oz butter (50 g)
Syrupy mixture for brushing (see below)
Jam
Devonshire cream

Grease and flour baking sheets. Sift flour and salt into a mixing bowl. Warm the milk to blood heat. Cream the yeast with the sugar. Melt the butter in the milk.

Pour all at once into the centre of the flour and mix to a soft dough.

Put into a floured bowl, cover with a damp cloth, and set to rise in a warm place until double in bulk.

Turn out the dough and divide into equal portions (14–18).

Knead into small balls with the palm of the hand. Place on the prepared baking tin. Prove for 10–15 minutes.

Brush with milk and place in a hot oven, 450°F (230°C) Gas 8, for 15–20 minutes.

When cooked, brush with a syrupy mixture to make them soft and sticky.

When cold, split and fill with Devonshire cream and jam.

Note: Syrupy mixture consists of 4 oz sugar (100 g), ⅛ pint milk (75 ml). Heat to 215°F (105°C).

Devon

Durham Yule Loaf

Traditional Recipe

1¾ lb plain flour (800 g)
2 oz butter (50 g)
2 oz lard (50 g)
6 oz sugar (175 g)
5 oz currants (150 g)
5 oz sultanas (150 g)
2 oz lemon peel (50 g)
½ teaspoon nutmeg (2½ ml)
¾ oz yeast (20 g)
½ pint warmed milk (300 ml)
1 egg

Rub butter and lard into the flour. Add the dry ingredients. Mix yeast with a little warm milk. Make a well in the centre and add yeast and beaten egg and the rest of the milk. Knead into soft dough, cover and allow to rise about 1 hour.

Turn on to a floured board, put into greased tins. Rise 15 minutes and bake in a moderate oven, 350°F (180°C) Gas 4, about 1 hour.

This quantity makes two 2 lb (1 kg) loaves. The recipe can be halved in which case use the whole egg.

Durham

Guernsey Biscuits

Type of Tea-cake

½ pint milk and hot water (300 ml)
   (a little more may be necessary)
1 oz yeast (25 g) creamed with
   2 teaspoons sugar (10 ml)
2 lb plain flour (900 g)
Good grating nutmeg
2 teaspoons salt (10 ml)
1 lb margarine (450 g) and small knob
   butter

Mix most of milk and water with creamed yeast, sprinkle with flour, cover and leave until ready.

Mix dry ingredients, rub in fat and make well in centre. Pour in yeast and more milk and water if required. Knead well, cover with cloth, place in warm place and leave to rise for 1½ hours.

Turn on floured board, knead lightly and form into balls, flatten or roll into biscuit shapes. Stand on greased baking tray in warm place for 15–20 minutes. Bake for 20 minutes, 400°F (200°C) Gas 6.

This should make 24 biscuits.

Hot Cross Buns

Add the yeast or dried yeast and sugar to the warm milk and leave for 5 minutes to become frothy. Add melted butter and beaten egg.

Warm and sieve flour and salt, add sugar, fruit and spice.

Put yeast mixture into mixing bowl and add warmed dry ingredients to make a soft dough and beat well until mixture leaves the sides of the bowl and hands clean. Leave to rise in a warm place covered with cloth or polythene. When doubled in size knead and shape into 12–16 buns. Put on baking trays and leave to prove 15–20 minutes covered in a greased polythene bag to prevent a skin forming.

Mark the tops with a soft pastry crust and bake in a hot oven, 400°F (200°C) Gas 6, for 20–25 minutes. Brush over with the glaze while buns are still hot.

NATIONAL FEDERATION OF WOMEN'S INSTITUTES *Yeast Cookery.*

1 oz yeast (25 g) or ½ oz dried yeast (15 g)
  plus 1 teaspoon sugar (5 ml)
½ pint milk (bare measure) (250 ml)
2 oz butter (50 g)
1 egg
1 lb flour (450 g)
1 teaspoon salt (10 ml)
1 oz sugar (25 g)
1½ oz chopped peel (40 g)
2 oz sultanas (50 g)
1 teaspoon mixed spice (10 ml)
Soft pastry for cross

Glaze
1 oz sugar (25 g) dissolved in
  1 tablespoon water (15 ml)

Lardy Cake

Sift together flour and salt and leave in a warm place. Cream the yeast with sugar, add the egg and warmed milk and mix with the flour to make a soft dough.

Leave in a warm place and when the dough has doubled its bulk roll out on to a floured board (about ½ inch or 1 cm thick). Divide the creamed filling into two portions and spread one-half on to two-thirds of the dough then fold into three as for flaky pastry and roll out again. Spread on the remainder of the filling, refold and roll out twice, finally shaping to fit an 8 inch (20 cm) cake tin. Allow to rise and bake in a hot oven, 400–425°F (200–220°C) Gas 6–7, for 30–35 minutes.

8 oz flour (225 g)
Pinch of salt
½ oz yeast (15 g)
1 teaspoon sugar (5 ml)
1 egg
¾ gill milk (100 ml)

For the Filling
2 oz lard (50 g)
2 oz sugar (50 g)
2 oz currants (50 g)

Northumberland and Durham

Malt Bread

As this is a sweet bread a big rise is not needed. A soft plain flour is used in this recipe. This quantity makes 2 small loaves.

Add the yeast to the warm water. Stand 5–10 minutes to become

1 oz fresh yeast (25 g) or 1 tablespoon
    dried yeast (15 ml) plus 1 teaspoon
    sugar (5 ml)
Approximately ¼ pint warm water
    (150 ml)
2 tablespoons black treacle (50 g)
4 tablespoons or 4 oz malt extract (100 g)
1 oz butter or margarine (25 g)
1 lb soft plain flour (450 g)
½ level teaspoon salt (2½ ml)
2–4 oz sultanas (50–100 g) (optional)

To Brush
Honey or milk and sugar syrup

frothy. Put the treacle, malt extract and margarine into a pan and warm them together. Allow to cool.

Sieve the flour and salt into a basin. Add the sultanas if used. Add the cooled malt mixture to the yeast liquid and then add both to the dry mix to form a soft dough.

Beat until the bowl becomes clean. Turn on to a lightly floured board and knead so that the dough becomes smooth and elastic.

Divide the dough into two pieces and then flatten them and roll each into a shape to fit the two 1 lb (½ kg) greased loaf tins. Put to rise inside loose fitting greased polythene bags. When risen bake in the centre of the oven at 400°F (200°C) Gas 6 for approximately 45 minutes.

The hot loaves can be brushed with honey or milk and sugar syrup.

NATIONAL FEDERATION OF WOMEN'S INSTITUTES *Yeast Cookery*.

Pulled Bread

Traditional Recipe

Westmorland

Knead some white bread dough, place it in a greased loaf tin and let it prove just as when making bread. When sufficiently risen, bake it in a hot oven for about 20 minutes, just long enough to set the dough. Turn it out of the tin and with two forks separate it into irregularly shaped pieces suitable for serving. Place them on a baking sheet and bake them in a moderate oven until crisp and lightly brown.

Rich Yeast Dinner Rolls

8 oz strong flour (225 g)
½ teaspoon salt (5 ml)
½ teaspoon sugar (5 ml)
½ oz margarine (15 g)
½ oz yeast (15 g)
3½–4 fl. oz milk (100 ml)
1 egg
Melted butter for brushing

Cumberland

Sieve flour and salt, add sugar and mix. Rub in margarine. Disperse yeast in warm milk. Make a well in the centre of the mixture. Add egg and liquid. Beat and knead to a clear dough. Allow to rise in a warm place until double in volume.

Weigh out 1 oz (30 g) pieces. Mould and put on a greased baking sheet to prove.

Bake in a hot oven, 425°F (220°C) Gas 7, for 8 minutes or until brown and cooked.

Brush over tops with melted butter.

This quantity makes 12 rolls.

Saffron Cake

Cut up saffron finely and place between greaseproof paper. Roll several times in order to bruise and infuse in 2 tablespoons (30 ml) of boiling water. Soak the saffron overnight. Strain and add the saffron water to the yeast liquid before mixing the dough.

Put the yeast or dried yeast and sugar in the lukewarm milk and water and leave for 5 minutes to become frothy. Add 1 cup (100 g) of the flour to the yeast liquid and mix together. Allow to sponge.

Rub the fats into the flour then add the salt, sugar, peel and fruit. Pour the yeast sponge and the saffron water into the rest of the ingredients and mix to a soft dough. Knead. Prove for about 2 hours, or until the dough is light. Divide into three and knead lightly before putting in greased 1 lb ($\frac{1}{2}$ kg) tins. Put to rise in a warm place for 15–20 minutes inside greased polythene bags or cover them to prevent a skin forming.

Bake at 375°F (190°C) Gas 5 for 30 minutes, reducing heat to 350°F (180°C) Gas 4 for a further 30 minutes.

1 dram saffron (1·8 g)
1 oz fresh yeast (25 g) or $\frac{1}{2}$ oz dried yeast (15 g) and 1 teaspoon sugar (5 ml)
$\frac{1}{2}$ pint lukewarm milk and water (300 ml)
2 lb strong plain flour (900 g)
6 oz lard (175 g)
6 oz margarine (175 g)
1 level teaspoon salt (5 ml)
6 oz caster sugar (175 g)
2 oz lemon peel (50 g)
$\frac{3}{4}$–1 lb currants (350–450 g)

Note for Beginners

Saffron is sold by chemists, usually in 1 dram amounts. If you just want to try one loaf the recipe can be divided by three. Rising is slow because the amount of yeast is fairly small and the mixture a rich one, so do not try to hurry the rising. Some recipes for saffron cake recommend only one rising, in the tin.

Cornwall

Sally Lunn

Put the yeast or dried yeast and sugar into the lukewarm milk and leave for 5 minutes. Sieve the flour and salt into a bowl. Melt the butter in a saucepan and add to the lukewarm milk, beat the egg and add this to the liquid mix. Make a well in the flour, add the liquid mix to form a dough with the hand. Beat thoroughly, leave to rise 30–40 minutes. Turn on to floured board, divide into two pieces, knead each till smooth and round, and place in greased round cake tin to $\frac{3}{4}$ inch (1 cm) from top, cover and set in a warm place for $\frac{1}{2}$–$\frac{3}{4}$ hour.

Bake in hot oven for 15 minutes, 425°F (220°C) Gas 7.

$\frac{1}{2}$ oz yeast (15 g) or $\frac{1}{4}$ oz dried yeast (10 ml) and $\frac{1}{2}$ teaspoon sugar (2$\frac{1}{2}$ ml)
1$\frac{1}{2}$ gills milk (200 ml)
12 oz flour (350 g)
$\frac{1}{2}$ teaspoon salt (5 ml)
1 oz butter (25 g)
1 egg

Note for Beginners

The cake tins for the Sally Lunn should be about 6 inch (15 cm) and fairly shallow; small sandwich tins are suitable.

NATIONAL FEDERATION OF WOMEN'S INSTITUTES *Yeast Cookery.*

Scotch Baps

½ oz dried yeast (1 level tablespoon) plus
   1 teaspoon sugar
   OR
1 oz fresh yeast (25 g) (if raised overnight
   use only ½ oz yeast)
½ pint milk and water mixed and warm
   (approximately) (250 ml)
1 lb strong plain flour (450 g)
2 oz butter or margarine (50 g)
2 teaspoons salt
1 egg

Put the yeast, warm milk and water, 1 teaspoon flour and sugar into a jug and leave about 5 minutes to become frothy. Rub butter or margarine into the flour and add the salt. Make a well, add the egg to the yeast liquid and mix to a *slack dough* adding extra warm liquid if required. Allow to prove until doubled in size. Knead on a board till firm to handle.

Divide into small pieces about the size of a duck egg (oval shape). Cover and put to rise until double size.

Bake at the top of a hot oven, 400°F (200°C) Gas 6, 15–20 minutes approximately.

These should not be glazed but floury on top. Makes about 12 baps.

NATIONAL FEDERATION OF WOMEN'S INSTITUTES *Yeast Cookery*.

Swedish Tea Ring

8 oz plain flour (225 g)
¼ teaspoon salt (2½ ml)
2 oz margarine (50 g)
1 oz sugar (25 g)
½ oz fresh yeast (15 g)
4 tablespoons milk (60 ml)
2 small eggs

Almond Paste
1 oz ground almonds (25 g)
1 oz caster sugar (25 g)
Little beaten egg

Glacé Icing
4 oz icing sugar (100 g)
A little water

Decoration
Cherries, angelica, flaked almonds

Durham

Sieve flour and salt into a warm bowl. Rub in margarine, add sugar. Dissolve yeast in a little tepid milk and add to beaten egg. Add to flour and mix to a soft dough. Knead. Leave to rise in warm place.

Divide mixture into two. Roll out to strips 15 inches (38 cm) long and 4 inches (10 cm) wide. Lay roll of almond paste along middle. Roll up and shape into ring. Rise on greased tray approximately 15 minutes.

Bake at 425°F (220°C) Gas 7 for 15 minutes approximately. When cool, ice with glacé icing and decorate with cherries, angelica and flaked almonds.

Yorkshire Tea Cakes

½ oz yeast (15 g) or 2 teaspoons dried
   yeast (10 ml) plus ½ teaspoon sugar
½ pint warm milk and water (300 ml)
1 lb flour (500 g)
1 level teaspoon salt
1 oz lard (25 g)
1 oz sugar (25 g)

Add the yeast or dried yeast and sugar to the warmed milk and water and leave for 5 minutes to become frothy. Sieve flour and salt into a warmed basin. Rub in the lard and add the sugar.

Mix to a light dough using the yeast liquid. Knead well until the mixture is no longer sticky. Cover and leave to rise in a warm place until doubled in size.

178

Knead once more, divide into five portions making each into a round cake $\frac{1}{2}$ inch (1 cm) thick. Place on warmed greased tray—enclose in a greased polythene bag or cover and prove until twice their original size.

Bake in a hot oven, 475°F (240°C) Gas 9, approximately 12 minutes. When ready brush over tops with butter or lard.

NATIONAL FEDERATION OF WOMEN'S INSTITUTES *Yeast Cookery*.

Alternative:
Add 1 oz currants (25 g) with the sugar. Shape the mixture into five cubes and flatten and roll to $\frac{1}{2}$ inch (1 cm) thick.   *Yorkshire*

HOME-MADE CONFECTIONERY
17

Apricotines

1 lb tin apricots (454 g)
Approximately ⅓ of juice from tin of
    apricots
6 oz granulated sugar (175 g)
2 teaspoons lemon juice (10 ml) or
    ¼ teaspoon tartaric acid (1 ml)
Granulated sugar to sprinkle on top

Cumberland

Sieve apricots with very little juice. Add sugar and lemon juice. Boil, stirring frequently, until the mixture is very thick and sets when dropped on a plate, about 20–30 minutes.

Pour at once into greaseproof sweet cases and sprinkle with granulated sugar. Keep in airtight box.

Makes 24 sweets.

Brown Nougat

2 oz shelled almonds (50 g)
2 oz icing sugar (50 g)
2 teaspoons lemon juice (10 ml)
Chocolate (optional)

Cumberland

180

Blanch, shred, chop and brown almonds, and keep them warm. Melt sugar (sieved if necessary) with lemon juice over gentle heat. Heat until golden brown.

Stir in almonds quickly and pour at once into a greased tin, about 6 inches (15 cm) square. Mark in squares before it sets.

Cut when cold, and wrap in waxed paper or coat with chocolate.

Butterscotch

Put ingredients in a thick saucepan and boil slowly until a nice golden colour, and a little sets hard when dropped into a cup of cold water—about 15–20 minutes.

Pour quickly into a buttered shallow tin (about 6 inches or 15 cm square), and leave to set. Break up and store in an airtight jar.

7 tablespoons sugar (200 g)
1 tablespoon vinegar (15 ml)
1 tablespoon water (15 ml)
2 tablespoons golden syrup (50 g)
4 oz butter (100 g)

Lincolnshire

Coffee Fudge

Put the sugar, milk and water into a heavy bottomed pan, heat very slowly until the sugar has dissolved. Add the butter and coffee. Bring to the boil and boil gently up to 328–400°F (170–200°C). Stir all the time or it will burn. Remove from the heat, add the nuts if used, and beat with a wooden spoon until thick and creamy.

You can use electric beaters if you do not add the nuts (the beaters knock them into crumbs). When it shows signs of setting pour into an oiled Swiss roll tin. When cool, mark into squares. When cold, cut.

Makes about 2 lb (1 kg).

1½ lb caster sugar (700 g)
½ pint evaporated milk (300 ml)
½ pint water (300 ml)
4 oz butter (100 g)
1 tablespoon instant coffee (15 ml)
    dissolved in 1 tablespoon water (15 ml)
2 oz chopped walnuts (50 g) can be added

Hampshire

Coffee Truffles

Mix everything very well together in a basin using a wooden spoon. Form into small balls with the hands. Roll some in sieved cocoa, some in chocolate vermicelli, some in nibbed almonds. A little rum improves them, naturally, if the occasion of both making and eating is suitable. Put in paper sweet cases.

Makes 2 dozen or more.

4 oz melted chocolate (100 g)
1 tablespoon instant coffee (15 ml)
    dissolved in the chocolate as it melts
2 egg yolks
6 oz icing sugar (175 g)
2 oz butter (50 g)
Rum (optional)

For Coating
Sieved cocoa
Chocolate vermicelli
Almond nibs

Hampshire

181

Marshmallows

½ oz gelatine (15 g)
¼ pint water (150 ml)
8 oz caster sugar (225 g)
Good pinch of salt
1 teaspoon vanilla essence (5 ml)
1 tablespoon chopped walnuts (30 ml)
1 tablespoon chopped cherries (30 ml)
Pink colouring
Icing sugar and cornflour for dusting

Cumberland

Soak the gelatine in half the water (use bowl or large basin). Boil the remainder of the water and sugar together for 4 minutes, this forms a syrup. Pour syrup over soaked gelatine. Add salt and vanilla essence. Whisk until the mixture becomes the thickness of cream and has turned white.

Pour half the mixture on to a dish which has been greased with margarine and dusted with cornflour. To this first dish add the walnuts and cherries.

Colour the remainder of the mixture with a little pink colouring and pour into a second dish. Leave to set. Turn out on to a board. Dust with a mixture of equal quantities of sifted icing sugar and cornflour. Cut into shapes and pack into boxes.

Marzipan

Uncooked

1 egg white
8 oz icing sugar (225 g)
½ teaspoon almond essence (2½ ml)
1 teaspoon lemon juice (5 ml)
8 oz ground almonds (225 g)

Lincolnshire

Whisk egg white and sifted icing sugar together, add essence and lemon juice. Stir in ground almonds. Store in polythene bag. Use for moulding marzipan sweets.

Stuffed Dates
Choose good quality dessert dates. Remove stones and fill cavity with marzipan. Put in paper cases.

Old-fashioned Cinder Toffee

2 tablespoons sugar (50 g)
1 tablespoon golden syrup (25 g)
1 teaspoon bicarbonate of soda (5 ml)

Cumberland

Heat the sugar and syrup slowly in a saucepan over a low heat until mixture 'toffees'. Smooth out the bicarbonate of soda on a saucer and add to the mixture when it is still boiling, whipping vigorously with a spoon. It will 'froth' up and should then be placed in a greased loaf tin and left to cool. While cooling keep it out of any draught. Break into pieces when cold.

Peanut Toffee

2 oz peanut butter (50 g)
2 oz golden syrup (50 g)
4 oz sugar (100 g)
1 tablespoon water (15 ml)
½ teaspoon vanilla essence (2½ ml)

Yorkshire

Boil all together, stirring well when the mixture starts to thicken, until a little sets hard in cold water. Pour into a greased tin about 5 inches (15 cm) square, and mark in squares before it sets.

Peppermint Creams

Whisk egg whites, add icing sugar (do not put essence or colouring directly on to egg whites). Beat well and then knead until smooth. Roll out and cut into shapes, dust with caster sugar if a rough surface is preferred or coat with chocolate.

2 egg whites
1 lb icing sugar (450 g)
2 teaspoons peppermint flavouring (10 ml)
Green colouring if desired
Caster sugar or chocolate coating

Yorkshire

Plum Pudding Candies

Pass the prepared fruits through a food mincer. Add the nuts finely chopped. Blend all thoroughly. Form into balls and roll in caster sugar.

2 oz stoned raisins (50 g)
2 oz stoned dates (50 g)
2 oz figs (50 g)
2 oz glacé cherries (50 g)
6 tinned apricot halves, well drained
2 oz finely chopped nuts (50 g)
Caster sugar

Yorkshire

Rum Truffles

Melt sugar, syrup, margarine, cocoa and jam in a pan. Slowly bring mixture to the boil, then leave to cool.

Meanwhile, sieve the sponge cake. Mix cake crumbs into the mixture; flavour with rum or rum essence. Divide the mixture into small pieces, coat each with vermicelli, roll into balls with the palm of the hand. Put into small sweet paper cases.

2 oz sugar (50 g)
1 tablespoon syrup (15 ml)
2 oz margarine (50 g)
1 level tablespoon cocoa (15 ml)
1 level tablespoon apricot or pineapple jam (15 ml)
6 oz stale sponge cake or biscuits (150–170 g)
Few drops rum or rum essence
Chocolate vermicelli or cocoa for coating
Small paper cases

Durham

Russian Caramel

Put all ingredients in pan together. Bring to boil and boil until stiff, stirring all the time, about 5 minutes. Pour into greased tin, about 6 inches (15 cm) square. When cold cut into shapes and put into sweet paper cases.

2 oz margarine (50 g)
Small tin condensed milk (150 ml)
1 dessertspoon sugar (25 g)
1 teaspoon vanilla essence (5 ml)
1 tablespoon treacle (25 g)

Durham

Salted Nuts

Any nuts
Butter and oil
Salt
Cayenne or paprika (optional)

Hampshire

Any nuts can be used for this, and they are so much cheaper to do yourself than to buy.

Blanch them, by taking their skins off. Then fry them in butter with a little oil added, for a minute or two. Drain them on kitchen paper and toss in salt while hot. Sprinkle the salt on greaseproof paper and shake the nuts up and down in it.

For a different flavour add a little cayenne or paprika to the salt.

Treacle Toffee

4 oz butter (100 g)
8 oz treacle (225 g)
1 lb pale soft brown sugar (450 g)
½ teacup cold water (90 ml)
1 teaspoon cream of tartar (5 ml)

Cheshire

Place all ingredients except cream of tartar in pan and dissolve. Add cream of tartar when it boils. Boil till it sets hard when dropped in cold water (about 15–20 minutes). Pour into buttered tins (two, about Swiss roll size). When cold break up and keep airtight in tin.

Truffles

¼ pint cream (125 ml)
1 lb melted chocolate (400 g)
Flavouring to taste
Cocoa

Herefordshire

Bring cream to boil and pour on to chocolate. Beat until it begins to set. Add flavouring and leave to cool. Then turn on to slab and roll into lengths. Cut into even sized pieces, form into balls and roll in cocoa. Very delicious. Makes 3–4 dozen balls.

Turkish Delight

½ pint hot water (250 ml)
1 lb granulated sugar (400 g)
1 saltspoon citric acid (¼ teaspoon)
Grated rind of 1 large or 2 small oranges
1½ oz powdered gelatine (40 g)
Pink colouring

Westmorland

Place water, sugar, acid, orange rind and gelatine in a saucepan, stir over gentle heat until dissolved. Bring to boiling point and boil for 20 minutes. Do not stir after it boils. Remove from heat and allow to cool 10 minutes. Pour half into a lightly buttered tin. Colour remainder pink and pour into another tin. Leave at least 24 hours. Cut into squares, and roll in a mixture of equal quantities of icing sugar and cornflour. Store in airtight tins with plenty of icing sugar between.

Unboiled Coconut Ice

Mix the coconut, milk and sugar and cream of tartar together and work to a stiff paste. Cut the paste in half. Colour one half pink, with considerable discretion. Roll each half separately to an oblong. Put on top of each other, having brushed the bottom half with egg white. Trim neatly and leave to set overnight.

4 oz desiccated coconut (100 g)
2 tablespoons sweetened condensed milk (50 ml)
3–4 oz caster sugar (75–100 g)
Pinch of cream of tartar
Little beaten egg white
Red colouring

Hampshire

Unboiled Fondant

Sieve icing sugar and add cream of tartar. Add cream and sufficient egg white to make a pliable consistency. Knead well together. Cut into 4 pieces.

8 oz icing sugar (200 g)
¼ teaspoon cream of tartar (1 ml)
1 dessertspoon cream (10 ml)
White of egg
Flavouring and colouring

Flavour:
1st piece with 6 drops peppermint essence.
2nd piece with raspberry essence.
3rd piece with strawberry essence and a little pink colouring.
4th piece with lemon essence and a little green colouring.

Mould or cut to shape with sweet cutters.

Cumberland

Uncooked Chocolate Orange Nut Fudge

Melt chocolate and butter in a bowl over hot water. Add evaporated milk, grated orange rind and nuts and mix well. Work in the sifted sugar until mixture is quite stiff. Turn into a Swiss roll tin approximately $7\frac{1}{2} \times 11\frac{1}{2}$ inches (19×29 cm). Leave to set. Cut into squares.

4 oz plain chocolate (100 g)
2 oz butter (50 g)
4 tablespoons evaporated milk (60 ml)
Grated rind of one orange
4 oz nuts (100 g), chopped
1 lb icing sugar (450 g)

Yorkshire

White Nougat

3 oz icing sugar (75 g)
2 oz honey (50 g)
1 egg white
½ teaspoon glucose (2½ ml)
2 oz almonds (50 g) (dried and warmed)
1 oz cherries (25 g)
¼ oz pistachios (5 g) (optional)
Sieved icing sugar
Rice paper

Cumberland

Line a tin approximately 6 inches square (15 cm) with rice paper. Cut piece for top.

Put sugar, honey, egg white, glucose into a pan. Whisk over gentle heat until thick and white. It should form a firm ball when dropped into cold water. Remove from heat. Add almonds (warmed), cherries and pistachios if used. Mix well.

Turn on to board with thick layer of icing sugar and press into shape of tin. Put in tin. Cover with rice paper. Press and put weight on top.

When cold, cut into size required and wrap.

BEVERAGES
18

Apple Ale

A Delicious Drink

Wash the apples and grate same, complete with skins, on a suet grater. Add the pulp to the water, and the cores too, to improve flavour.

Stir the apple water every day for a week and then strain.

Add sugar, ginger (well bruised), cinnamon and cloves, stir until the sugar is dissolved, and leave until the following day.

Then strain through a clean tea cloth, pour into bottles, cork lightly and leave for a week, when it will be ready for drinking.

To make a gallon (4½ l) use:
1 gallon cold water (4½ l)
2 lb apples (1 kg) (any kind)
1½ lb sugar (700 g)
1 oz root ginger (25 g)
½ level teaspoon cinnamon (2½ ml)
¼ level teaspoon cloves (2½ ml)

Devon

Apple Toddy

Wipe the apples and cut up roughly without peeling. Place the pieces in a casserole with the water, put on the lid and simmer slowly until the apples are thoroughly softened. Press through a sieve to pulp the apples, add the honey and bicarbonate of soda and sip slowly while hot.

2 large apples
1 pint water (600 ml)
1 tablespoon honey (15 ml)
½ teaspoon bicarbonate of soda (2½ ml)

This is a children's drink and the bicarbonate of soda is added to make the drink fizz which probably makes it more interesting for young folk.

Serves 4 or more.

NATIONAL FEDERATION OF WOMEN'S INSTITUTES *Home Made Wines, Syrups and Cordials.*

Blackcurrant Shake

¼ pint milk (150 ml)
2 tablespoons blackcurrant syrup or
  cordial (30 ml)
1 brickette vanilla ice-cream (1½ oz or
  40 g)

Cumberland

Mix the milk and flavouring in a jug. Add the brickette and beat with a rotary whisk, till frothy. Pour into a tall glass and serve with a straw.

Cider Cup

8 oz loaf sugar (200 g)
½ pint water (300 ml)
1 lemon
1 pint chilled cider (600 ml)
½ glass sherry or rum (45 ml)
1 pint soda water (600 ml)
3 or 4 slices red-cheeked apple
Sprigs of mint or borage

Somerset

Dissolve sugar in the water. Add thinly peeled lemon rind. Bring to the boil. Strain into a jug. Chill. Add cider. Strain in lemon juice. Stir in sherry or rum. When required add soda water, apple, and a sprig or two of mint or borage. Makes about 2¾ pints (1½ l).

Note: If able to buy sparkling cider, use instead of still cider and double the remaining ingredients.

Cider Fruit Cup

1 tin pineapple juice (500 ml)
½ pint pear, apple, cherry or apricot
  juice (300 ml)
1 pint concentrated orange squash
  (600 ml)
4 pints cider (2¼ l)
1 pint fizzy lemonade (300 ml)

Gloucestershire

Put all ingredients together in a large bowl, add cider and lemonade just before the Cup is to be served. Ice if liked.

Makes about 7½ pints (4 l).

Cider Toddy

Heat the cider, bruised ginger and a twist of lemon peel in an aluminium, stainless steel or enamelled saucepan until bubbles just begin to rise in the liquid. Quickly remove from the heat, stir in the honey and strain into a warmed glass. This is excellent for drinking just before bedtime. Drinking it in bed and taking two Aspirins is said to prevent a cold. Even if this is a false hope it certainly induces sleep.

1 glass dry cider (250 ml)
$\frac{1}{4}$ oz root ginger (10 g or 1 small piece)
Lemon peel
1 dessertspoon honey (10 ml)

NATIONAL FEDERATION OF WOMEN'S INSTITUTES *Home Made Wines, Syrups and Cordials.*

Fruitade

Put fruit into preserving pan, allowing 1 quart ($1\frac{1}{4}$ l) water to every pound of fruit (450 g). Heat them up and strain through a jelly bag.

Add juice of 1 lemon and $\frac{1}{4}$ lb sugar (100 g) to every quart ($1\frac{1}{4}$ l) of juice. Stir till sugar is dissolved. Delicious served with a piece of ice in the glass.

Black currants, red currants, raspberries etc.
Lemon juice
Sugar

Gloucestershire

Ginger Beer

Peel lemons, cut fruit into slices. Place in a bowl with the sugar, cream of tartar and ginger, cover with the boiling water. When lukewarm, add the yeast (well creamed). Leave in a warm place overnight, strain through muslin, then bottle in screw-topped bottles.

The ginger beer is now ready for drinking, but will keep for several weeks.

2 lemons
$1\frac{1}{2}$ lb granulated sugar (700 g)
$\frac{1}{2}$ oz cream of tartar (15 g)
1 oz bruised root ginger (25 g)
6 quarts boiling water ($6\frac{1}{2}$ l)
$\frac{1}{2}$ oz yeast (15 g)

Gloucestershire

Ginger Drink

Put all the ingredients except the sugar in a large pan and bring to the boil. Add the sugar, stir till it is dissolved, then boil for 15 minutes. Strain and bottle when cold.

Dilute with water to taste. A refreshing drink.

Makes about 2 pints undiluted ($1\frac{1}{4}$ l).

1 oz root ginger (25 g)
1 quart water ($1\frac{1}{4}$ l)
$\frac{1}{2}$ teaspoon tartaric acid (5 ml)
1 or 2 chillies
1 lb loaf sugar (450 g)

Westmorland

Grapefruit Cordial

2 grapefruit
1 orange
1½ pints boiling water (900 ml)
1½ lb sugar (700 g)
1 oz tartaric acid (25 g)

Cumberland

Wash fruit and peel rind thinly. Cut fruit into small pieces, removing white and pips. Cut up rind and pour over all the boiling water. Add sugar and tartaric acid.

Allow to stand overnight and strain. Dilute to taste.

Makes just under 3 pints (1½ l) undiluted.

Honey Coffee

1 breakfast cup hot milk (200 ml)
1 teaspoon coffee essence (5 ml or more to taste)
1 dessertspoon honey (10 ml)

West Kent

Combine and drink while hot.

Hot Lemon Toddy

1 lemon
1 teaspoon glycerine (5 ml)
1 dessertspoon honey (10 ml)
Boiling water

Put the lemon juice, glycerine and honey in a warmed tumbler and fill up with boiling water. Serve with a thin twist of lemon peel floating on the surface.

NATIONAL FEDERATION OF WOMEN'S INSTITUTES *Home Made Wines, Syrups and Cordials.*

Iced Coffee

Extra strong freshly made coffee is essential for this. You cannot, incidentally, make good coffee unless you buy top quality beans or ground coffee in the first place.

Make the coffee, strain it and let it get cold and put it in the refrigerator. Do not put ice cubes into it. Keep it in the refrigerator until you want it, and serve it with chilled whipped cream. You may add a little milk to the chilling coffee but do not try to chill coffee with cream in it. Hand bar syrup with it if sweetening is wanted.

Bar Syrup

Melt 1 lb (½ kg) caster sugar very gently over a low heat with a teacup of water (150 ml) until all the sugar has completely vanished. It will keep indefinitely stored in a bottle.

Hampshire

Lemonade

Squeeze and grate lemons, add all together and pour on boiling water. Stir well and bottle when cold. Dilute to taste.

This quantity makes 2¼ pints (1¼ l) of undiluted lemonade.

2 lemons
1½ lb sugar (700 g)
1 oz citric acid (25 g)
1½ pints boiling water (900 ml)

Durham

Lemonade or Orangeade

Remove the rind thinly from the lemon or oranges and squeeze out the juice. Place the rind, juice and sugar in a jug and pour on the boiling water. Cover till cold. Strain and serve in a glass.

Makes just under ¾ pint (400 ml).

1 lemon or 2 oranges
4 lumps sugar
½ pint boiling water (300 ml)

Cheshire

Mint Lemonade

Peel the lemons finely and pound the rind with the flesh, mint leaves and sugar. Add water, stir well and leave for 1 hour. Strain through fine muslin, serve with bits of lemon peel and a sprig of mint in each glass.

Makes just over 1 pint (650 ml).

Handful of fresh mint leaves
5 tablespoons sugar (150 g)
3 lemons
1 pint water (600 ml)
Lemon peel and mint to garnish

Cumberland

Orange Squash

Cut away the outside of the orange peel thinly then extract the juice. Place peelings in the liquidizer with enough of the water to fill the goblet. Switch to top speed for 30 seconds. Pour into saucepan with the rest of the water.

Bring to the boil, add sugar, citric acid and orange juice. Lower the heat, stirring until sugar is dissolved. Pour through a strainer and bottle in hot sterilized bottles. Dilute with water or soda water. Colour as required.

Makes 5¼ pints (3 l).

3 oranges
4 pints water (2¼ l)
3 lb sugar (1½ kg)
1½ oz citric acid (40 g)
Orange food colour
Water or soda water for diluting

Cumberland

Pineapple Fizz

1 pint boiling water (600 ml)
12 oz sugar (350 g)
2 lemons
A tin of pineapple juice (19 fl. oz or 540 ml) (or crushed pineapple)
3 bottles soda water (10–12 fl. oz size or 284–340 ml)

Cumberland

Pour boiling water over sugar and boil for 5 minutes. Add lemon juice and pineapple, leave until cold.

Strain and add the soda water. Children just love this.

Makes about 3½ pints (2 l).

Pussyfoot

1 small piece orange
1 small piece lemon
4 drops grenadine syrup
1½ tablespoons orange squash (25 ml)
1½ tablespoons lemon squash (25 ml)
Soda water
1 dessertspoon gin (10 ml) (optional)

Put the pieces of fruit in a tumbler, add the grenadine and leave for a few minutes. Measure in the orange and lemon squash and add soda water to taste. Serve after chilling. This makes a drink for one person. It is even more pleasant if made in a 1 pint (600 ml) tumbler, a dessertspoonful of gin added before filling the tumbler with soda water.

NATIONAL FEDERATION OF WOMEN'S INSTITUTES *Home Made Wines, Syrups and Cordials.*

Rhubarb Cordial

2 lb rhubarb (1 kg)
4 oz white sugar (100 g)
2 cloves
¼ oz root ginger (2 medium-sized pieces)
1 quart water (1¼ l)

Gently simmer the chopped rhubarb, sugar, water, cloves and bruised ginger in a saucepan until the rhubarb is soft, replacing any water that boils away. Strain well and serve from a warmed glass jug decorated with a few mint leaves.

NATIONAL FEDERATION OF WOMEN'S INSTITUTES *Home Made Wines, Syrups and Cordials.*

Summer Punch

4 oranges
1 grapefruit
3 lemons
4 oz sugar (100 g)
1 quart soda water (1¼ l)
Slices of fresh fruit

Cumberland

Squeeze juice from fruit. Dissolve sugar in a little water. When cold add to fruit juice. Add slices of fruit.

Add soda water just before serving.

Makes about 2½ pints (1½ l).

The Cardinal

Melt the barley sugar in the hot water and combine with the other ingredients. Warm up and infuse for a while. Strain before serving.

Makes 3 pints (1¾ l).

4 oz barley sugar (100 g) (quite essential)
1 pint hot water (600 ml)
1 quart cheap red wine (1¼ l)
A good powdering of freshly grated nutmeg
2–3 inches of cinnamon stick (5–7 cm)
3 slices tangerine, de-pipped
A few cracked cardamom seeds
A blade or two of mace

Hampshire

Three Fruit Punch

Dissolve the sugar in hot water. When cool add to the juices of fruits and chill.

A few slices of orange and several cherries frozen in the cubes improves the appearance of this punch.

Makes 1½ pints (900 ml).

7 oz granulated sugar (200 g)
½ pint hot water (300 ml)
2 lemons
2 oranges
2 grapefruit

Cumberland

Treacle Posset (1)

Heat the milk until near boiling point, then add the treacle and lemon juice. Boil slowly until the curds separate, strain and serve hot as a remedy for a cold.

1 pint milk (600 ml)
2 tablespoons treacle (30 ml)
1 lemon

Treacle Posset (2)

Heat the milk and dissolve the treacle in it, serve hot.

For each person use:
1 teaspoon black treacle (5 ml)
1 glass milk

NATIONAL FEDERATION OF WOMEN'S INSTITUTES *Home Made Wines, Syrups and Cordials.*

White Wine Cup

13½ fl. oz dry white wine (400 ml)
A little fruit in season or from a can
A little sugar and water syrup or syrup
    from can to taste
6¾ fl. oz soda water (200 ml)
¾ fl. oz brandy (40 ml) (optional)
A little decoration to float on top of the
    fruit cup, e.g. borage flowers, eau-de-
    cologne mint leaves, thinly sliced
    cucumber or lemon

Sugar and Water Syrup
1 lb granulated sugar (450 g)
½ pint water (300 ml)
1 teaspoon liquid glucose (if syrup to be
    stored for some time add glucose)
    (5 ml)

Cambridgeshire

Put the wine, fruit and syrup into a 2 lb (1 kg) Kilner jar, shake, chill. Add the soda water and brandy, shake and serve in a glass bowl or jug or glasses with the decoration floating on top.
    Sufficient for 6–8 small glasses.

Sugar and Water Syrup
Dissolve the sugar in the water, add the glucose and boil to 220°F (105°C). Cool slightly, pour into a hot jar and tie down with paper. Store in a cool place. Use cold for the wine cup.

Yard of Flannel

1 quart of barley wine (1¼ l)
1 teaspoon powdered ginger (5–10 ml)
4 oz 'pieces' brown sugar (100 g)
¼ pint rum (150 ml)
4 eggs very well beaten

Hampshire

Serve this hot or cold. If hot be careful not to cook the eggs. Heat the other ingredients first, remove from the stove and add the rum and then the beaten eggs, still beating as you go.
    Enough for 12–16 glasses.

PRESERVES
19

The material for jams and chutneys has come from two National Federation of Women's Institutes publications, *Preservation* and *Unusual Preserves*. That on crystallizing comes from a Yorkshire publication *Crystallization of Fruit and Flowers*.

Information on drying herbs will be found in Chapter 8, 'Herbs and Flavourings'.

Metric conversions are given with all the recipes. The figures have been adjusted to give the same proportions of fruit, sugar and other ingredients as in the original recipes; but these have not been re-tested using the metric weights and measures.

Jam Making

General Method

1 Simmer fruit (adding water and extra acid when necessary) until the skins are tender and the volume has decreased by one-third when water has been added. The time will vary from a few minutes for a small quantity of, say, raspberries to 30–45 minutes for a large quantity of, say, black currants.
2 Take a pectin test, add liquid pectin if necessary to obtain a satisfactory result.
3 Remove pan from heat and add warmed sugar.
4 Stir thoroughly to dissolve sugar.

5 Bring quickly to boiling point.
6 Boil rapidly until setting point is reached, 5–20 minutes. Remove scum if any.
7 Transfer jam to warmed jars, and fill to the brim.
8 Place fitting wax circles on the surface of the hot jam.
9 Cover jars when hot or cold (if left until cold, cover jars with a clean cloth).
10 Label jam with kind of jam and date. Store in a dark dry ventilated place.

Notes

Fruit

Use dry fresh fruit slightly under-ripe. Fruit may be divided into three groups according to the amount of pectin contained.

Good Pectin Content	Medium Pectin Content	Poor Pectin Content
Black and red currants	Early blackberries	Strawberries
Cooking apples	Greengages	Pears
Gooseberries	Loganberries	Rhubarb
Damsons	Fresh apricots	Cherries
Some plums		Medlars
Quince		Late blackberries
		Elderberries
		Tomatoes
		Marrows

Acid

Acid is added to fruit before it is cooked, to help extract pectin, to improve colour, and to prevent crystallization. It must be added to fruits with a poor acid content, and to any vegetable jams. The quantity of acid to be added is as follows:

> To 4 lb of fruit (2 kg) —
> 2 tablespoons lemon juice (1 average lemon) OR
> $\frac{1}{2}$ level teaspoon citric or tartaric acid OR
> $\frac{1}{4}$ pint red currant or gooseberry juice (150 ml)

Pectin Test

The setting property of jam is dependent on its pectin content. To test for this:
1 Take 1 teaspoon of juice from pan, and place in a glass. Cool.
2 Add 3 teaspoons of methylated spirits.
3 Shake gently together.
   If plenty of pectin is present, a clear jelly-like clot is formed.
   If a medium amount of pectin is present, several small clots will be present.
   If a poor amount of pectin is present, no real clot will be formed, and if after further cooking no clot is formed, additional pectin should be added. The quantity to be added is 2–4 liquid ounces per pound of fruit (50–100 ml per 500 g of fruit).

Pectin may be made as follows:
1 Simmer unpeeled sliced apples, red currants, or gooseberries in an equal volume of water.
2 Cook for 25 minutes, mashing down.
3 Strain through scalded jelly bag.
4 Use immediately OR
5 Sterilize in small vacuum jars at boiling point for 5 minutes.

Note: Sterilized juice, when opened, loses its setting properties quickly. Use before 24 hours have elapsed.

Sugar
Lump, granulated or preserving may be used. It must be thoroughly dissolved before the jam or jelly is brought to the boil.

Setting Point
A keeping jam should have 60 per cent added sugar content, i.e. three parts sugar to five parts jam.
   To determine whether this point has been reached, either of the following tests may be used, temperature or weight test.

Temperature Test
1 Stir jam.
2 Dip sugar thermometer in hot water.
3 Submerge bulb fully in jam.
4 When it registers 220°F or 221°F (105°C) jam is cooked.

Weight Test
1 Note weight of pan and spoon BEFORE preserving has begun.
2 When jam weighs 10 lb (5 kg) for every 6 lb sugar used (2·5 kg), jam is at setting point.
3 To find final weight, multiply the quantity of sugar used by 10, divide by 6.

   Example: 3 lb sugar = $3 \times 10 \div 6$ = 5 lb jam ($1·5$ kg = $1·5 \times 10 \div 6$ = $2·5$ kg).

Flake Test
The set of the jam can be determined by the following test:
1 Dip clean wooden spoon in boiling jam.
2 Allow the cooling jam to drop from spoon.
3 If drops run together and form a flake or 'curtain' it is sufficiently cooked.

Note: For jam with whole fruit, i.e. strawberry, leave to cool in pan for 10 minutes. Stir gently and fill jars, this prevents the fruit rising.

Recipes

Apple and Pineapple Jam

6 lb cooking apples (3 kg)
2 pints tinned pineapple juice (1¼ l),
    including that from 1 tin pineapple
    pieces
2 lemons (juice)
6 lb sugar (3 kg)

Peel, core and cut up apples (tying peel and cores in muslin bag and hanging them in pan). Place apples, pineapple juice and lemon juice in pan and cook until tender. Remove bag of peel after squeezing out juice. Add sugar and pineapple and boil rapidly until setting point is reached—approximately 10 minutes. Finish.

Apple Ginger

4 lb granulated sugar (2 kg)
3 pints water (1¾ l)
4 lb apples (2 kg)
2 oz ground ginger (50 g)

Make a thick syrup of the sugar and water by boiling them together. Pare, core and cut apples into thin pieces and boil in the syrup until transparent. Then add the ginger, boil for another 5 minutes, bottle and seal.

    Useful either as a preserve or for tart fillings.

Dried Apricot Jam

2 lb apricots (1 kg)
6 pints water (3½ l)
6 lb sugar (3 kg)

Wash the apricots, cut up small and soak in the water for 24 hours. Then make the jam by the general method.

    Yield 10 lb (5 kg) jam.

Fresh Apricot Jam

6 lb fresh apricots (3 kg)
6 lb sugar (3 kg)
1 pint water (600 ml)

Fruit must be just ripe for best results. Make by the general method, removing stones.

    Yield 10 lb (5 kg) jam.

Black Currant Jam

4 lb black currants (2 kg)
3 pints water (1¾ l)
6 lb sugar (3 kg)

Use the general method.

    Yield 10 lb (5 kg) jam.

Gage Plum

Use the general method.
  Yield 10 lb (5 kg) jam.

6 lb gages (3 kg)
1 pint water (600 ml)
6 lb sugar (3 kg)

Glencar Jam

Cut up figs very finely, also rhubarb and peel; put all together with sugar and let it stand for 24 hours; then boil till it sets.

1 lb dried figs (500 g)
4 lb rhubarb (2 kg)
6 oz candied lemon peel (175 g) or rind and juice of 1 lemon
4 lb sugar (2 kg)

High Dumpsie Dearie Jam

Cook the fruit separately, in a little water, till soft and tender, then add warmed sugar to the proportion of 1 lb to 1 pint, together with the grated lemon rind and ginger. When the sugar is dissolved, heat and bring to boiling point. Test for set at the end of 10 minutes' boiling. Finish in usual way.

Equal quantities of apples, pears and plums
1 lb sugar (500 g) to 1 pint cooked fruit (600 ml)
Lemon rind and root ginger for flavouring

Mulberry Jam

Simmer the mulberries in their own juice until they are tender; simmer the peeled, cored and cut apples separately, until they are tender. Add to the mulberries and stir. Add sugar, bring to the boil, test for set. Finish in the usual way.

3 lb ripe mulberries ($1\frac{1}{2}$ kg)
1 lb apples (500 g)
$3\frac{1}{2}$ lb sugar ($1\frac{3}{4}$ kg)

Pear, Apple and Quince Jam

Peel and core the fruits and cut into pieces. Retain peel and cores and tie them in a muslin bag with the lemon rind. Simmer fruit in water (adding the muslin bag and its contents) until completely tender. Remove muslin bag and squeeze out the juice. Add the warmed sugar and allow it to dissolve, then add the lemon juice and boil rapidly until set. Finish.

2 lb cooking apples (1 kg)
2 lb cooking pears (1 kg)
$1\frac{1}{2}$ lb quinces (750 g)
Rind and juice of 1 lemon
2 pints water ($1\frac{1}{4}$ l)
6 lb sugar (3 kg)

Raspberry Jam

Use the general method.
  Yield 10 lb (5 kg) jam.

6 lb raspberries (3 kg)
6 lb sugar (3 kg)

Rhubarb and Orange Jam

6 oranges
Juice of 2 lemons
1 quart finely cut rhubarb (1¼ l)
3 lb loaf sugar (1½ kg)

Peel oranges, remove as much of the white pith as possible, divide them and take out the pips, slice the pulp into a preserving pan; add the rind of half the oranges cut into thin slices, simmer with the lemon juice.

Peel the rhubarb, cut it into thin pieces, and add to orange pulp. Add warmed sugar, allow it to dissolve, then bring to boiling point; test after 10 minutes. Finish.

Rhubarb and Rose-petal Jam

Rhubarb
Lemon juice
Sugar
Scented rose-petals, red if possible

To each 1 lb (500 g) prepared rhubarb add the juice of 1 lemon and 1 lb (500 g) sugar. Cover the cut up rhubarb with the sugar and lemon juice and leave to stand overnight.

Chop up two handfuls of scented rose-petals, red if possible, to each 1 lb (500 g) of fruit, and cook all together until set. This is a delicious jam and a lovely colour.

Two ounces (50 g) angelica, fresh or crystallized, can be used in place of rose-petals if preferred.

Strawberry Jam

7 lb hulled strawberries (3½ kg)
6 lb sugar (3 kg)
Juice of 4 lemons

Use the general method.
Yield 10 lb (5 kg) jam.

Green Tomato Jam

Rind of 1 sweet orange
2 lb green tomatoes (1 kg)
1½ lb sugar (750 g)

Shred the orange as for marmalade (short shreds) and cook in AS LITTLE WATER AS POSSIBLE until tender. Cut up the tomatoes and add to the cooked orange rind; simmer for about ¾ hour. Add sugar, dissolve, and boil fast for 20 minutes, or until it sets. Finish in usual way.

Ripe Whortleberry Jam

2 lb whortleberries (1 kg)
Juice of 1 lemon
1½ lb sugar (750 g)

Wash fruit in cold water, drain thoroughly. Put in preserving pan. Crush with wooden spoon, add lemon juice, simmer until fruit is soft and thick. Add warmed sugar, dissolve, bring to boil. Boil until setting point is reached. Pot and cover.

Chutneys

Equipment

Only enamel-lined, monel metal, stainless steel or aluminium pans should be used. Avoid anything that may give a metallic flavour.

Use nylon or hair sieves, stainless steel knives, wooden spoons. Clean, dry, warm jars or bottles must be used. Covers must be vinegar resistant, i.e. a ceresin disc under a metal top; unless cover is plastic coated.

General Method

1 Chop or mince the fruits and vegetables.
2 Cook in a closed pan with a very small amount of water (a pressure cooker is recommended).
3 Combine the cooked mixtures with spices and half the required amount of vinegar, cook for 45 minutes (approximately).
4 Dissolve the sugar in the remaining vinegar, add to that in the pan and simmer the whole amount, very slowly until the required consistency is reached, i.e. when a wooden spoon is drawn through the mixture it leaves a clean path and no trace of free (unabsorbed) liquid.
5 Fill dry hot jars to the brim.
Cover with vinegar-resistant lids and store in cool dark place.

Note: Chutney needs to mature. Store jars at least 6 months.

Apple Chutney

Use the general method.
Yield about 5½ lb (2¾ kg) chutney.

3½ lb apples (1¾ kg)
8 oz sultanas (250 g)
4 oz crystallized ginger (100 g)
1 oz garlic (25 g)
1 pint vinegar (600 ml)
½ teaspoon mixed spice (2½–5 ml)
½ teaspoon cayenne pepper (2½–5 ml)
½ teaspoon salt (2½–5 ml)
½ teaspoon ground coriander (2½–5 ml)
1½ lb sugar (750 g)

Apricot Chutney

Hot

Soak apricots for 48 hours.
Chop or mince raisins, onions and apricots and cook in ½ pint (300 ml) of water in which the apricots were soaked, for about

8 oz dried apricots (250 g)
1 lb stoned and chopped raisins (500 g)
1 lb onions (500 g)
2 pints vinegar (1¼ l)
1 lb sugar (500 g)
1 tablespoon salt (15 ml)
1 dessertspoon cayenne (10 ml)
2 oz ground ginger (50 g)
1 oz coriander seed (25 g)
2 tablespoons made mustard (30 ml)

30 minutes. Add half the vinegar, simmer till tender, then leave to get cold.

Next day, add the rest of the ingredients except mustard (spices should be put in a muslin bag) and the rest of the vinegar, and simmer for 2 hours. Remove the muslin bag, add the mustard, simmer for a further 10 minutes, and pot. It is necessary to stir frequently when the chutney is nearly cooked as it becomes thick.

Banana Chutney

Hot

2 lb large onions (1 kg)
8 oz crystallized ginger (250 g)
1 lb dates (500 g)
16 ripe bananas
1 tablespoon salt (15 ml)
1 oz pickling spice in bag (25 g)
Vinegar
1 lb black treacle (500 g)

Chop onions finely, mince ginger and dates, slice bananas. Place in saucepan with salt and bag of spices. Cover all with vinegar. Boil for 5 minutes—take spice bag out. Add treacle and cook in the oven—or over an even heat until a brown colour.

This is a specially good recipe.

Date and Apple Chutney

Mild and Sweet

2 lb dates (1 kg)
2 lb apples (1 kg)
1 lb onions (500 g)
1 teaspoon ground ginger (5–10 ml)
1 teaspoon mustard (5–10 ml)
1 teaspoon salt (5–10 ml)
¼ teaspoon cayenne pepper (1–2½ ml)
1 pint vinegar (600 ml)
8 oz brown sugar (250 g)

Use the general method.

Note: This chutney is quickly made.

Gooseberry Chutney

3 lb gooseberries (1½ kg)
8 oz eschalots or onions (250 g)
6 oz stoned raisins (175 g)
1 pint vinegar (600 ml)
½ oz mixed spice (15 g)
½ oz crushed mustard seed or mustard
    (15 g)
1 oz salt (25 g)
½ teaspoon cayenne pepper (2½ ml)
½ oz paprika pepper (15 g)
10 oz sugar (275 g)

Use the general method.
    Yield 4 lb (2 kg) chutney.

Orange Chutney

Peel and mince onions and cook in a little water; peel and core the apples; mince orange peel and flesh (having removed pith), apples, chillies and dried fruit. Put ingredients, except sugar, in a pan with one-third of the vinegar, and simmer till thick. Add a second one-third of the vinegar, and simmer till thick. Add the rest of the vinegar, and the warmed sugar, and simmer till thick; pot and cover.

1 lb onions (500 g)
3 lb apples (1½ kg)
3 lb sweet oranges (1½ kg)
Minced chillies, the number depending on taste—about one dozen would make a moderately hot one
1 lb sultanas or raisins (500 g)
2 teaspoons ground ginger (10–20 ml)
2 dessertspoons salt (20–40 ml)
4 pints vinegar (2¼ l)
2 lb sugar (1 kg)

Red and Green Pepper Chutney

Prepare vegetables, discarding seeds of peppers. Mince or chop finely all fruit and vegetables. Put in pan with spices (those that are whole in a piece of muslin) and one-third of the vinegar, and simmer till thick. Add a second one-third of the vinegar, and simmer till thick. Add the rest of the vinegar, and the warmed sugar, and simmer till thick; pot and cover.

1 lb red and green peppers, mixed (500 g)
2 lb green tomatoes (1 kg)
2 lb sour apples (1 kg)
1½ lb onions (750 g)
1 oz salt (25 g)
1½ oz mixed (40 g more or less as liked) chillies, cloves, allspice, root ginger, mustard seed, peppercorns
1½ pints vinegar (900 ml)
1 lb sugar (500 g)

Prune Chutney

All-the-year-round Chutney

Soak prunes for 48 hours; remove stones.

Put prunes and onions through mincer. Put one-third of the vinegar and all other ingredients except sugar into a pan (spices in muslin bag) and simmer till thick. Add a second one-third of the vinegar, and simmer till thick. Add the rest of the vinegar, and the warmed sugar, and simmer till thick; pot and cover.

2 lb prunes (1 kg)
1 lb onions (500 g)
1 pint vinegar (600 ml)
2 oz salt (50 g)
1 teaspoon ground ginger (5–10 ml)
1 teaspoon cayenne pepper (5 ml)
2 oz mustard seed (50 g)
1 oz mixed pickling spice (25 g)
1 lb sugar (500 g)

Rhubarb Chutney

Use the general method.
Yield about 3 lb (1½ kg) chutney.

2½ lb rhubarb (1¼ kg)
8 oz onions (250 g)
½ oz ground ginger (15 g)
¼ oz salt (5 g)
½ oz curry powder (15 g), best quality
¾ pint vinegar (450 ml)
1 lb sugar (500 g)

Green Tomato Chutney

2 lb green tomatoes (1 kg)
1 lb apples (500 g)
8 oz shallots (250 g)
1 lb raisins or sultanas (500 g)
1 oz garlic (25 g)
½ teaspoon salt (2½ ml)
½ teaspoon cayenne (2½ ml)
½ teaspoon cardamom (ground)
   (2½–5 ml)
½ teaspoon ginger (2½–5 ml)
¾ pint vinegar (450 ml)
12 oz brown sugar (350 g)

Use the general method.
   Yield about 3½ lb (1¾ kg) chutney.

Ripe Tomato and Marrow Chutney

4 lb tomatoes, blanched (2 kg)
1 lb marrow, peeled (500 g)
8 oz onions (250 g)
½ oz salt (15 g)
Pinch of cayenne
½ teaspoon paprika (2½–5 ml)
¼ teaspoon ground cinnamon (1–2 ml)
¼ teaspoon ground allspice (1–2 ml)
¼ teaspoon ground mace (1–2 ml)
½ pint vinegar (300 ml)
12 oz white sugar (350 g)

Use the general method.
   Yield 3½ lb (1¾ kg) chutney.

Note: This chutney is quickly made.

Sloe Chutney

2 lb sloes (1 kg)
1 lb brown sugar (500 g)
8 oz stoned raisins (250 g)
1 stick of cinnamon
1 teaspoon cloves (10 ml)
½ pint vinegar (300 ml)

Put the sloes in a casserole in the oven till they are soft. Rub through a sieve and add the other ingredients (spices in a muslin bag). Boil gently for ½ hour. Put in small jars and cover to avoid evaporation.
   Improves with keeping.

Three Fruit Chutney

8 oz marrow (250 g)
8 oz cooking apples (250 g)
8 oz cooking pears (250 g)
1 oz chopped onions (25 g)
½ pint vinegar (300 ml)
½ teaspoon flour (5 ml)
½ teaspoon dry mustard (5 ml)
¼ oz cayenne pepper (5 g)
¼ oz turmeric (5 g)
¼ oz ground ginger (5 g)
4–6 oz white sugar (100–150 g)

Prepare marrow, sprinkle with salt and leave overnight.
   Pour off liquid, steam and mash with a fork. Cook apples, pears and onion in as little water as possible till soft, then mash with a fork. Put one-third of vinegar and all ingredients except sugar into a pan, and simmer till thick. Add a second one-third of the vinegar and simmer till thick. Add the rest of the vinegar and the warmed sugar, and simmer till thick; pot and cover.

Crystallization of Fruit and Flowers

Candied Fruits

The most suitable fruits are those which have a pronounced flavour, as delicate flavours are frequently masked by the large quantity of sugar absorbed. Pineapples, apricots, peaches and pears which are among the most successful are, for reasons of cost in this country, generally prepared from canned fruits. Among the fresh fruits suitable are fleshy plums, greengages and apricots, angelica, orange and lemon peel may also be used.

From Canned Fruits
The can of fruit should be opened and the syrup drained and measured. For every pound (500 g) of drained fruit the syrup must be made up to $\frac{1}{2}$ pint (300 ml), with water. Usually there is sufficient juice.
    Now follow the processing table below:

Sugar Syrup—Sufficient for 1 lb (500 g) of Fruit
To each $\frac{1}{2}$ pint (300 ml) of syrup drained from the fruit, add $\frac{1}{2}$ lb (250 g) of sugar, or preferably $\frac{1}{4}$ lb (125 g) sugar and $\frac{1}{4}$ lb (125 g) glucose. Dissolve sugar slowly in fruit syrup, add glucose and bring to boil.

For 1 lb (500 g) Drained Fruit

1st day	Make the syrup as above and whilst boiling pour over the fruit. See that the fruit is immersed—leave until the next day.
2nd day	Drain off the syrup, add 2 oz (50 g) sugar to the syrup, bring to the boil and pour over the fruit—leave until next day.
3rd day	Repeat the process as on 2nd day.
4th day	Repeat the process again.
5th day	Drain off the syrup from the fruit and this time add 3 oz (75 g) sugar and when dissolved, add the fruit and simmer for 3–4 minutes. Leave 2 days.
7th day	Repeat the process as on 5th day. Leave 4 days. If the syrup is still thin, repeat the process of the 5th day yet again, until the thickness of run honey.
11th day (or later)	After leaving 4 days, drain off the syrup and place fruit on a cake rack over a plate to catch the syrup and dry off, by placing in a cool oven, 120°F (50°C), with the oven door slightly open until dry. Drying can be intermittent and can be done also in an airing cupboard, or in the sun during the summer. The fruit is sufficiently dry when the surface is no longer sticky.

From Fresh Fruit
Fresh fruit should be firm and sufficiently ripe so that the flavour is good. Small crab apples, apricots and fleshy plums should be punctured in numerous places with a silver fork. After preparing the fruit it should be placed in sufficient boiling water to cover it and cooked until tender. For 1 lb (500 g) of drained fruit, measure $\frac{1}{2}$ pint (300 ml) of the liquid in which the fruit has been cooked. Usually it is easier to work with halved plums. Care must be taken not to lose the shape of the fruit.

For 1 lb (500 g) Drained, Cooked Fresh Fruit

1st day   Add either 6 oz (175 g) sugar or 2 oz (50 g) sugar and 4 oz (125 g) glucose to the fruit juice.

Continue as for canned fruit, but repeat the process for 3 more days, then add the 3 oz (75 g) sugar as on the 5th day and continue adding 2 oz (50 g) sugar from there.

Crystallized Finish

Take pieces of candied fruit and dip each one quickly into boiling water. Drain off any excess moisture, then roll each piece in some fine granulated sugar.

Glacé Finish

To give a glacé finish to the candied fruit, fresh syrup should be made consisting of 1 lb (500 g) of sugar dissolved in ¼ pint (150 ml) of water. The fruit should be dipped in boiling water for 20 seconds and drained. A small quantity of syrup should be poured into a hot cup and the pieces of fruit quickly dipped into it with a fork and placed on a wire tray. As soon as the syrup is cloudy a fresh portion of hot syrup should be taken. The glacéd fruit should then be dried, but the temperature should not be more than 120°F (50°C).

Candied Angelica

The stalks should be picked in April when they are young and tender and the colour bright. The stalks should be placed in a basin and a boiling brine, ¼ oz (5 g) salt to 2 quarts (2¼ l) water, poured over them. They should be soaked for 10 minutes, rinsed in cold water, then placed in a pan of fresh boiling water and boiled for 5–7 minutes. They should then be drained and scraped to remove the outer skin. The angelica should then be candied as directed previously for fruit.

Candied Peel (1)

Orange, lemon or grapefruit peel requires cooking for about 1 hour, changing the water three times (grapefruit peel needs several changes of water). It is then drained and can be candied as directed previously for fruit.

Candied Peel (2)

Put the peel into a saucepan with sufficient water to cover it. Simmer gently for about 2 hours until the peel is quite tender, replenishing water as necessary. Add the sugar, 2 oz (50 g) to each orange or lemon peel, stir until this has dissolved and bring to the boil. Simmer for 20 minutes with saucepan lid on. Put on one side to cool without a lid on the pan. Next day reboil the syrup and simmer for a few minutes. On the third day simmer gently until the peel has absorbed nearly all the syrup. Drain the peel and dry. Any remaining syrup can be poured into the hollow of the peel before drying.

Candied Peel (3) *Crystallized Orange Peel*

Use only oranges with thick rough skins (Jaffa types). Wash well and peel in quarters, removing any white skin from the pith. Soak in a brine solution, 6 oz (175 g) salt to 1 pint (600 ml) water, until ready to use. In this way one can collect orange skins as the oranges are eaten, over about 14 days.

Rinse well, then put peel in saucepan with sufficient water to cover, bring to the boil, drain, repeat this three times, the last time allowing the peel to cook until tender (test with the head of a pin). Weigh drained peel and use equal weight sugar to fruit. Dissolve sugar in water in saucepan (approximately ½ pint (300 ml) water to ½ lb (250 g) sugar). Boil for 2 minutes.

Add peel to syrup, boil gently for 20 minutes with saucepan lid on pan. Leave now 2–4 days. Simmer again 20 minutes without lid. Leave again 2–3 days, and now simmer until only a quarter of the syrup is left when you *boil hard*, shaking the pan from time to time to prevent peel burning.

When most of the syrup is cooked away, lift out peel gently, dip in boiling water, place on waxed paper on cooling rack and allow to dry. Dip in sugar and put in jar but *do not seal*.

Marrons Glacés

Snip the tops of the chestnuts, put a few at a time in boiling water and scald for about 2½ minutes. Peel them carefully while hot, removing all the brown inner skin. Put the peeled chestnuts into cold water in a large pan and bring gradually to simmering point and simmer very gently until the nuts are tender but not broken. Make a syrup from 1 lb (500 g) sugar, the glucose and just over ½ pint (300 ml) of water (about 12 fl. oz or 350 ml) in a pan large enough to hold the chestnuts. Bring the syrup to the boil, add the drained chestnuts, and bring the syrup back to boiling point. Remove from the heat, but leave if possible in a warm place. Next day, reboil the syrup with the chestnuts in the pan without the lid and leave covered overnight.

Repeat this on the third day with the addition of 6–8 drops of vanilla essence added before heating the syrup. Lift the chestnuts out carefully and drain on a wire rack.

For the glacé finish follow the directions given previously. If the chestnuts are to be kept for any length of time, they should be wrapped in aluminium foil to prevent them from hardening.

2 lb sweet chestnuts (1 kg)
1 lb granulated sugar (500 g)
1 lb glucose or dextrose (500 g)
Water
Vanilla essence
1 lb additional sugar (500 g) for glacé finish

Packing
The fruit should be packed in cardboard or wooden boxes, waxed paper being used as a lining to separate the layers. If desired it may be stored in jam jars or fruit bottles by tying papers or cloth over the top. The container must not be sealed or air-tight as the fruit may ferment or become mouldy under these conditions.

207

Crystallized Flowers

Crystallized flowers have become very popular as decorations for cakes, party sweets, etc. The method is simple and with care the flowers will last for months, keeping a fresh natural colour.

Method

Place 1 teaspoonful of gum arabic (crystals *not* powder) in a small screw top bottle, cover with 1 tablespoon of rose or orange water. Leave for 2 or 3 days to dissolve into a sticky glue, shaking the bottle occasionally.

Using a small soft brush, cover the petals, calyx and as much stem as is needed of the flower with the gum arabic solution. Big loose flowers are best taken apart, when each petal is dealt with separately and the flowers made up again when wanted. The painting MUST be done very thoroughly, as bare spots shrivel and will not keep.

Dredge lightly two or three times with caster sugar until each flower is well covered, and dry off in a warm place on muslin or sugared greaseproof paper. Difficult flat blooms can be placed on the edge of a shelf, held down by something over their stems. Twenty-four hours in the linen cupboard is usually long enough for the flowers to become stiff and dry.

Store in the DARK, preferably in a cardboard box.

The following crystallize very satisfactorily: Primroses, violets, pansies, forget-me-nots, mimosa, cowslips, plum and apple blossom, rose leaves, sweet peas, lilies of the valley and mint leaves, etc. A little vegetable colouring in the gum arabic solution will give the flowers a more cheerful appearance, but care should be taken not to use too much, when the result is most unnatural.

Never crystallize poppies, buttercups, nightshade, foxgloves, laburnum or lupins.

Edible Frosting

Using the same gum arabic solution, brush on a warm plate and dry off in a cool oven.
The solution dries and chips off as frost for cake decorations.

HOME FREEZING
20

This chapter has been compiled from books published by Denbighshire, Leicestershire, West Kent and Yorkshire.

The true value of a home freezer is:
1   To provide variety of food at all seasons.
2   To facilitate buying at low prices, e.g. special offers, bulk buying, seasonal prices.
3   To eliminate waste.
4   To serve as a labour-saving appliance.
5   To preserve home produce at peak condition.
6   To facilitate entertaining.

One could go on listing points of value—the scope is limited only by the capacity of the appliance and the requirements, ideas and ability of the owner.

When choosing a home freezer, initial cost, accommodation, time, available produce and general usage are all points that must be considered. A well stocked freezer need not only contain meat, poultry and vegetables, but also snacks readily prepared, fully prepared meals for holiday times, picnic meals and a week's stock of bread, cakes and scones.

It is worth while to calculate how often various foods are likely to be served over a period of a month. Where there is a garden or farm it may be possible to calculate how much produce can be expected for preservation for winter use or on the other hand, how much is required.

All manufacturers will supply specific directions for the care and maintenance of their freezers.

Very little supplementary equipment other than the packaging materials is required.

Equipment for Packing and Labelling
Correct packaging need not be costly but it is absolutely essential for good results. All food must be sealed in moisture- and vapour-proof wrappings or containers to prevent evaporation and consequent 'freezer burn' or drying out. Materials that are brittle at low temperatures are not suitable for wrapping. Polythene and moisture- and vapour-proof cellulose tissue bags are inexpensive and suitable materials. These can be sealed with a warm iron or, more conveniently, by twisting the open end of the bag, doubling it over in a swan's neck and securing firmly with fine string, plastic covered bell wire or specially made seals. Aluminium foil is suitable and can be double-folded to give a seal. With all thin packaging materials there is danger of puncturing, and an overwrap of brown paper or stockinet (mutton cloth) is advisable.

Plastic and waxed containers are more expensive. If the lids are a good fit, no further seal will be required, but a special frost-resisting tape is available for looser fitting lids. Glass preserving jars can be used but are fragile at low temperatures and poor conductors of cold.

Even-shaped packets pack more compactly than odd ones; cubes much more tightly than tubs. If rigid containers are in short supply, the packaged food can be frozen in a suitable container and removed when frozen to the required shape. This will leave the container free for shaping further packages.

Greaseproof, waxed and brown papers are not suitable.

Most frozen food wrappings and containers can be re-used if carefully washed and dried after use.

Much time can be wasted unless packages are marked. Tie-on labels should be used and chinagraph (wax) or lead pencil is better than ink, which tends to smudge. Full details of the contents of each package will be most helpful when required for use. Coloured pencil can be used to indicate contents at a glance, e.g. green for peas, red for strawberries.

It is usually possible to buy wire mesh baskets to fit into the freezer and these are most convenient for keeping foods of the same kind together. A cheaper alternative is to use net bags.

A stock chart hung near the freezer will be invaluable if kept up-to-date.

The Quantity to Freeze at One Time
The quantity of food frozen at one time should be limited as it is essential that the food freezes as quickly as possible. Some freezers have a separate compartment for freezing new additions which can then be transferred to general storage. Air spaces should be allowed between packets of food which should be packed in contact with a refrigerated surface.

Not more than 10 per cent of the cubic capacity of a freezer should be frozen at once, e.g. if a freezer has a capacity of 150 lb, 15 lb of unfrozen produce is the maximum that should be placed in the freezer in any one day.

Storage Life
Most fresh products will store for 12 months. It should not be necessary to keep them for

longer as fresh supplies will then be ready for freezing. Pork, cured meats, sausages and cooked bakery products should be eaten preferably within 6 months and uncooked bakery products within 3 months.

Accidental Thawing and Power Cuts

Should a power failure occur, *do not open the freezer*. The food in it will keep perfectly for 12–72 hours—the fuller the freezer the longer it will take to thaw.

Check that the switch has not been inadvertently turned off before telephoning for help; avoid this by the use of sticky tape over the switch.

It is wise to have emergency plans in case anything goes wrong. Local shopkeepers or friends' freezers may have spare space for your food, or you may find a local supplier of dry ice; 15 lb dry ice in a 6 cubic foot freezer should protect the food for 2 or 3 days.

Provided ice is still present, partially thawed food can be frozen again—except shellfish, rissoles and similar foods. If doubtful it is better to cook the food and re-freeze when cooked.

Useful General Notes

1   See food is always cooled to at least room temperature before putting into the freezer. If possible, chill foods before putting them in the freezer.
2   Allow air space between packs for rapid freezing. When food is frozen it can be moved and stacked closely.
3   For successful results the freezer should run at 0°F ($-10°$C).
4   Pack food in family meal quantities.
5   Don't keep food in the freezer any longer than necessary and certainly no longer than the recommended storage period.
6   Food does not improve in freezer storage.
7   Handle food quickly to cut down deterioration. Deal with small quantities at a time.
8   Observe the basic rules of hygiene.
9   Limit additions of foods to the freezer to the quantities advised by the manufacturer of the freezer.
10 Freeze quickly, thaw slowly.

Freezing Fresh Foods

Meat

Meat should be hung as required before freezing and frozen in joints of up to 4 lb (2 kg). Large pieces of meat take a long time to freeze and are difficult to utilize. Surplus fat should be removed, bones trimmed and the joint shaped so there are no awkward edges. Overwrap any bones protruding with greaseproof. Several chops or steaks can be packed together with a double fold of greaseproof paper between each one. This makes it possible to open the pack and take out as many chops or steaks as required. Boned meat stores economically and stock from the bones freezes well. Liver can be wrapped in small parcels before putting into bags or muslin.

Cured meat is not usually frozen as it keeps satisfactorily at normal temperatures. If it is desired to freeze it, it should be matured before putting into the freezer.

Sausages can be frozen but care must be taken to cut down salt and spices in the recipe; keep only 2–4 weeks.

When freezing made-up dishes avoid spices and onion and reduce the salt content.

Poultry and Game

Game should be hung before freezing and all poultry and game should be prepared for cooking before freezing. Stuffing should not be put into the carcass and giblets should be wrapped so that they do not mark the bird. Chicken livers make a good separate pack for savouries if not required with the giblets. When shank bones or feet are likely to protrude, they should be wrapped in greaseproof paper and tied close to the body before the bird is packed. An overwrap of mutton cloth is useful. Whole carcasses are bulky and halved or jointed birds are recommended if they are to be finally used in that form.

Rabbits and hares are better jointed and each joint wrapped separately, then packed together but take care to avoid air pockets.

Fish

Fish should be frozen as soon as possible after being caught. It should be very well washed after gutting. Cut again into usable pieces or steaks or fillets, packing a number of steaks or fillets together with greaseproof paper between each piece. Dip white fish in a salt solution—4 oz (100 g) salt per quart (1¼ l) of water, to improve texture.

The head and fins are removed from small fish which are packed whole.

Boil lobsters and crabs before freezing.

Fish has a comparatively short freezer life and should be used within 6 months.

Fruit

Most fruits freeze well. Fresh, good quality fruit should be picked over and, if necessary, rinsed in small quantities of ice-cold water.

Dessert fruit is usually frozen with dry sugar, 4–6 oz (100–150 g) per 1 lb (450 g) or syrup, ½–1 lb (225–450 g) sugar per pint (600 ml) water.

Pears and peaches are subject to discoloration and should be kept under water containing ½ oz (15 g) salt and ½ oz (15 g) citric acid per quart (1¼ l) during preparation; a rigid container is preferred for storage and the syrup should cover the fruit. A crumpled up piece of greaseproof paper under the lid will keep the fruit submerged and allow the necessary head space.

Good cooking apples can be sliced, dipped in fast boiling water for 2–3 minutes, cooled in very cold water and packed unsweetened.

Purées, sweetened with 1 part sugar to 3–4 parts purée, freeze excellently. When cooled down, put into moisture/vapour-proof bags and shape in oblongs or pack into trays to freeze. Remove from box or trays when frozen as packages store in much less room.

Soft fruits can be frozen in 2–3 lb (1–1½ kg) batches for jam and jelly-making later. This saves work in the busy summer months and gives bright-coloured and fresh flavoured jam as required throughout the year.

Recommended Soft Fruits

Blackberries   —Cultivated or wild, if large, juicy and ripe.
Cherries   —Black varieties.
Loganberries   —Red ripe.
Raspberries   —Early red, Lloyd George, Malling Promise, Norfolk Giant.
Strawberries   —Cambridge Prizewinner, Cambridge Vigour, Royal Sovereign, if sliced.
Whortleberries —Wild or cultivated Blueberries.

Vegetables

Good quality summer vegetables freeze excellently. Leafy salad plants are not suitable for freezing; celery loses its crispness. Tomatoes can be frozen but the final product is no better than if canned or bottled. It is a waste of freezer space to store vegetables that keep well otherwise.

   To control spoilage and off-flavours, vegetables require to be scalded. This important process is carried out as follows: The vegetables are prepared in the usual way. A large saucepan containing at least 4 pints (2¼ l) of boiling water will be required and also a quantity of cold water containing ice—a supply of ice can be easily obtained if cake tins half-filled with cold water are placed in the freezer 2–3 hours before required. About ½ lb (225 g) of the prepared vegetable is placed in a straight-sided mesh basket or a net or butter muslin bag and plunged into the fast boiling water. The coldness of the vegetables will take the water off the boil and it is essential that the source of heat be sufficient to reboil the water within 1 minute. The scalding time is reckoned from the moment of reboiling, according to the times following. As soon as the scalding time is completed, the basket or bag is drained and transferred to the ice-cold water. When the vegetables are cold they are ready for packing and freezing. The scalding and cooling water can be used for subsequent batches provided the quantity of boiling water remains sufficient and the cooling water is kept cold with added ice.

Vegetable	Preparation	Scalding Time (minutes)
Asparagus	Grade for size, cut into 6 inch (15 cm) lengths	2 (thin) 4 (thick)
Beans		
Broad	Pod	3
French	Wash, string if necessary	2–3
Runner	Wash, string and slice	2–3
Corn on the Cob	Use when just mature, remove silk and husk, wrap cobs individually	4–6
Peas	Use in prime condition, pod	1–2
Spinach	Wash carefully, remove stems, blanch in 3 oz (75 g) batches	2½

Corn on the cob should be thawed before cooking, but other vegetables are placed frozen in a small quantity of boiling water. Cooking time is about half as long as with fresh vegetables. Corn on the cob should be cooked in unsalted water and seasoned when tender.

Recommended Vegetables

Asparagus	
Beans	
Broad	—All varieties when young.
Dwarf	—Divil Fin Precoce, Granada, Perpetual, Tender Green, The Prince, The Victory.
Runner	—Cockham Dene Improved, Kelvedon Wonder, Scarlet Emperor, White Monarch.
Broccoli	—Green Sprouting (Calabrese), Purple Sprouting, White Sprouting.
Brussels Sprouts	—Small firm sprouts preferred. Cambridge varieties, Noisette, Sanda.
Carrots	—Shorthorn varieties with good orange colour, young, Amsterdam Forcing, Early Nantes, Perfect Gem.
Cauliflower	—Divide into sprigs. Majestic.
Peas	—Early June, Kelvedon Wonder, Lincoln, Newburgh Gem, Onward, Perfected Freeze, Peter Pan, Phenomenon, Thomas Laxton.
Spinach	—Giant Savoy Leaf, Goliath, New Zealand, Perpetual, Prickly New Giant, Zenith XXX.
Sweet Corn	—Canada Cross, Earliking, Golden Bantam, John Innes.
Mushrooms	—Very fresh. Do not blanch.

Herbs

See Chapter 8, 'Herbs and Flavourings'.

Dairy Produce

Butter

Butter freezes well if closely wrapped, but tends to become rancid as all fat does.

Cheese

Mature cheese, closely wrapped in foil, freezes well but must be thoroughly thawed before use. There is a tendency for the texture to become rather crumbly. Grated cheese is a useful standby.

Cream

Will freeze quite well but tends to become granular and needs beating very hard on thawing to reduce to smoothness.

Eggs

They should not be frozen in the shell, but if broken and packed in containers add 1 teaspoon of sugar or $\frac{1}{2}$ teaspoon of salt per egg. Egg whites freeze very easily, better than egg yolks. Hard boiled eggs are not successful as the whites become rubbery.

Milk

This is inclined to separate unless homogenized milk is used.

Freezing Ready Cooked Foods

A wide range of pies (meat or fruit), cakes and breads can be wrapped and frozen either raw or cooked. Many savoury dishes freeze well.

When packed meals have to be prepared regularly, it is a great convenience for the housewife to pack sandwiches, pasties, etc., in daily packs and freeze them until required.

Many complicated sauces can usefully be made in bulk and frozen in small containers, but seasonings and flavourings tend to intensify when frozen so under-season to start with and adjust after thawing.

Goods for short-term freezing, say for use in two weeks, can be stored well wrapped in wax paper. Goods to be stored for any longer period should be packaged as for fresh produce.

INDEX

INDEX OF COUNTY RECIPES